Do-It-Yourself

Java Games

Do-It-Yourself Java Games

An Introduction to Java Computer Programming

2nd Edition

by Annette Godtland

Godtland Software Corporation, Publishing Division
Rochester, Minnesota

Creative and Thoughtful Solutions

Copyright

Library of Congress Control Number: 2015917874

ISBN: 978-1518789137

Printed in the United States of America

Second Edition – 2015

Published by:
Godtland Software Corporation, Publishing Division
Rochester, MN

Table of Contents

Introduction...1
Setup..2
    Create a Java Work Folder...2
    Download and Install Java...2
    Download and Install Eclipse..2
    Download DIYJava.zip...3
    Set up Eclipse..3
Project 1 – Hello World..8
    Lesson 1.1 – Java Projects and Packages..8
    Lesson 1.2 – Classes, Superclasses and Programs...14
    Lesson 1.3 – Variables and Strings..23
    Lesson 1.4 – Joining Strings, the Escape Character..26
Project 2 – ASCII Art...30
    Lesson 2.1 – Print Typeable Characters...30
    Lesson 2.2 – Export a Program..36
    Lesson 2.3 – Share a Program...38
Project 3 – Name Game...41
    Lesson 3.1 – Reuse Strings..41
Project 4 – Silly Story..45
    Lesson 4.1 – Input a String...45
Project 5 – Name Game Revisited..49
    Lesson 5.1 – If Statements, Strings that are Equal or Contain Letters....................................49
Project 6 – Choose an Adventure...55
    Lesson 6.1 – Long Strings...55
    Lesson 6.2 – Switch Statements...57
    Lesson 6.3 – Methods...60
    Lesson 6.4 – Switch Default..63
    Lesson 6.5 – Reuse Methods...65
Project 7 – Finish the Name Game...70
    Lesson 7.1 – Methods with Parameters..70
    Lesson 7.2 – While Loops...74
    Lesson 7.3 – Infinite Loops...76
Project 8 – Calculator..79
    Lesson 8.1 – Integer Data Type and Addition..79
    Lesson 8.2 – Convert a String to an Integer...83
    Lesson 8.3 – Methods that Return a Value...87
    Lesson 8.4 – Try/Catch Blocks and Exceptions..90
    Lesson 8.5 – Integer Subtraction, Multiplication, and Division..92
    Lesson 8.6 – Double Data Type...95

Lesson 8.7 – Extend the DIYWindow Class...98
Project 9 – Guess My Number..102
Lesson 9.1 – Comparing Numbers...102
Lesson 9.2 – Generate Random Numbers...107
Lesson 9.3 – Increment Integers...108
Project 10 – Temperature Converter..112
Lesson 10.1 – Order of Operation..112
Project 11 – Ten Little Chocolates..117
Lesson 11.1 – For Loops..117
Project 12 – Word Scramble..122
Lesson 12.1 – Comments...122
Lesson 12.2 – String Length and Substring..125
Lesson 12.3 – Print to the Console...128
Lesson 12.4 – Arrays..130
Lesson 12.5 – Static Methods..134
Project 13 – Secret Code..138
Lesson 13.1 – Write to a File...138
Lesson 13.2 – Read from a File, Catch Multiple Exceptions....................................142
Lesson 13.3 – Methods with Multiple Parameters..146
Lesson 13.4 – Index of Characters in a String...147
Lesson 13.5 – Boolean Data Type..151
Lesson 13.6 – Case without Break...155
Lesson 13.7 – System Exit...157
Lesson 13.8 – Data File with the Jar File..157
Project 14 – Word Mastermind...159
Lesson 14.1 – Prompt for Yes or No..159
Lesson 14.2 – Replace Characters in a String..162
Lesson 14.3 – Instance Variables...167
Lesson 14.4 – Convert a String to Uppercase..172
Lesson 14.5 – Empty Array...176
Lesson 14.6 – Static Final Variables..180
Project 15 – Hangman..184
Lesson 15.1 – Switch Statement with Integers..184
Lesson 15.2 – Character Data Type..191
Lesson 15.3 – Index of Next Character..194
Lesson 15.4 – Check User Input...197
Lesson 15.5 – Read All Lines of a File, Null Values..200
Lesson 15.6 – Array Lists..202
Project 16 – Crazy Eights..207
Lesson 16.1 – Objects, Card..207
Lesson 16.2 – Constructors...211

Lesson 16.3 – Modulo..212
Lesson 16.4 – Other Card Methods...216
Lesson 16.5 – Deck...220
Lesson 16.6 – Hand..225
Lesson 16.7 – Crazy Eights: Setup...232
Lesson 16.8 – Crazy Eights: Your Turn..235
Lesson 16.9 – Crazy Eights: Computer's Turn...240
Lesson 16.10 – Crazy Eights: Taking Turns...243
Lesson 16.11 – Crazy Eights: Playing Eights...245
I Hope You Enjoyed this Book..253
Questions, Comments, or Suggestions..253
Other Books I've Written..253
Appendix A - Glossary...256
Appendix B - Completed Listings..270
Appendix C – Install Required Software and Files..380
Create a Java Work Folder Detailed Instructions..380
Download and Install Java Detailed Instructions..380
Download and Install Eclipse Detailed Instructions...381
Download DIYJava.zip Detailed Instructions...382

Introduction

Do you like playing computer games? Do you enjoy solving puzzles? If so, you may enjoy computer programming.

Are you a hands-on kind of person? Would you rather start on a project right away instead of first reading long chapters about how things work? Do you lose interest if too much technical information is presented at a time? If so, this may be the right computer programming book for you.

This book teaches Java programming as you create projects (computer games) in small, manageable steps. You will create games like: Choose an Adventure, Secret Code, Hangman, Crazy Eights, and many more.

The lessons in each project are presented using a "try-it" approach: do the steps shown and see what happens. You'll be given programming tasks, each followed by a program code listing. The listings have fill-in blanks to allow you to write much of the program code yourself. But don't worry if you are unsure of how to fill in the blanks; see *Appendix B – Completed Listings*, for answers.

Don't skip any lessons–each lesson explains a new programming technique, most of which are used again in later lessons. Doing all the lessons will make later lessons easier.

Appendix A - Glossary has definitions of Java programming terms. The first use of each term in the glossary, like "listing" and "code" used above, will be underlined.

Several different approaches can often accomplish the same programming task. You don't have to use the code shown in the answer if your code does what was asked or if you like what your code does better. Feel free to experiment with the code and see what happens. Half the fun of programming is making programs do whatever you want.

Go to *http://youtu.be/oogkS7bUhA4* to watch a video demonstration of the Word Mastermind, Hangman, and Crazy Eights programs you will create when you do the lessons in this book.

Do-It-Yourself Java Games was updated to a second edition to work in Windows 10 and Java 8.

Setup

The first step in Java programming is to install and set up a couple needed programs. If you want more detailed setup instructions, see *Appendix C – Install Required Software and Files*. Once this short setup is complete, you'll write your first Java program.

Create a Java Work Folder

First, create a folder on your computer for all your Java work. I called mine *java* and put it in my user folder, *c:\Users\Annette*. Therefore, my Java <u>work folder</u> is *c:\Users\Annette\java*.

If more than one person will create Java programs on your computer, you should create a different work folder for each of you. This book puts every action you are to take in a numbered list, like this:

1. Create a Java work folder on your computer.

See *Appendix C – Install Required Software and Files* if you want more detailed instructions for how to create a work folder.

Download and Install Java

The free Java Development Kit is required for creating Java programs.

1. Download the latest version of the *Java Development Kit (JDK)* for *Java Standard Edition (SE)* from *http://www.oracle.com/technetwork/java/javase/downloads/index.html*. See *Appendix C – Install Required Software and Files* if you're unsure of which version to download.

2. Double-click the downloaded file to install it.

Download and Install Eclipse

You'll use the free Eclipse Java development environment to enter your Java program code and to create your programs.

1. Download the latest version of *Eclipse IDE for Java Developers* from *http://www.eclipse.org/downloads/*.

2. <u>Extract</u> the files from the downloaded .<u>zip file</u> to your computer. I put mine in my user folder, *c:\Users\Annette*. If more than one person will create Java programs on your computer, extract the files again into a different folder for each additional person.

3. Create a <u>shortcut</u> to the *eclipse.exe* file in the *eclipse* directory you just extracted. My file

was in *c:\Users\Annette\eclipse*. Paste this shortcut for starting Eclipse onto your desktop. If more than one person will create Java programs on your computer, create and rename a shortcut for each of you. For example, I renamed mine *Eclipse for Annette*.

See *Appendix C – Install Required Software and Files* if you want more detailed instructions for how to download and install Eclipse or to create a shortcut.

Download DIYJava.zip

There are a few more files needed for the lessons.

1. Download *DIYJava.zip* for free from *http://www.godtlandsoftware.com/DIYJava/*.

2. Extract the files from *DIYJava.zip* into your Java work folder.

See *Appendix C – Install Required Software and Files* if you want more detailed instructions for how to download DIYJava.zip.

Set up Eclipse

Now that everything is installed, set up Eclipse.

1. Double-click your *Eclipse* shortcut. The *Workspace Launcher* window should appear:

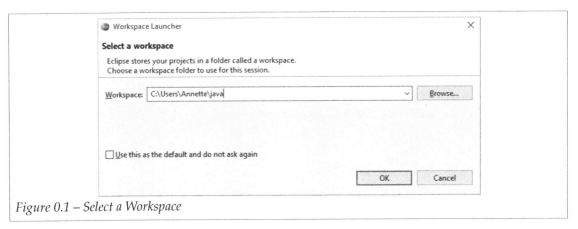

Figure 0.1 – Select a Workspace

2. Click the *Browse...* button to find your Java work folder, as shown in Figure 0.1, and then click *OK*. The *Welcome to the Eclipse IDE for Java Developers* window should appear.

3. Click *Workbench* to open the main Eclipse window.

Workbench

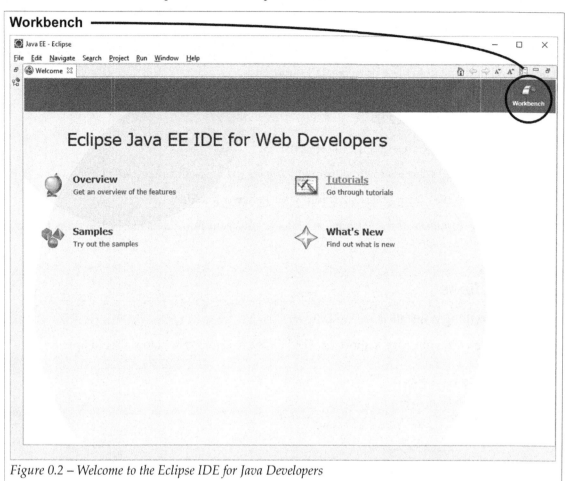

Figure 0.2 – Welcome to the Eclipse IDE for Java Developers

Use the Java perspective:

1. Click *Window / Perspective / Open Perspective / Java.*

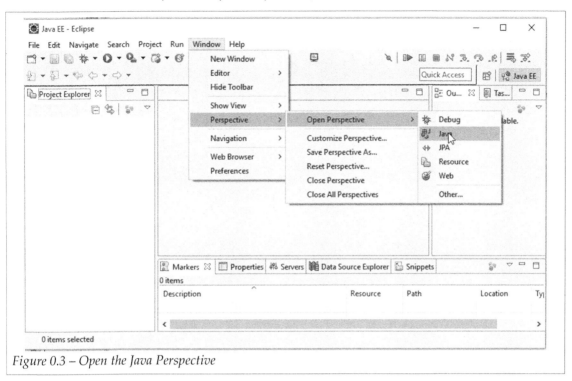

Figure 0.3 – Open the Java Perspective

Make more room for writing code:

    1.   Close the *Task list*, as shown:

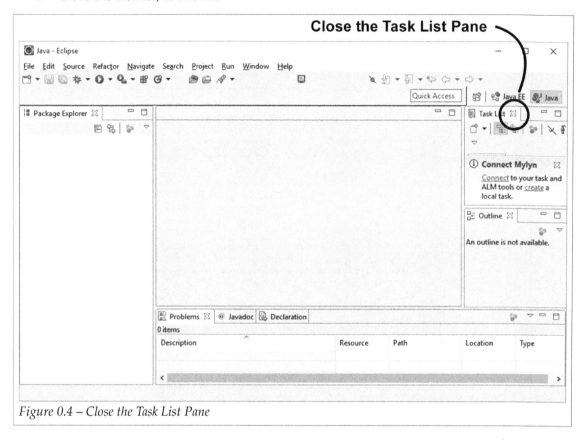

Figure 0.4 – Close the Task List Pane

2. Move the *Outline* tab to the bottom of the *Package Explorer* pane.

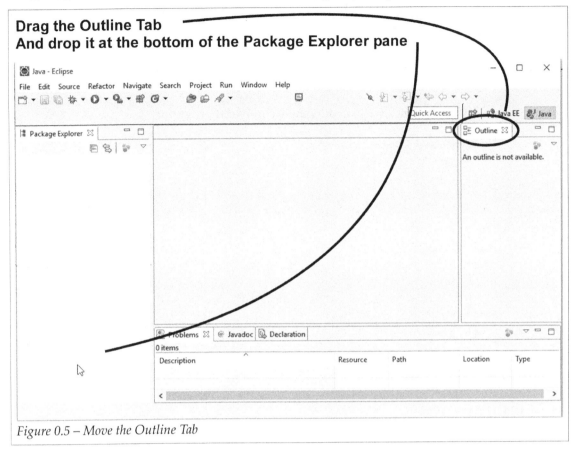

Figure 0.5 – Move the Outline Tab

You now have everything you need to create your first program!

Project 1 – Hello World

Traditionally, everyone's first program prints "Hello World". This first program demonstrates how to create, save, and <u>run</u> a program. It also shows the basic structure used in all Java programs.

Here's a screenshot of the window created by the Hello World program:

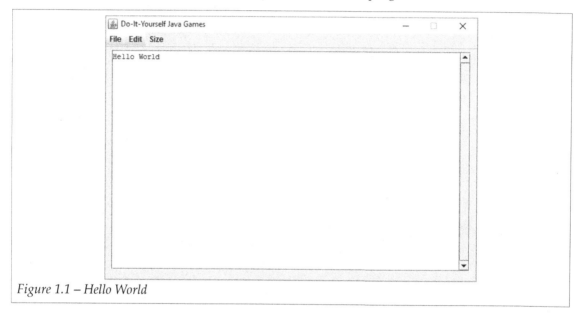

Figure 1.1 – Hello World

Lesson 1.1 – Java Projects and Packages

Programs are first organized by <u>Java projects</u>, then by <u>packages</u> within the Java projects. You'll create a Java project for each program in this book.

Packages hold program files that are usually used together. Because the programs in this book will be small, most of the Java projects you create will have only one package.

In this lesson, you'll create one Java project and one package for your first program.

Try It

Create your first Java project, called *Hello World*:

1. If Eclipse is no longer open:

1. Double-click the *Eclipse* shortcut you created on your desktop.

2. Click *OK* to use your Java work folder as your workspace.

2. Right-click in the *Package Explorer* pane and choose *New / Java Project*.

3. Name the Java project *Hello World*, and select *Use Default JRE* if it is 1.7 or higher, then click *Next*. See Figure 1.2. If the default JRE is less than 1.7, select the option to *Use an execution environment JRE* of 1.7 or higher.

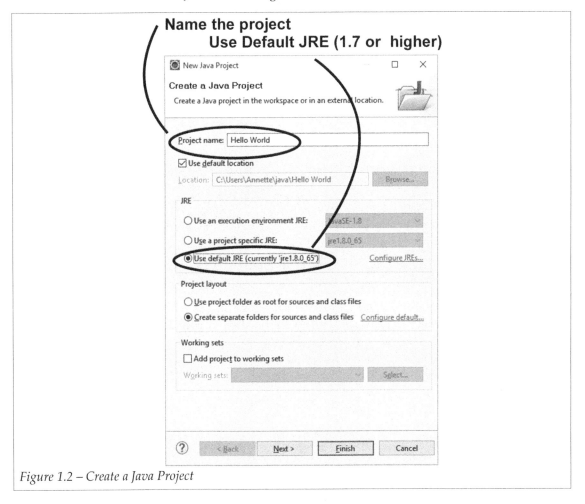

Figure 1.2 – Create a Java Project

4. Click *Libraries*, then click *Add External JARs....*

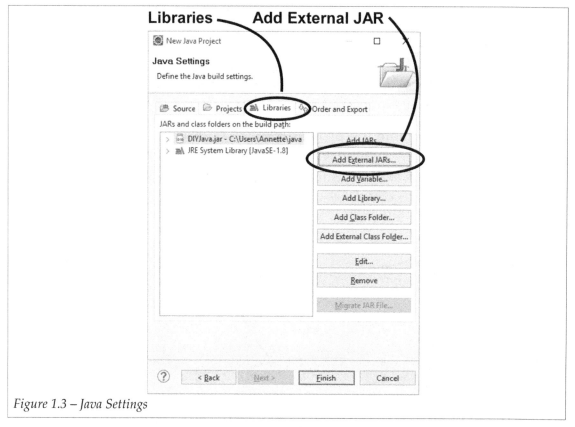

Figure 1.3 – Java Settings

5. Browse to and select *DIYJava.jar*, which you installed in your Java work folder, and click *Open*.

6. Click *Finish*.

The *Package Explorer* pane now lists one project (*Hello World*) with the added <u>JAR file</u> (*DIYJava.jar*).

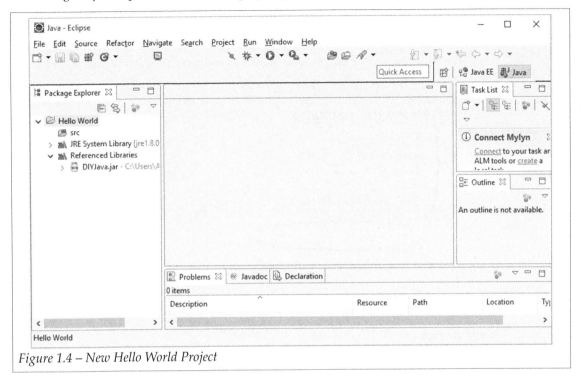

Figure 1.4 – New Hello World Project

Create a package for your Hello World program in the *Hello World* project:

1. Right-click on the *Hello World* project and choose *New / Package*.

2. Name the package _____._____.*helloworld*, as shown in the image below. Use your own name as part of the package name. I used *annette.godtland.helloworld* for my package name.

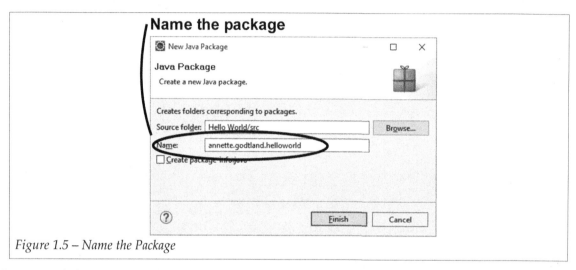

Figure 1.5 – Name the Package

3. Click *Finish*.

The *Package Explorer* pane now shows the package you created in your *Hello World* project.

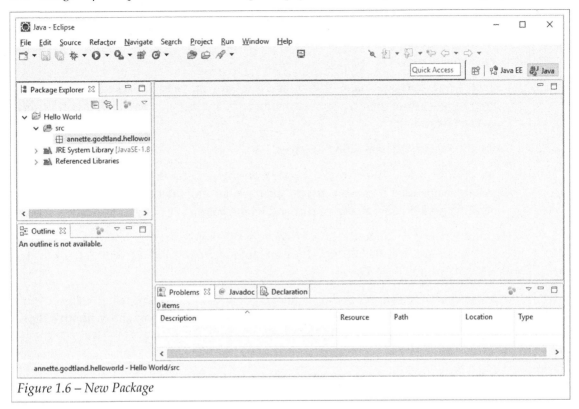

Figure 1.6 – New Package

Key Points and More

- Right-click in the *Package Explorer* pane to create Java projects and packages.

- Create a different Java project for each program.

- Eclipse will create a folder on your computer named the same as the Java project. Give your Java project a name you want for the folder on your computer.

  - You now have a folder called *Hello World* in your Java work folder.

  - For example, capitalize the first letter of each word and put a space between each word like the *Hello World* project.

- Add *DIYJava.jar* to the Java projects you create with the help of this book.

  - *DIYJava.jar* is an external JAR file.

  - *DIYJava.jar* makes it easy to write programs that print text to a window.

- Organize your program files into packages in Java projects.

- Put program files that are usually used together into one package.

  ◦ Because your programs will be small, most of your programs will have only one package.

- Package name rules:

  ◦ Make your package name different from anyone else's package names. Java programmers traditionally use their name or business name as the first part of their package name.

  ◦ Use all lowercase letters with no spaces.

  ◦ Use periods between different categories in the package name. For example, if the package name identifies who created the package and what the package will be used for, put a period between the creator and its purpose.

- Make sure when you create the Java Projects in this book that you are using JRE 1.7 or higher. Once you select the JRE level for creating a project, Eclipse will default to that option for all future Java Projects.

- Java projects are for Eclipse; packages are for Java. Because you're using Eclipse, you'll use both Java projects and packages. If you were to create Java programs without Eclipse, you would probably use only packages.

Lesson 1.2 – Classes, Superclasses and Programs

Java programs are made from one or more classes. Classes contain the actual program code: the instructions that, when run in sequence, perform a desired task.

Every class must name some other class as its superclass. For example, programs intended to run in a window must name some type of window class as its superclass.

In this lesson, you'll create your first class: a program that runs in a *DIYWindow*.

Try It

Create your first class using the *DIYWindow* class as its superclass:

1. Right-click on your package in the *Package Explorer* pane and choose *New / Class*.

2. Enter *HelloWorld* for the class name, as shown in the image below. (Hint: there's no space between "Hello" and "World".)

3. Click *Browse* for *Superclass*.

   1. Enter "diy" for the *type*, select *DIYWindow*, as shown in Figure 1.7, and click *OK*.

4. For *Which method stubs would you like to create?*, select these options, as shown in Figure 1.7

    1. *public static void main (String[] args)*.

    2. *Constructors from superclass*.

    3. It doesn't matter if the third option, *Inherit abstract methods*, is selected or not.

5. Click *Finish* to create the class.

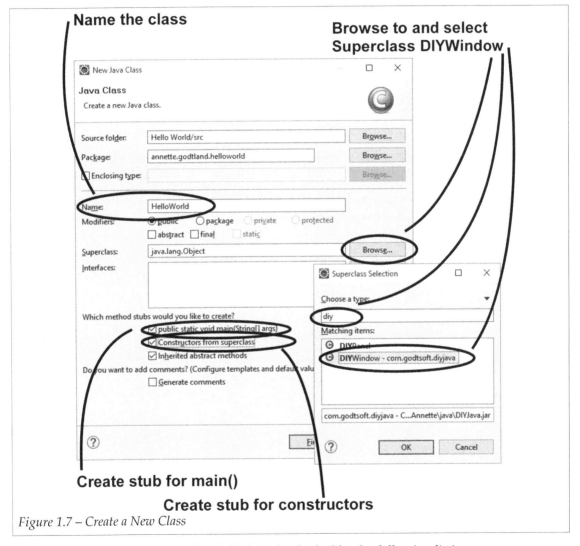

Figure 1.7 – Create a New Class

Eclipse will create code for a *HelloWorld* class that looks like the following listing.

Listing 1-1, from HelloWorld.java

```java
package annette.godtland.helloworld;

import com.godtsoft.diyjava.DIYWindow;

public class HelloWorld extends DIYWindow {

    public HelloWorld() {
        // TODO Auto-generated constructor stub
    }

    public static void main(String[] args) {
        // TODO Auto-generated method stub

    }

}
```

Eclipse adds <u>comment</u> code you don't need. Comments are lines that begin with // or groups of lines that begin with /* and end with */.

1. Remove the automatically-<u>generated</u> comment lines from this class, where it says *(Code was removed from here.)* in the following listing.

Listing 1-2, from HelloWorld.java

```java
package annette.godtland.helloworld;

import com.godtsoft.diyjava.DIYWindow;

public class HelloWorld extends DIYWindow {

    public HelloWorld() {

        (Code was removed from here.)

    }

    public static void main(String[] args) {

        (Code was removed from here.)

    }

}
```

Remove the automatically-generated comments from the program code for every class you create for this book. You'll add your own comments in later lessons.

Refer to *Appendix B - Completed Listings* to see how to complete the code. However, you'll learn more if you try to complete the code yourself before you look up the answer.

The <u>block of code</u> that starts as *public static void main* is called the <u>*main()* method</u>. The block of code that starts as *public HelloWorld()* is called the constructor.

Now, add your first lines of code:

1. Add code to the constructor and *main()* method exactly as shown here. Changes to make to code are always shown bold in the listings.

Listing 1-3, from HelloWorld.java

```
package annette.godtland.helloworld;

import com.godtsoft.diyjava.DIYWindow;

public class HelloWorld extends DIYWindow {

   public HelloWorld() {
      print("Hello World");
   }

   public static void main(String[] args) {
      new HelloWorld();
   }

}
```

1. Press *Ctrl-S* to save the program.

2. Click the *Run* button to run the program. See Figure 1.8.

Figure 1.8 – The Run Button

What happened?

A window should open that displays "Hello World". See Figure 1.9.

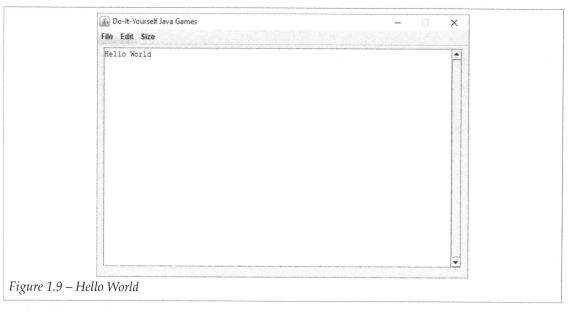

Figure 1.9 – Hello World

1. What would you have to change in your class to make it say hello to *you*?

Listing 1-4, from HelloWorld.java

```
    . . .

public HelloWorld() {
   print("Hello _____");
}
    . . .
```

1. Save the program and run it.

What happens if you make a mistake?

1. Type the word "print" incorrectly and save the program.

Listing 1-5, from HelloWorld.java

```
    . . .

public HelloWorld() {
   printttt("Hello Annette");
}
    . . .
```

What happened?

Many error indicators appear. See Figure 1.10.

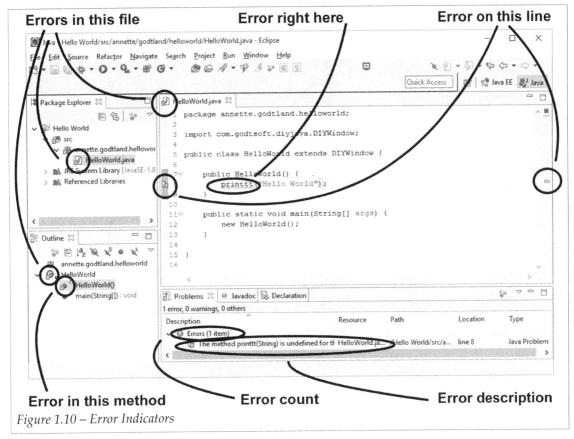

Errors in this file

Error right here

Error on this line

Error in this method

Error count

Error description

Figure 1.10 – Error Indicators

1. Double-click the Error count in the *Problems* pane of Eclipse to see the list of errors found.

2. Double-click on the Error description in the *Problems* pane to move your cursor to the line with the error.

3. Rest your cursor on the actual error (where it says *Error right here* in Figure 1.10). Eclipse will list ways to fix the problem, as shown in Figure 1.11. This feature of Eclipse is called <u>Quick Fix</u>.

Quick Fixes

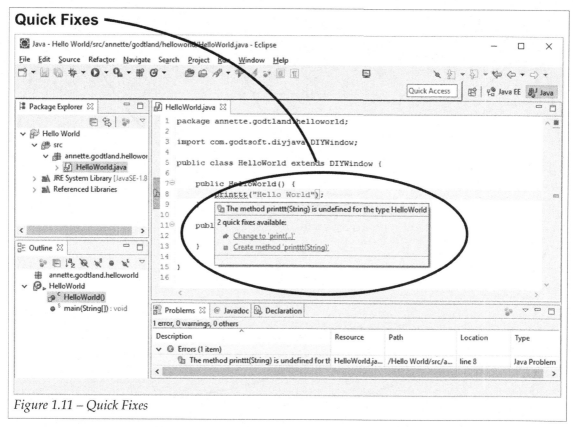

Figure 1.11 – Quick Fixes

4. Click the quick fix called *Change to "print(...)"*.

That action will fix the error for you.

1. Save changes.

All error indicators should disappear.

Now, print more:

1. Change the code to make your program say this:

```
Hello, earthling.
Take me to your leader.
```
Listing 1-6, from HelloWorld.java

```
   . . .

public HelloWorld() {
    print("_____");
    print("_____");
}
```

...

Throughout the lessons, unless there are <u>syntax errors</u>, save changes and run the program after every code change.

Did it print the correct lines? If not, fix the code and try again.

1. What do you think you would have to print to put a blank line between the two sentences, as shown below. (Hint: you want nothing printed on that line.)

```
Hello, earthling.

Take me to your leader.
```
Listing 1-7, from HelloWorld.java

```
   . . .

public HelloWorld() {
   print("Hello, earthling.");
   print(___);
   print("Take me to your leader.");
}
   . . .
```

Key Points and More

-   Java programs are made up of classes. Every program requires a *main()* method in one of its classes.

    ◦   The *main()* method must be written as *public static void main(String[] args)*. Later lessons will explain what all those words mean.

-   Multiple classes are often used together to create one program. However, most of the programs in this book will be made of only one class.

-   Every class must have a superclass. Any class can be used as a superclass. You'll create your own superclass in a later lesson.

-   Classes with the same superclass are considered to be of the same type. For example, the main class you create for every program in this book will use the *DIYWindow* class as its superclass. So every program in this book will be a type of *DIYWindow*.

-   To create classes, right-click in the *Package Explorer* pane.

    ◦   Class names can contain numbers, letters, dollar signs, and underscores. Dollar signs and underscores are usually not used.

    ◦   Blanks or periods aren't allowed in class names.

- Class names cannot start with a number.

- Class names typically start with an **uppercase** letter.

- If the class name includes more than one word, the first letter of each word is usually uppercase, and the rest of the letters are lowercase.

- Classes can have one or more constructors.

  - The class constructor is named the same as the class and must be <u>declared</u> as *public*. Constructors will be explained more in later lessons.

  - A constructor is <u>called</u> by using *new* followed by the name of the constructor and parentheses. For example, *new HelloWord()* in the *main()* method calls the HelloWorld constructor.

- Blocks of code are enclosed in curly brackets, { }, and each line of code ends with a semicolon, *;*.

  - Every Java program runs the *main()* method first.

  - The *main()* method calls the class constructor in all the programs in this book. Therefore, the *main()* method will run first, followed by the class constructor.

  - Each <u>statement</u> within the curly brackets, is run, one at a time, in the order it appears in the code.

  - Blank lines between lines of code have no effect on how the code runs. Blank lines are added to make the code easier for you to read.

- *print()* statements print the text in the parentheses to a window.

  - Each *print()* statement prints on a new line.

  - To print a blank line, use *print()* with empty parentheses.

  - The *print()* method is part of *DIYWindow*, which is in *DIYJava.jar*. That's why you added the external JAR file, *DIYJava.jar*, to the project, and why you chose *DIYWindow* as the superclass for the HelloWorld class.

- Comments are lines that begin with // or a group of lines that begin with /* and end with */.

  - Remove the automatically-generated comments Eclipse creates when you create a class.

  - You'll add your own comments in later lessons.

- Press *Ctrl-S* to save your program.

- Click the *Run* button to run your program. The *Run* button looks like a typical play button.

- Unless you have syntax errors or are told not to, save and run your program after you make the changes from each code listing.

- Refer to *Appendix B - Completed Listing* to see how to complete the code. However, you may complete the listing differently if your code does the same thing or if you like what your code does better.

- The same options won't be used for every class you create. Be sure to follow the instructions exactly as written when you create each class.

- The displayed window uses a default font size of 12. The window menu has an option to change the size of the font after the window is opened. To change the default font size used for any of the programs in this book, add the following line of code to the to the beginning of the constructor:

```
setFontSize(__);
```
- For example, to change the default font size for HelloWorld to 18, use:

```
public HelloWorld() {
  setFontSize(18);
  print("Hello, earthling.");
  print();
  print("Take me to your leader.");
}
```
  - None of the programs in this book change the default font size. Add the setFontSize line of code to the constructor of any program for which you want to change the default font size.

Lesson 1.3 – Variables and Strings

Variables are named pieces of <u>data</u>. String <u>variables</u> hold sequences of character data (text). You can save, use, and reuse text if you put it in a <u>string</u>.

Try It

1. Replace the code in the class constructor with the following code. Type the code exactly as shown.

Listing 1-8, from HelloWorld.java

```
    . . .

  public HelloWorld() {
    String word1 = "Jeff's";
    String word2 = "awesome";
```

```
    String word3 = "dog";
    print(word1);
    print(word2);
    print(word3);
  }
    . . .
```

What did it print?

1. Reverse the contents of the first 2 print statements.

Listing 1-9, from HelloWorld.java

```
    . . .

public HelloWorld() {
    String word1 = "Jeff's";
    String word2 = "awesome";
    String word3 = "dog";
    print(word2);
    print(word1);
    print(word3);
  }
    . . .
```

Notice that the words are printed in the order of the print statements.

1. Rearrange the lines as shown.

Listing 1-10, from HelloWorld.java

```
    . . .

public HelloWorld() {
    String word1 = "Jeff's";
    print(word1);
    String word2 = "awesome";
    print(word2);
    String word3 = "dog";
    print(word3);
  }
    . . .
```

What did it print?

1. Switch the first 2 lines as shown.

Listing 1-11, from HelloWorld.java

```
    . . .
```

```
public HelloWorld() {
   print(word1);
   String word1 = "Jeff's";
   String word2 = "awesome";
   print(word2);
   String word3 = "dog";
   print(word3);
}
   . . .
```

You receive a syntax error in the first print statement that says:

`word1 cannot be resolved to a variable.`

1. Move all the string code back at the beginning of the constructor as shown.

2. Add a statement to print *word2* more than once as shown.

Listing 1-12, from HelloWorld.java

```
   . . .

public HelloWorld() {
   String word1 = "Jeff's";
   String word2 = "awesome";
   String word3 = "dog";
   print(word2);
   print(word1);
   print(word2);
   print(word3);
}
   . . .
```

What did it print?

Key Points and More

- Variables are pieces of data to which you give a name.

- To declare a variable, give the type, such as *String*, a name, such as *option*, and a value, such as "Yes", like this:

`String option = "Yes";`

  ◦ Variable names can contain numbers, letters, dollar signs, and underscores. Dollar signs and underscores are usually not used.

  ◦ Blanks and periods aren't allowed in variable names.

  ◦ Variable names must not start with a number.

- Variable names typically start with a **lowercase** letter. (Hint: this is different from class names, which start with an uppercase letter.)

- Variable names are usually all lowercase. However, if the variable name contains more than one word, the first word usually starts lowercase, and all other words start uppercase. For example:

```
String myName = "Annette";
```

- Variables can be declared in any order, but they must be declared before they can be used.

- String variables are often referred to as simply "strings".

- Declare a variable by type only once. All other uses of the variable shouldn't include its type. For example:

```
String option = "Yes";
option = "No";
```

- Assign a new value to a string from text between a pair of double-quotes or from another string. For example, after these three lines of code are run in sequence, *winner* would have the value of "Annette":

```
String winner = "Unknown";
String player1 = "Annette";
winner = player1;
```

Lesson 1.4 – Joining Strings, the Escape Character

A plus sign is used to join strings. The <u>escape character</u> is used to allow special characters in strings.

Try It

1. Add a new string variable, called *statement*, which joins *word1*, *word2*, and *word3*, and print its value.

Listing 1-13, from HelloWorld.java

```
    . . .

public HelloWorld() {
    String word1 = "Jeff's";
    String word2 = "awesome";
    String word3 = "dog";
    String statement = word1 + word2 ___ word3;
    print(statement);
}
    . . .
```

1. Add a space between each word. (Hint: a space should be typed as a space between quotes, " ".)

Listing 1-14, from HelloWorld.java

```
    . . .

public HelloWorld() {
    String word1 = "Jeff's";
    String word2 = "awesome";
    String word3 = "dog";
    String statement = word1 + ___ + word2 + ____ + word3;
    print(statement);
}
    . . .
```

You can split a string into two lines by using the new line symbol, "\n".

1. Replace all the code in the constructor and type the code exactly as shown.

Listing 1-15, from HelloWorld.java

```
    . . .

public HelloWorld() {
    String greeting = "Hello, Annette.\nHow are you?";
    print(greeting);
}
    . . .
```

1. How would you change the greeting string so it contains a blank line between the two lines of text, like in the listing below? (Hint: a second new line must be started.)

```
Hello Annette.

How are you?
```

Listing 1-16, from HelloWorld.java

```
    . . .

public HelloWorld() {
    String greeting = "Hello, Annette._____How are you?";
    print(greeting);
}
    . . .
```

1. Replace all the code in the constructor, exactly as shown, and try to include quotes as part of what's printed, like this:

```
Annette said to say "hi".
```
Listing 1-17, from HelloWorld.java

```
    . . .

  public HelloWorld() {
    print("Annette said to say "hi".");
  }
    . . .
```

What happened? You received an error. Add the escape character (backslash \) before each double-quote you want in a string. Otherwise Java thinks the quotes are there to begin or end the string.

How do you remember which slash, \ or /, is called a backslash? A backslash, \, is a slash whose top falls backwards, and a forward slash, /, is a slash whose top falls forward. In Java, a backslash is the escape character, and a forward slash is the division symbol. Division will be covered in a later lesson.

1. Add escape characters (backslashes) before each double-quote that surrounds 'hi'.

Listing 1-18, from HelloWorld.java

```
    . . .

  public HelloWorld() {
    print("Annette said to say \"hi\".");
  }
    . . .
```

But what if you want to include a backslash, \, in a string? Put the escape character (backslash) before each backslash you want in a string.

For example, to print "http:\\", use:

```
print("http:\\\\");
```

1. Use escape characters where needed to change the code so it prints the following line. (Hint: not all the fill-in blanks need the escape character.)

```
My user folder is "c:\Users\Annette".
```
Listing 1-19, from HelloWorld.java

```
    . . .

  public HelloWorld() {
    print(__"My user folder is __"c:__\Users__\Annette__".__");
  }
    . . .
```

Key Points and More

- Use the plus sign to join strings together.

- Use the escape character (a backslash \) in strings to handle special characters:

  - *n* in a string will cause anything that follows it to be printed to a new line.

  - \\" can be used to include a double-quote in a string.

  - \\ \\ can be used to include a backslash in a string.

Project 2 – ASCII Art

It's time to become a little creative. You'll learn to produce some drawings in this ASCII Art program and then share your finished program with others if you so choose.

Here's a screenshot of the ASCII Art program:

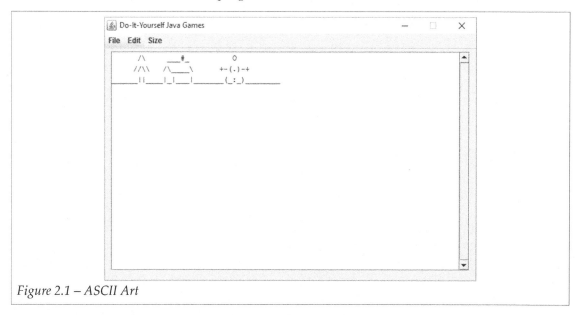

Figure 2.1 – ASCII Art

Lesson 2.1 – Print Typeable Characters

ASCII stands for American Standard Code for Information Interchange. ASCII is a standard numeric code for each character that can be displayed on an electronic device. This ensures that all electronic devices show the same character for each code.

ASCII Art is a picture made from the characters that can be typed on a computer keyboard.

Try It

As you create programs, remember that the Java project name, package name, and class name are very similar but have slight differences:

- Java project name - start each word with a capital letter; use a space between each word.

- Package name - use all lowercase letters; remove spaces between words.

- Class name - start each word with a capital letter; remove spaces between words.

Start writing the next program:

1. Create a new *Java project* called *ASCII Art* and add *DIYJava.jar* to the project.

2. Create a new *package* called _____._____.*asciiart* in the project.

3. Create a new *class* called *ASCIIArt,* with superclass *DIYWindow* and with a stub for *main()* and its constructors.

4. Add code to *main()* to call the *ACIIArt* constructor.

Listing 2-1, from ASCIIArt.java

```
package annette.godtland.asciiart;

import com.godtsoft.diyjava.DIYWindow;

public class ASCIIAart extends DIYWindow {

    public ASCIArt() {
    }

    public static void main(String[] args) {
        new _____;
    }
}
```

1. Add code to the constructor to print a large "H".

Listing 2-2, from ASCIIArt.java

```
    . . .

    public ASCIIArt() {
        print("H   H");
        print("H   H");
        print("HHHH");
        print("H   H");
        print("H   H");
    }
    . . .
```

1. Change the program to print your initials in large letters. My initials are AMG.

Listing 2-3, from ASCIIArt.java

```
    . . .
```

```
public ASCIIArt() {
    print("_____");
    print("_____");
    print("_____");
    print("_____");
    print("_____");
}
    . . .
```

You can create more than just initials with the characters on your keyboard. For example:

```
@@@@@@@
 |       |
 |  (o) (o)
C          )
 |      ___|
 |      /
/        \
```

1. Change the code to print the above image. (Hint: use the escape character to print a backslash, \.)

Listing 2-4, from ASCIIArt.java

```
    . . .

public ASCIIArt() {
    print("_____");
    print("_____");
    print("_____");
    print("_____");
    print("_____");
    print("_____");
    print("_____");
    print("_____");
}
    . . .
```

Here are more images you can create from typeable characters.

Winter scene:

```
    /\          __#_              O
   //\\     /\___\        +-(.)-+
_____||____|_|__|_____(_:_)_____
```

Ballroom dancing:

```
   O         O          O      O
   \|__   __|/      __|/    \|__
  _/|__   __|\_     _/|_    _|\_
```

The art of fencing:

```
/\O__/   /\O___      O__/     O         O
   |        |       <|      <|\__     <|>
 _/\_     _/\_      _/\_     _/\_    _/\_
```

Bicycle riders:

```
_____  __@        __@          __@         __~@
_____  _ `\<,_     _`\<,_      _`\<,_      _`\<,_
____  (*)/ (*)   (*)/ (*)    (*)/ (*)    (*)/ (*)
~~~~~~~~~~~~~~~~~~~~~~~~~~~~~~~~~~~~~~~~~~~~~~~~~~~~
     ~~O
  -   /\,
  -  -|~(*)
  -  (*)
^^^
      _____
```

Unicycle rider:

```
       -o
   o      `o
   '
   \_Q_/
    I
   /T\
   \|/
_____=0=_____
```

Boats and ships:

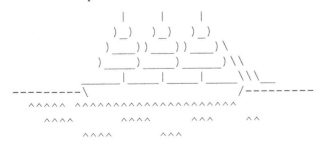

```
   .    o  ..
  o  .  o  o.o
       ...oo
          __[]__
       __|_o_o_o\__
       \"""""""""""/
        \.  ..   . /
 ^^^^^^^^^^^^^^^^^^^^^^
            4
         _____
      _  \ \ \ \ \
     <'\ /_/_/_/
      ((____!___/)
       \0\0\0\0\/
        ~~~~~~~~~~~
```

Penguin:

```
   __
  ( o>
  ///\
  \V_/_
```

Whale:

```
            .-'
 '--./ /     _.---.
 '-,   (__..-`    \
    \           .    |
     `,.___.   ,'__.--/
       '._/_.'___.-`
```

Cat:

```
         /\_/\
    ____/ o o \
   /~____  =ø= /
  (_____)__m_m)
```

Dinosaurs:

```
                 __
               / _)
        _/\/\/\_/ /
      _|         /
     _|  (  |  ( |
    /__.-'|_|--|_|
```

```
                 __
               / _)
        _.----._/ /
       /         /
    __/  (  |  ( |
   /__.-'|_|--|_|
```

```
             /‾‾)
   .-^^^-/ /‾
 __/     /
<__.|_|-|_|
```

Houses:

```
        @ @ @
        []___
       /    /\___
(~)   /_/\_// ____/\
 |    |  || |||__|||
```

```
   []___
  /    /\
 /____/__\
|[][]||||
```

Castle:

```
           |ZZzz
   |Zzz    |      |Zzz
  /_\ /\  | /\ /_\
  |*|_||/_\||_|*|
  |.....|*|.....|
__~|  .. !~!  .. |~___
.*.|___|_|___|.*.
```

Birthday cake:

```
      iiiiiiiiii
     |:H:a:p:p:y:|
   __|_____|__
  |^^^^^^^^^^^^^^^^|
  |:B:i:r:t:h:d:a:y:|
  |                |
  ~~~~~~~~~~~~~~~~~~~
```

Space ship:

```
                          _
 ‾‾‾‾‾‾‾‾‾‾‾‾‾‾‾‾‾‾‾‾‾    _-_‾
 \=============_=_/  ___.---'---·._____
      \_ \   \----·_____.----/
       \ \  / /    ‾`-_-'
    __,--`._-'..'-_
   /_____       ||
         `--._____,-'
```

1. Make some of your own designs using typeable characters.

Listing 2-5, from ASCIIArt.java

```
   . . .

public ASCIIArt() {
    print("_____");
    print("_____");
    print("_____");
    print("_____");
    print("_____");
    print("_____");
    print("_____");
    print("_____");
}

   . . .
```

Key Points and More

- Very nice pictures can be made using just typeable characters.

- Don't forget to use the escape character if you want to print a double-quote or a backslash.

Lesson 2.2 – Export a Program

You must <u>export</u> a finished program if you want to run it without Eclipse or if you want to run it on a different computer.

If you export your program, it will be made into a JAR file (a Java ARchive file) on your computer. JAR files have names that end with ".jar". To run the program, double-click on the JAR file.

Try It

1. Right-click on the *ASCII Art* project in the *Package Explorer* pane and choose *Export*.

2. Select *Runnable JAR File*, as shown in Figure 2.2, and click *Next*.

3. Select the *ASCIIArt Launch configuration*, as shown in Figure 2.2.

4. Enter *ASCIIArt.jar* for the *Export destination*, as shown in Figure 2.2.

5. Select the option to *Package required libraries into generated JAR*, as shown in Figure 2.2.

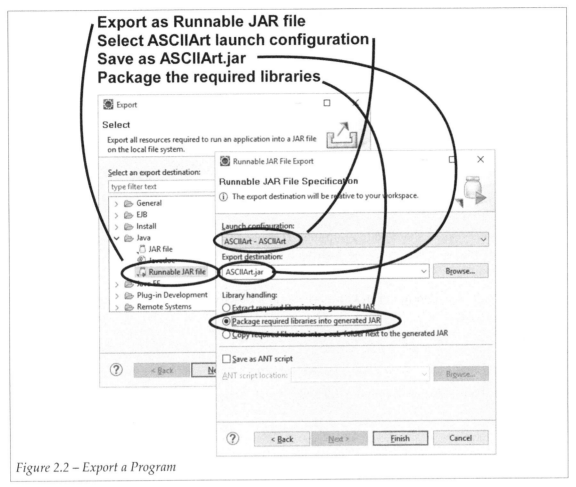

Figure 2.2 – Export a Program

6. Click *Finish* to complete the export.

To run your program without Eclipse:

7. Find *ASCIIArt.jar* in your Java work folder.

8. Double-click *ASCIIArt.jar*.

Key Points and More

- Export the program as a JAR file if you want to run the program outside of Eclipse or on a different computer.

- You can save different versions of your program in different JAR files. For example, you might want different JAR files for different ASCII Art images. Use all the same export options but name a different *Export destination* for each version of the program.

- Your exported JAR file can be run on any Windows, Mac, Linux, or Solaris computer with the *Java Runtime Environment* installed.

  ◦ The *Java Runtime Environment* is already installed on most computers for running other programs.

  ◦ The *Java Runtime Environment* was included in the *Java Development Kit* you installed. Therefore, it too is already installed on your computer.

  ◦ Anyone can download and install just the *Java Runtime Environment*, without the *Java Development Kit*, from *http://java.com/en/download/index.jsp*.

Lesson 2.3 – Share a Program

There are many ways to share your programs. This lesson tells you how to share your program using *Google Drive* and *Facebook*. The instructions assume you already have both Google and Facebook accounts.

See the *Key Points and More* at the end of this lesson for other ways to share your program.

Try It

1. Go to Google Drive at *http://drive.google.com* and log in to your account.

2. Click the *new* button, as shown in Figure 2.3, and choose *File upload*.

Figure 2.3 – Upload a File

3. Browse to and select the JAR file you want to share.

4. After upload is complete, right-click on the uploaded JAR file and choose *Share*.

5. Click the *Advanced* link in the lower right corner of the window. See Figure 3.4.

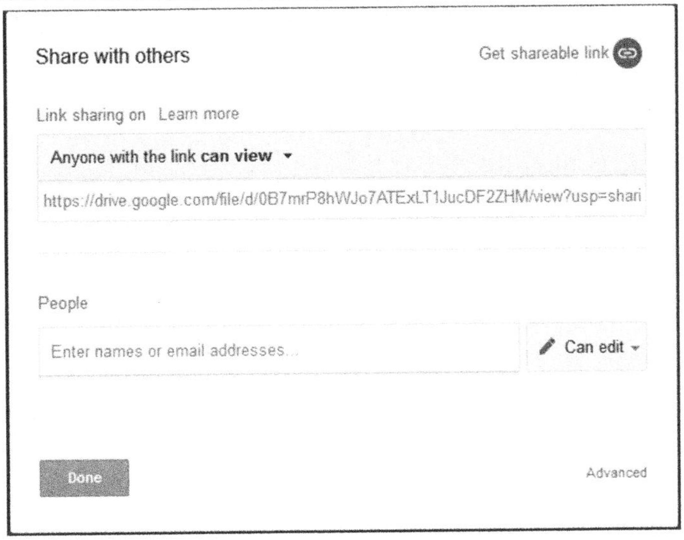

Figure 2.4 – Advanced Link

6. Click the *Share link via Facebook* button, as shown in Figure 2.5:

Sharing settings

Link to share

https://drive.google.com/file/d/0B7mrP8hWJo7ATExLT1JucDF2ZHM/view?usp=sharing

Share link via:

Figure 2.5 – Share Link Via Facebook

7. Write a *Facebook* entry to tell about your link.

Key Points and More

- To share your programs, do one of these:
    - Send the JAR file to friends attached to an e-mail.
    - Put the JAR file on the Web, then share a link to it.
- To put your JAR file on the Web, do one of these:
    - Put it on your own website.
    - Put it on Google drive – *http://drive.google.com.*
    - Put it in Drop Box – *https://www.dropbox.com/.*

- Put it in FilesAnywhere – *https://www.filesanywhere.com/*.

- To share a link with friends, do one of these:
  - Send the link in an e-mail.
  - Post the link on Facebook.
  - Post the link on Google Plus.
  - Tweet the link in Twitter.

- When someone clicks the link to your JAR file, they should download the file then double-click the downloaded file to run your program.

- The *Java Runtime Environment* must be installed on the computer in order for your program to run.

- The *Java Runtime Environment* is already installed on most computers to run other programs. If a computer doesn't have the *Java Runtime Environment*, it can be installed for free from *http://java.com/en/download/index.jsp*.

Project 3 – Name Game

The Name Game program will print different messages for different names.

Here's a screenshot of the Name Game program:

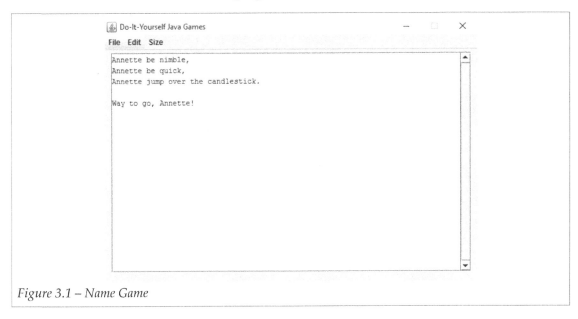

Figure 3.1 – Name Game

Lesson 3.1 – Reuse Strings

A string variable can be set once, then used many times in a program. String variables make it easy to change a word or phrase used many times in a program.

Try It

Start writing the next program:

1. Create a new *Java project* called *Name Game* and add *DIYJava.jar* to the project.

2. Create a new *package* called _____._____.*namegame* in the project.

3. Create a new *class* called *NameGame,* with superclass *DIYWindow* and with a stub for *main()* and its constructors.

4. Add code to *main()* to call the *NameGame* constructor.

Listing 3-1, from NameGame.java

```
package annette.godtland.namegame;

import com.godtsoft.diyjava.DIYWindow;

public class NameGame extends DIYWindow {

    public NameGame() {
    }

    public static void main(String[] args) {
        new _____;
    }
}
```

1. Print the "Jack be Nimble" nursery rhyme:

```
Jack be nimble,
Jack be quick,
Jack jump over the candlestick.
```
Listing 3-2, from NameGame.java

```
    . . .

    public NameGame() {
        print("_____");
        print("_____");
        print("_____");
    }
    . . .
```

1. Add code to put Jack's name into a string called *name*.

2. Change the code to print *name* joined with " be nimble."

Listing 3-3, from NameGame.java

```
    . . .

    public NameGame() {
        String name = "Jack";
        print(name + " be nimble,");
        print("Jack be quick,");
        print("Jack jump over the candlestick.");
    }
    . . .
```

1. Change the code to use *your* name with " be nimble,".

Listing 3-4, from NameGame.java

```
    . . .

public NameGame() {
    String name = "_____";
    print(name + " be nimble,");
    print("Jack be quick,");
    print("Jack jump over the candlestick.");
}
    . . .
```

1. How would you change the rest of the lines so they also use your name instead of Jack's?

Listing 3-5, from NameGame.java

```
    . . .

public NameGame() {
    String name = "Annette";
    print(name + " be nimble,");
    print(_____);
    print(_____);
}
    . . .
```

1. Add code after the nursery rhyme to print a blank line after the nursery rhyme.

2. Add code to print "Way to go, _____!", using your name. (Hint: use the string variable.)

Listing 3-6, from NameGame.java

```
    . . .

public NameGame() {
    String name = "Annette";
    print(name + " be nimble,");
    print(name + " be quick,");
    print(name + " jump over the candlestick.");
    print(_____);
    print(_____);
}
    . . .
```

Key Points and More

- Put text into a string variable if you want to use it more than once in the program.

- String variables allow you to easily change a program to run with different data.

Project 4 – Silly Story

Next, you'll write a program to create a silly story based on a nursery rhyme.

Here's a screenshot of the Silly Story program:

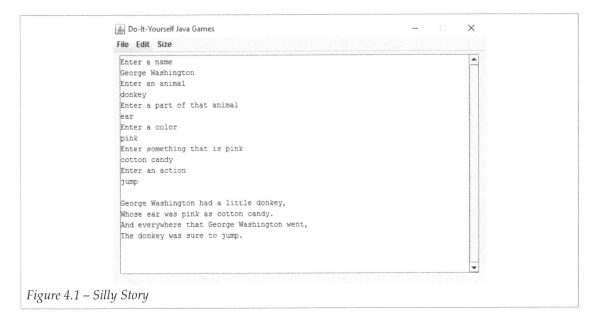

Figure 4.1 – Silly Story

Lesson 4.1 – Input a String

In the previous program you had to write the program code to assign a different value to a string variable. Instead, you can ask the <u>user</u> to enter a value when the program is running.

Try It

Start writing the next program:

1. Create a new *Java project* called *Silly Story* and add *DIYJava.jar* to the project.

2. Create a new *package* called _____._____.*sillystory* in the project.

3. Create a new *class* called *SillyStory,* with superclass *DIYWindow* and with a stub for *main()* and its constructors.

4. Add code to *main()* to call the *SillyStory* constructor.

5.   Print the words to the nursery rhyme, "Mary Had a Little Lamb" in the constructor:

```
Mary had a little lamb,
Whose fleece was white as snow.
And everywhere that Mary went,
The lamb was sure to go.
```

Listing 4-1, from SillyStory.java

```
package annette.godtland.sillystory;

import com.godtsoft.diyjava.DIYWindow;

public class SillyStory extends DIYWindow {

    public SillyStory() {
        print("Mary had a little lamb,");
        print("_____");
        print("_____");
        print("_____");
    }

    public static void main(String[] args) {
        new _____;
    }
}
```

The previous lesson showed you how to easily change a word every time it appears in a program.

1.   Now, replace Mary's name with your name in this story.

Listing 4-2, from SillyStory.java

```
    . . .

    public SillyStory() {
        String name = "_____";
        print(_____ + " had a little lamb,");
        print("Whose fleece was white as snow.");
        print("And everywhere that " + _____ + " went,");
        print("The lamb was sure to go.");
    }
    . . .
```

1.   Enter code, exactly as shown, so the user can enter a name.

Listing 4-3, from SillyStory.java

```
    . . .
```

```
public SillyStory() {
    String name = input();
    print(name + " had a little lamb,");
    print("Whose fleece was white as snow.");
    print("And everywhere that " + name + " went,");
    print("The lamb was sure to go.");
}
    . . .
```

1. When you run the program, type a name and press the *Enter* key.

Make the program easier to use:

1. Tell the user to enter a name before the code waits for <u>input</u>.

2. Print a blank line before the code prints the story.

Listing 4-4, from SillyStory.java

```
    . . .

public SillyStory() {
    print(_____);
    String name = input();
    print(____);
    print(name + " had a little lamb,");
    print("Whose fleece was white as snow.");
    print("And everywhere that " + name + " went,");
    print("The lamb was sure to go.");
}
    . . .
```

What else could you replace?

1. Replace: "lamb" with any animal, "fleece" with a part of the animal, "white" with any color, "snow" with something that color, and "go" with an action.

Listing 4-5, from SillyStory.java

```
    . . .

public SillyStory() {
    print("Enter a name");
    String name = input();
    print("Enter an animal");
    String animal = input();
    print(_____);
    _____ animalPart = _____;
    print(_____);
    _____ color = _____;
```

```
    print(_____);
    _____ thing = _____;
    print(_____);
    _____ action = _____
    print();
    print(name + " had a little " + _____ + ",");
    print("Whose " + _____ + " was " + _____ + " as " + _____ + ".");
    print("And everywhere that " + name + " went,");
    print("The " + _____ + " was sure to " + _____ + ".");
    }
    ...
```

This is the end of the Silly Story program. Export it if you want to run your Silly Story program without Eclipse:

1. Right-click on the *Silly Story* project and choose *Export*.

2. Select *Runnable JAR File*.

3. Select *SillyStory* for the *Launch configuration*.

4. Enter *SillyStory.jar* for the *Export destination*.

5. Select the option to *Package required libraries into generated JAR*.

6. Click *Finish* to complete the export.

Key Points and More

- To create a silly story, replace words in a known story, or your own made up story, with text the user enters for those words.

- Use *input()* to ask for input from the program's user.

  - First, use *print()* to tell the user what you want entered.

  - Put the data entered from *input()* into a string.

- *input()* is a method in the *DIYWindow* class, which is in *DIYJava.jar*. Methods will be explained more in the next lessons.

Project 5 – Name Game Revisited

The Name Game program will be a little more fun if the user can enter any name, and the program prints different messages for different names.

Here's a screenshot of the revisited Name Game program:

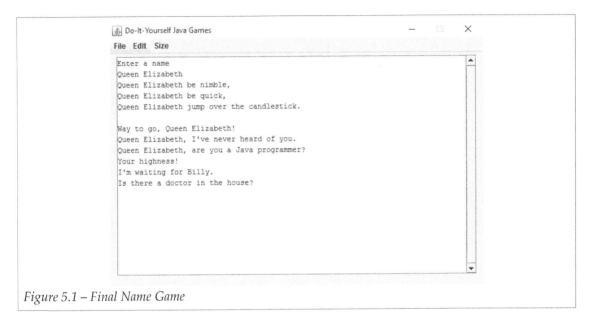

Figure 5.1 – Final Name Game

Lesson 5.1 – If Statements, Strings that are Equal or Contain Letters

If statements let you run one block of code if a condition is true, and another if it's false.

In this lesson, you'll check if a string is equal to, starts with, ends with, or contains another string. You'll then print different messages for different names.

Try It

Go back to the Name Game program.

1. How do you tell the user to enter a name, then wait for him/her to input a name?

Listing 5-1, from NameGame.java

```
    . . .
    public NameGame() {
        print(_____);
        String name = _____;
        print(name + " be nimble,");
        print(name + " be quick,");
        print(name + " jump over the candlestick.");
        print("");
        print("Way to go, " + name + "!");
    }
    . . .
```

Which of the two strings do you think this code would print?

```
if (true) {
    print("I like dogs.");
}
else {
    print("I like cats.");
}
```

If you guessed "I like dogs", you guessed right.

Can you guess what would make it print "I like cats."?

```
if (_____) {
    print("I like dogs.");
}
else {
    print("I like cats.");
}
```

If you guessed "false", you guessed right.

These are called *if* statements.

Comparing the value of *name* with "Jack" will result in either a true or false condition.

1.   Add code exactly as shown.

Listing 5-2, from NameGame.java

```
    . . .

    public NameGame() {

        . . .

        print("Way to go, " + name + "!");

        if (name.equals("Jack")) {
            print(name + ", your jumping skills are famous!");
```

```
        }
        else {
            print(name + ", I've never heard of you.");
        }
        . . .
```

_____

1. Run the program more than once, sometimes entering "Jack" and other times enter a different name.

2. Add another *if* statement to say something special if *name* is your name.

Listing 5-3, from NameGame.java
_____

```
    . . .

    public NameGame() {

        . . .

            print(name + ", I've never heard of you.");
        }

        if (name.equals("_____")) {
            print(name + "_____");
        }
        else {
            print(name + "_____");
        }
        . . .
```
_____

Other common string tests are: *startsWith()*, *endsWith()*, and *contains()*. For example, to check if *name* starts with "A", use:

```
if (name.startsWith("A"))
```

You could also use an *if* statement without an _else_ block like this:

```
if (name.startsWith("A")) {
    print("Go to the front of the line.");
}
```

If *name* doesn't start with "A", the above code won't print anything.

1. Print "Your highness!" if the person is a king. (Hint: check if the name starts with "King".)

Listing 5-4, from NameGame.java
_____

```
    . . .

    public NameGame() {
```

```
    . . .
      print(name + ", are you a Java programmer?");
    }

    if (name.startsWith("_____")) {
      print("Your highness!");
    }
    . . .
```

To check if a string does **not** meet the criteria, put a <u>not operator</u>, !, in front of the test. For example, to check if *name* is **not** Annette, use:

```
if (!name.equals("Annette"))
```

    1.   Print "I'm waiting for Billy." if the name isn't *Billy*.

Listing 5-5, from NameGame.java

```
    . . .

  public NameGame() {

        . . .

      print("Your highness!");
    }

    if (_____) {
      print("I'm waiting for Billy.");
    }
    . . .
```

If a string value contains more than one word, it should have a space between the words.

    1.   How would you check if the user entered only a first or last name? (Hint: check whether *name* has a blank character in it.)

Listing 5-6, from NameGame.java

```
    . . .

  public NameGame() {

        . . .

      print("I'm waiting for Billy.");
    }

    if (____name.contains(" ")) {
```

```
        print("Don't you have a first and last name?");
    }
        . . .
```

You can also check for more than one condition. Use the <u>exclusive or operator</u>, ||, to test for one condition **or** another, and use the <u>exclusive and operator</u>, &&, to test for one condition **and** another.

1. Change the code that printed "Your highness!", to now print the same for either a king or a queen.

Listing 5-7, from NameGame.java

```
    . . .

public NameGame() {

        . . .

    if (name.startsWith("King") || name.startsWith("_____")) {
        print("Your highness!");
    }
        . . .
```

Write code that will:

1. Let the user know there may be a medical emergency if the name is a doctor (starts with "Dr.") but isn't "Dr. Frankenstein".

2. Otherwise, if the name is "Dr. Frankenstein", tell the user no help is needed.

3. Otherwise, ask if there's a doctor in the house.

Listing 5-8, from NameGame.java

```
    . . .

public NameGame() {

        . . .

    print("Don't you have a first and last name?");
    }

    if (_____) {
        print("Doctor, this may be a medical emergency!");
    }
    else if (_____) {
        print("Doctor Frankenstein, no help is needed here.");
```

```
}
else {
   print("Is there a doctor in the house?");
}
   . . .
```

Key Points and More

- An *if* statement is the word "if" followed by a condition in parentheses, which is followed by a block of code in curly brackets. This block of code may also be followed by the word "else" and another block of code in curly brackets. This is all part of the *if* statement.

- *if* checks for a condition, which is either true or false.

  - If true, the block of code within curly brackets immediately after the condition is run.

  - If false, the block of code within the curly brackets immediately after the word *else*, is run.

    - You can use an *if* statement without an *else* block.

    - You can use an *else if* condition and block if you want to test for another condition when the prior condition is false.

- Use the not operator, !, to check for the opposite of the condition.

- Use the exclusive and operator, &&, between conditions to check if both conditions are true.

- Use the exclusive or operator, ||, between conditions to check if at least one of the conditions is true.

- Use these methods to check strings for different conditions:

  - Use *equals()* to check if a string is the same as the string in the parentheses.

  - Use *startsWith()* to check if a string starts with the string in the parentheses.

  - Use *endsWith()* to check if a string ends with the string in the parentheses.

  - Use *contains()* to check if a string contains the string in the parentheses.

- Call methods by entering the variable name followed by a period and the method name.

Project 6 – Choose an Adventure

Next, you'll create a program that starts an adventure story where the reader chooses what should happen next.

Here's a screenshot of the Choose an Adventure program:

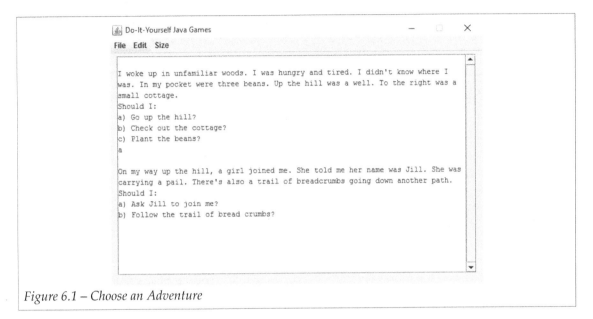

Figure 6.1 – Choose an Adventure

Lesson 6.1 – Long Strings

Sometimes strings are so long they don't fit into the Eclipse edit window very well. This lesson will show you how to enter the long paragraphs of text for the Choose an Adventure program.

Try It

Start writing the next program:

1. Create a new *Java project* called *Choose an Adventure* and add *DIYJava.jar* to the project.

2. Create a new *package* called _____._____.chooseanadventure in the project.

3. Create a new *class* called *ChooseAnAdventure,* with superclass *DIYWindow* and with a stub for *main()* and its constructors.

4. Add code to *main()* to call the *ChooseAnAdventure* constructor.

Listing 6-1, from ChooseAnAdventure.java

```
package annette.godtland.chooseanadventure;

import com.godtsoft.diyjava.DIYWindow;

public class ChooseAnAdventure extends DIYWindow {

    public ChooseAnAdventure() {
    }

    public static void main(String[] args) {
        new _____;
    }
}
```

This is the start of the adventure story:

I woke up in unfamiliar woods. I was hungry and tired. I didn't know
where I was. In my pocket were three beans. Up the hill was a well. To
the right was a small cottage.

To print the start of the story, you could use a print statement like this:

print("I woke up in unfamiliar woods. I was hungry and tired. I didn't
know where I was. In my pocket were three beans. Up the hill was a
well. To the right was a small cottage.");

But Eclipse doesn't wrap long lines very nicely. So, instead, join shorter Strings together.

1. Create a String called *story*.

2. Add one sentence to *story* at a time.

3. Print *story*.

Listing 6-2, from ChooseAnAdventure.java

```
    . . .

    public ChooseAnAdventure() {
        String story = "I woke up in unfamiliar woods.";
        story = story + " I was hungry and tired.";
        story = story + " _____ ";
        story = story + " _____ ";
        story = story + " _____ ";
        story = story + " _____ ";
        print(_____);
    }
    . . .
```

Adventure stories need options. Options for this first situation are:

```
Should I:
a) Go up the hill?
b) Check out the cottage?
c) Plant the beans?
```

1. Print the above options after the story.

Listing 6-3, from ChooseAnAdventure.java

```
    . . .

  public ChooseAnAdventure() {

      . . .

    print(story);
    print("_____");
    print("_____");
    print("_____");
    print("_____");
  }
    . . .
```

Key Points and More

- Put as much as you want in each string.

- This lesson kept strings very short so they fit better both in Eclipse and in this book.

- Split the text wherever you want. Strings don't have to be split into sentences.

Lesson 6.2 – Switch Statements

A *switch* statement lets you run a different block of code for each expected value of a variable.

Try It

Ask the user what to do.

1. Ask for input from the user, and put his/her answer into a string called *choice.*

Listing 6-4, from ChooseAnAdventure.java

```
    . . .

  public ChooseAnAdventure() {

      . . .
```

```
print("c) Plant the beans?");
String _____ = _____;
```

. . .

You could write a long *if* statement to check if *choice* is equal to *"a"*, else if *choice* is equal to *"b"*, else if *choice* is equal to *"c"*. However, there's another type of code that checks if a value is equal to one of several choices. It's called a *switch* statement.

The usual *switch* statement looks like this:

```
switch(_____) {
case _____ :
         _____;
         _____;
  break;
case _____ :
         _____;
         _____;
  break;
case _____ :
         _____;
         _____;
  break;
}
```

To fill in the details of the *switch* statement:

- **switch** – put the variable to be checked for the different values in the parentheses. For example, if you want to check if the variable *reply* is "Yes" or "No", use:

```
switch(reply) {
```

- **case** – create one *case* and its value for each expected value. For example, if one of the expected values is "Yes", use:

```
case "Yes" :
```

- **:** – place one or more lines of code after the colon to be run when the variable has the value of that *case*.

- **break;** – put a *break* statement at the end of the code for the *case*. The program will then skip to the end of the *switch* statement.

1. Add a *switch* statement to:

    1. Print "Going up the hill." if the user enters "a".

    2. Print "Checking the cottage." if the user enters "b".

    3. Print "Planting beans." if the user enters "c".

Listing 6-5, from ChooseAnAdventure.java

```
    . . .

public ChooseAnAdventure() {

    . . .

    String choice = input();

    switch(choice) {
    case "____" :
       print("_____");
       break;
    case "____" :
       print("_____");
       break;
    case "____" :
       print("_____");
       break;
    }
    . . .
```

If you got the following syntax error, it means you did not set the correct option when you created the project:

```
Cannot switch on a value of type String for source level below 1.7.
Only convertible int values or enum variables are permitted
```

1. If you got the above syntax error, use Quick Fix and choose *Change project compliance and JRE to 1.7* to fix the error.

Key Points and More

- Use a *switch* statement to run different code for each expected value of a variable.

- A typical *switch* statement has:

  - The word *switch* with the variable that can have one of several different values.

  - A *case* label for each expected value.

  - Code for each *case* label.

  - A *break* statement at the end of each *case*'s code.

- A *switch* statement will run only the code whose *case* equals the value of the *switch* variable.

- Make sure when you create the Java Projects in this book that you select use JRE 1.7 or higher. Once you select the JRE level for creating a project, Eclipse will default to that option for all future Java Projects.

Lesson 6.3 – Methods

A method is a named block of code that can be called from anywhere in a program. You can create as many methods as you want.

Try It

1. Type the code exactly as shown below to create a method called *goUpTheHill()*.

Listing 6-6, from ChooseAnAdventure.java

```
      . . .
   }

   private void goUpTheHill() {

   }

   public static void main(String[] args) {

      . . .
```

1. In *goUpTheHill()*, print "Going up the hill."

Listing 6-7, from ChooseAnAdventure.java

```
      . . .

   private void goUpTheHill() {
      print("_____");
   }
      . . .
```

1. Next, create methods to check the cottage and plant the beans.
2. Have each method print a message.

Listing 6-8, from ChooseAnAdventure.java

```
      . . .
   }

   private void _____() {
      print("_____");
```

```
}
private void _____() {
    print("_____");
}

public static void main(String[] args) {

    ...
```

Notice that each method was added to the list in the *Outline* pane.

1. Click the *Sort* button in the *Outline* pane, as shown in Figure 6.2.

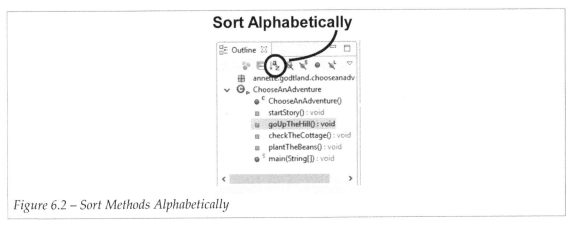

Figure 6.2 – Sort Methods Alphabetically

main() and the constructor will be listed first. All other methods will be listed alphabetically.

You can click the method name in the *Outline* pane to go to that method in your code.

1. Now replace the *print()* statements in the *switch* statement with calls to the correct methods.

Listing 6-9, from ChooseAnAdventure.java

```
    ...

public ChooseAnAdventure() {

    ...

    switch(choice) {
    case "a" :
        goUpTheHill();
        break;
    case "b" :
        _____;
```

```
        break;
    case "c" :
            _____;
        break;
    }
}
    . . .
```

If you run the program and enter a, b, or c, it should print the right message.

In the next lesson you'll need to run the code in the constructor again. Java doesn't allow you to call a constructor more than once. However, code in other methods can be called more than once. So move the code from the constructor to its own method.

1. Create a new method called *startStory()*.

2. Cut all the code from the constructor and paste it into *startStory()*.

3. Call *startStory()* from the constructor.

Listing 6-10, from ChooseAnAdventure.java

```
        . . .

public ChooseAnAdventure() {
    startStory();
}

private void startStory() {
    String story = "I woke up in unfamiliar woods.";

        . . .
}
    . . .
```

Key Points and More

- Methods are named blocks of code.

- Methods follow the same name conventions as variables:

  - Method names can contain numbers, letters, dollar signs, and underscores. Dollar signs and underscores aren't usually used.

  - Blanks or periods aren't allowed in method names.

  - Method names must not start with a number.

  - Method names usually start with a **lowercase** letter.

- Method names are usually all lowercase. However, if the method name contains more than one word, the first word usually starts lowercase, and all other words start uppercase.

- Methods always have parentheses after their name.

- Use methods to help organize your code. Put code that completes a task into its own method.

- You can create as many methods as you want.

- This lesson covered methods with empty parentheses. In later lessons you'll create methods with variables in those parentheses.

- Private methods can only be used by the class in which the method is <u>defined</u>. The methods you just created will only be used within the same class. So they are declared with the word *private*. In later lessons you'll create methods that can be used by other classes.

- Methods that <u>return</u> no value are defined as *void*. The methods you just defined return no value, so they are declared with the word *void*. In later lessons you'll create methods that return values.

- If you click the method name in the *Outline* pane, you'll be taken to that method in the code.

Lesson 6.4 – Switch Default

A *switch* statement can have a *default* case to run if none of the other *cases* in the *switch* statement match the *switch* variable.

Try It

What happens if the user enters something other than "a", "b", or "c"? The program ends without printing any messages. That's not really what you would want the program to do.

Switch statements have an optional *default* case after all the other *cases*:

```
switch(_____) {
case _____ :
    _____;
    _____;
  break;
case _____ :
    _____;
    _____;
  break;
```

```
default :
        _____;
        _____;
}
```

Code in the *default* case will only run if no other *case* matches the switch variable.

So what should the program do if the user enters something other than "a", "b", or "c"? It should repeat the same options.

1. Add the *default* case and have it call *startStory()*.

Listing 6-11, from ChooseAnAdventure.java

```
    . . .

public void startStory() {

        . . .

    case "c" :
        plantTheBeans();
        break;
    default :
        _____;
    }
        . . .
```

If you run the program now, and enter something other than "a", "b", or "c", it will repeat the story and options.

Next, make the story easier to read:

1. Print a blank line at the beginning of *startStory()*.

Listing 6-12, from ChooseAnAdventure.java

```
    . . .

private void startStory() {
    print(____);
    String story = "I woke up in unfamiliar woods.";

        . . .
```

Key Points and More

·   Add the optional *default* case to a *switch* statement if you want code to run when no other *case* matches the *switch* variable.

- Put the *default* case after the last case of the *switch* statement.

- The *default* case doesn't need a *break* statement.

Lesson 6.5 – Reuse Methods

In this lesson you'll reuse methods by calling them more than once from different places in a program.

Try It

Add more to the story. If the user chooses to go up the hill, continue with:

```
On my way up the hill, a girl joined me. She told me her name was Jill.
She was carrying a pail. There's also a trail of breadcrumbs going down
another path.
Should I:
a) Ask Jill to join me?
b) Follow the trail of bread crumbs?
```

1. Replace the code in *goUpTheHill()* with code to print the above story and options.

2. Use a *switch* statement:

   1. If the user enters "a", call *goWithJill()*.

   2. If the user enters "b", call *followBreadCrumbs()*.

   3. If the user enters anything else, call *goUpTheHill()* again.

3. Create the methods *goWithJill()* and *followBreadCrumbs()*.

   1. Each method should just print a message for now.

Listing 6-13, from ChooseAnAdventure.java

```
    . . .

private void goUpTheHill() {
    print();
    String story = "_____";
    story = story + "_____";
    story = story + "_____";
    story = story + "_____";
    print(_____);
    print("_____");
    print("a)_____");
    print("b)_____");

    String choice = _____;
```

```
        switch (_____) {
        case _____ :
            _____;
            break;
        case _____ :
            _____;
            break;
            _____ :
            _____;
        }
    }
    . . .

    private void plantTheBeans() {
        print("Planting the beans.");
    }

    _____ goWithJill() {
        print(_____);
    }

    _____ followBreadCrumbs() {
        print(_____);
    }

    public static void main(String[] args) {
        new ChooseAnAdventure();
    }
    . . .
```

Did you notice the code is very similar for each new part of the story?

If the user chooses to go with Jill, continue the story with:

```
I was so much enjoying listening to Jill's stories. I didn't notice the
branch across the path. I fell down.
What happened next?
a) I broke my crown and Jill came tumbling after.
b) The beans fell out of my pocket and immediately sprouted a bean
stalk.
```

1. Replace the code in *goWithJill()* to print the story and call *brokeMyCrown()* and *sproutedABeanStalk()*.

2. Add the new methods *brokeMyCrown()* and *sproutedABeanStalk()*.

Listing 6-14, from ChooseAnAdventure.java

    . . .

```
private void goWithJill() {
    _____;
    _____;
    _____;

        . . .

    _____;
    _____;
}
    . . .

private void _____  {

    _____
}

private void _____  {

    _____
}

public static void main(String[] args) {
    new ChooseAnAdventure();
}
    . . .
```

Methods can be called more than once. For example, if the user chooses to follow the bread crumbs, have an option to go with Jill:

```
I followed the bread crumbs for awhile. Jill had to go to her
grandmother's house. Before she left, Jill warned me about the cottage
in the woods.
Should I:
a) Go with Jill?
b) Check out the cottage in the woods?
```

1. Replace the code in *followBreadCrumbs()* with the above story. Call the two methods you already created: *goWithJill()* and *checkTheCottage()*.

Listing 6-15, from ChooseAnAdventure.java

```
    . . .

private void followBreadCrumbs() {
    _____;
    _____;
    _____;

        . . .

    _____;
    _____;
```

```
    }
    . . .
```

The reason this program was in this book was to introduce you long strings, *switch* statements, and methods. By now, you should know how to write the code to continue this Choose an Adventure story on your own. Here are some ideas for further adventure:

Broke my crown:

```
I was in real trouble now! The crown is all I had that identified me as
a prince! A frog hopped across the path. There was an interesting
cottage by the pond.
Should I:
a) Kiss the frog?
b) See if anyone is in the cottage?
```

Check the cottage:

```
There are 3 bowls of porridge, 3 comfortable chairs, and 3 soft beds. I
was hungry and worn out.
Should I:
a) Eat the porridge?
b) Sit in one of the chairs?
c) Take a nap in one of the beds?
```

Plant the beans:

```
I planted the beans and immediately a bean stalk sprouted. Maybe if I
climbed the stalk I could get high enough to see my way out of the
woods.
Should I:
a) Climb the beanstalk?
b) Cut the beanstalk down?
```

Climb the beanstalk:

```
I climbed the beanstalk. It went up into the clouds. Below I could see
a trail of bread crumbs on one of the paths. Someone must have been
through here before.
Should I:
a) Follow the breadcrumbs?
b) See what else is at the top of the beanstalk?
```

1. Add more to the story to make your own adventure.

This is the end of the Choose an Adventure program.

1. Export your Choose an Adventure program if you want to run it without Eclipse.

Key Points and More

- Methods make it easy to reuse code. If the same code will be used in more than one place in your program, put it into a method. Then call the method from all the places that use that code.

Project 7 – Finish the Name Game

The Name Game would be better if you let the user run it again and again with different names.

Here's a screenshot of the final Name Game program:

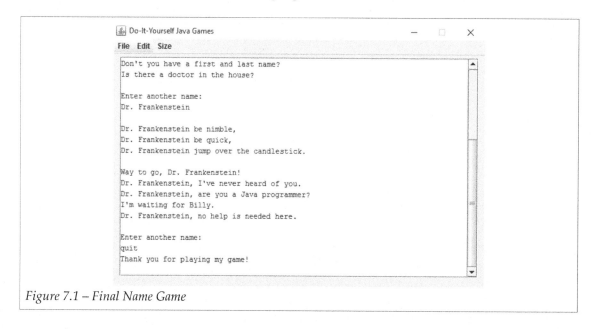

Figure 7.1 – Final Name Game

Lesson 7.1 – Methods with Parameters

Sometimes you want to run the same code again, but with different data. To do this, <u>pass</u> the data into a method as a <u>parameter</u>.

In this lesson, you'll create a method to expect a name as the parameter. The method will then print messages for the name.

Try It

Go back to the *NameGame* program.

1. Move all the code that checks the name and prints the messages, into a method called *checkName()*.

2. Call *checkName()* from where you removed the code from the constructor.

Listing 7-1, from NameGame.java

```
   . . .

public NameGame() {
   print("Enter a name:");
   String name = input();
   checkName();

      (Code was removed from here.)
}

private void checkName() {
   print(name + " be nimble,");
   print(name + " be quick,");
   print(name + " jump over the candlestick.");
   print();
   print("Way to go, " + name + "!");

      . . .

   if (name.startsWith("Dr.") && !name.equals("Dr. Frankenstein")) {
      print("Doctor, this may be a medical emergency!");
   }
   else if (name.equals("Dr. Frankenstein")) {
      print("Dr. Frankenstein, no help is needed here.");
   }
   else {
      print("Is there a doctor in the house?");
   }
}
   . . .
```

This will result in many syntax errors. The syntax errors say:

```
name cannot be resolved
```
In other words, Java doesn't know what *name* is.

Look at the blocks of code in your program:

Listing 7-2, from NameGame.java

```
   . . .

public NameGame() {
   print("Enter a name:");
   String name = input();
   checkName();
}
```

```
   private void checkName() {
      print(name + " be nimble,");

      . . .

   }
      . . .
```

---

name is declared inside the constructor. But *print(name + " be nimble,");* is in a block of code, outside the constructor.

    1.   Declare *name* inside *checkName()*.

Listing 7-3, from NameGame.java

```
      . . .

   private void checkName() {
      String name = "";
      print(name + " be nimble,");

      . . .

   }
      . . .
```

This made the syntax errors go away, but if you run the program now, it won't print the entered name.

How can you tell *checkName()* to use the same name the user entered in the constructor? You pass it as a parameter.

For example, when you used the *print()* method, you passed a string as a parameter, like this:

```
print("Hello World");
```
The *print()* method is defined in *DIYWindow* to expect a string as a parameter, like this:

```
public void print(String s) {
   . . .
}
```

    1.   Pass *name* as a parameter when you call *checkName()*.

    2.   Change *checkName()* to expect a string called *name*. (Hint: you define a method to expect a string the same way *print()* was defined to expect a string. Hint: call the variable *name* instead of *s*.)

    3.   Remove *String name = "";* added to *checkName()* in the last step.

Listing 7-4, from NameGame.java

```
   . . .

public NameGame() {
   print("Enter a name:");
   String name = input();
   checkName(_____);
}

private void checkName(_____) {

   (Code was removed from here.)

   print(name + " be nimble,");
   print(name + " be quick,");
   print(name + " jump over the candlestick.");


   . . .


}
   . . .
```

Key Points and More

- If your code has a value you want a method to use:
  - Pass that value as a parameter when you call the method.
  - Define the method to expect that type of value as a parameter, giving both the variable type and variable name.
    - The variable type defined in the method declaration must be the same type as the variable passed in.
    - The variable name defined in the method declaration may be different from the name of the variable passed in.
  - The value of the parameter sent will be assigned to the new variable defined as the method parameter.
  - The method can then use the new variable in its code.
- Parameters are only copies of the variables.
  - A method changes only the variable that was defined as a parameter. It doesn't change the original variable in the code that called the method.
  - If the method must change the value of the original variable, you should return the

value or use <u>instance variables</u> instead of parameters. These techniques will be covered in later lessons.

Lesson 7.2 – While Loops

A <u>while loop</u> repeats a block of code while a condition is true.

Try It

1. Add code exactly as shown and see what happens when you run it.

Listing 7-5, from NameGame.java

```
    . . .

public NameGame() {
    while (true) {
        print("Enter a name:");
        String name = input();
        checkName(name);
    }
}
```

Make it easier to read each set:

1. Add a blank line before and after it checks the name.

Listing 7-6, from NameGame.java

```
    . . .

public NameGame() {
    while (true) {
        print("Enter a name:");
        String name = input();
        print(__);
        checkName(name);
        print(__);

    . . .
```

Now your program writes messages to names again and again. What if you want it to quit asking names and then do something else? For example, print "Thank you for playing my game!" when the user decides to quit.

1. Add a print statement after the *while* loop to print "Thank you for playing my game!"

Listing 7-7, from NameGame.java

```
    . . .

  public NameGame() {
     while (true)

        . . .
     }
     print("_____");

        . . .
```

That change creates a syntax error:

```
Unreachable code
```

Your program has a loop that never ends. It never quits asking for a name and it never reaches the print statement after the loop. How can you make it end the loop?

Think about the earlier lessons when you used *if* statements to check if something was true or false. You could replace the word *true* in the *while* loop with a condition that would return true or false.

1. Add a condition to repeat the block of code until the user enters "quit" for the name. (Hint: repeat while *name* isn't "quit".)

Listing 7-8, from NameGame.java

```
    . . .

  public NameGame() {
     while (_____)
        print("Enter a name:");

        . . .
```

That was an unfair task. Even if you typed the correct condition:

```
while (!name.equals("quit")) {
```

you'll receive a syntax error. It doesn't know the variable called *name*.

Inside the loop, *name* is declared as a string:

```
String name = input();
```

But now you're trying to use *name* in the *while* statement before it was declared. Variables must be declared before you use them.

Change the code to do these things in this order:

1. Tell the user to enter a name.

2. Wait for the user to enter the name and put it in a new string called *name*.

3. Continue the loop as long as *name* doesn't equal "quit":

   1. Print a blank line.

   2. Check *name*.

   3. Print a blank line.

   4. Tell the user to enter another *name*.

   5. Wait for the user to enter a name and put it in *name*.

Listing 7-9, from NameGame.java

```
    . . .

public NameGame() {
    print("_____");
    String name = _____;
    while (!name.equals("quit")) {
        print();
        checkName(name);
        print();
        print("_____");
        name = _____;
    }
    print("Thank you for playing my game!");
}
    . . .
```

Now the program should print "Thank you for playing my game!" when the you enter "quit".

This is the end of the Name Game program.

1. Export your Name Game program if you want to run it without Eclipse.

Key Points and More

- The *while* loop will keep repeating the code in the curly brackets while a condition is true.

- Variables must be declared before they can be used in the while condition.

- Variables declared outside the *while* loop can be used in the loop. But variables declared in the loop can not be used outside the loop.

Lesson 7.3 – Infinite Loops

An <u>infinite loop</u> is one that never end. Some infinite loops run so fast you can't stop the loop by clicking the Window's close button. There's another way to stop a program stuck in such a loop.

Try It

Make the while loop into an infinite loop that never ends:

1. Remove the line of code that takes input from the user and puts its value into *name*.

Listing 7-10, from NameGame.java

```
    . . .

  public NameGame() {
     print("Enter a name:");
     String name = input();
     while (!name.equals("quit")) {
        print();
        checkName(name);
        print();
        print("Enter another name");

           (Code was removed from here.)


     }
        . . .
```

Now when you run the program, it will repeat the loop using the same name and never ends.

You might be able to stop the program if you click the Window's close button. If not, you can click the *terminate* button in the *Console* pane, as shown in Figure 7.2, to exit the program.

If the *Console* pane is not shown:

1. Click *Window / Show View / Console*.

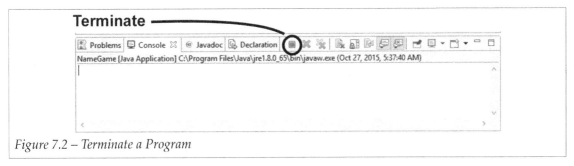

Figure 7.2 – Terminate a Program

1. Run the program then click the *Terminate* button to exit the program.

After you've used the *Terminate* button, fix the infinite loop.

1. Ask for the name from the user.

Listing 7-11, from NameGame.java

```
    . . .

public NameGame() {
    print("Enter a name:");
    String name = input();
    while (!name.equals("quit")) {
        print();
        checkName(name);
        print();
        print("Enter another name");
        name = _____;
    }

    . . .
```

Key Points and More

- An infinite loop is a loop that never ends.

- A tight infinite loop is an infinite loop that never pauses. An infinite loop that calls *input()* inside the loop pauses for the user to enter a value. Such an infinite loop wouldn't be a tight infinite loop.

- Everyone will at some time create a tight infinite loop in a program by accident.

- A tight infinite loop running on a computer slows down all programs running on the computer.

- If an infinite loop runs too fast, you might not be able to stop the program by clicking the Window's close button.

- To end any program running in Eclipse, even one caught in a tight infinite loop, click the *Terminate* button in the *Console* pane.

- If you can't end a program running *outside* of Eclipse, reboot the computer. You should never export a program to run outside of Eclipse if it has code that runs in a tight infinite loop.

Project 8 – Calculator

Next, you'll create a Calculator program. So far, you've been using just string data. But computers are even better at using numbers. In the next several lesson, you'll learn about different kinds of numbers, how to declare them, and <u>calculations</u> you can do with them.

Here's a screenshot of the Calculator program:

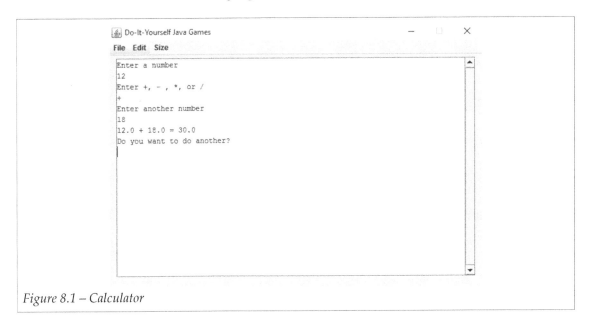

Figure 8.1 – Calculator

Lesson 8.1 – Integer Data Type and Addition

<u>Integers</u> are <u>whole numbers</u>: not <u>decimal numbers</u> and not <u>fractions</u>. Integers can be added together to return a sum or added to a string to be inserted in the string.

You'll use integers to create a simple calculator in this lesson.

Try It

Start writing the next program:

1. Create a new *Java project* called *Calculator* and add *DIYJava.jar* to the project.

2. Create a new *package* called _____._____.*calculator* in the project.

3. Create a new *class* called *Calculator*, with superclass *DIYWindow* and with a stub for *main()* and its constructors.

4. Add code to *main()* to call the *Calculator* constructor.

Listing 8-1, from Calculator.java

```
package annette.godtland.calculator;

import com.godtsoft.diyjava.DIYWindow;

public class Calculator extends DIYWindow {

    public Calculator() {
    }

    public static void main(String[] args) {
        _____;
    }
}
```

Numbers are typed into programs without quotes.

1. Print the number 5.

Listing 8-2, from Calculator.java

```
    . . .

    public Calculator() {
        print(5);
    }
    . . .
```

Numbers can be put into variables. In Java, declare integer variables as *int*. For example, to declare an integer called score and give it a value of 21, use:

```
int score = 21;
```

1. Declare an integer called *a* and assign it an <u>initial</u> value of 5.

2. Print *a*.

Listing 8-3, from Calculator.java

```
    . . .

    public Calculator() {
        int a = 5;
        print(a);
```

```
    }
    . . .
```

You can also join an integer to a string.

1. Add a description to the printed value.

Listing 8-4, from Calculator.java

```
    . . .

    public Calculator() {
        int a = 5;
        print("a is " + a);
    }
    . . .
```

1. Declare another integer variable, *b*, with a value of 7.

2. Print *b* with a description like you did for *a*.

Listing 8-5, from Calculator.java

```
    . . .

    public Calculator() {
        int a = 5;
        print("a is " + a);
        int b = _____;
        print(_____);
    }
    . . .
```

Between strings, a plus sign joins the strings. Between numbers, a plus sign adds the numbers together.

1. Add a third integer to the program, *c*, and assign it the sum of 5 and 7.

2. Print *c* with a description like you did for *a* and *b*.

Listing 8-6, from Calculator.java

```
    . . .

    public Calculator() {
        int a = 5;
        print("a is " + a);
        int b = 7;
        print("b is " + b);
        int c = 5 + 7;
```

```
    print(_____);
}
    . . .
```

___

1. Because 5 and 7 are stored in variables, what do you think you could change so *c* is a sum of what's in variables *a* and *b*?

Listing 8-7, from Calculator.java

___

```
    . . .

public Calculator() {
    int a = 5;
    print("a is " + a);
    int b = 7;
    print("b is " + b);
    int c = _____  +  _____;
    print("c is " + c);
}
    . . .
```

___

Key Points and More

*   Whole numbers (not decimal numbers and not fractions) are called integers. Declare integers as *int*.

*   Integers can be added together to create a sum.

*   Integers can be added to a string.

    ◦   If you add an integer to a string, it will put that number in that position of the string.

*   You should usually use int integers when your code needs integers. However, int variables can only hold values between -2,147,483,647 and 2,147,483,647. If you want larger integers, or if your integer will always be smaller and you want to reduce the amount of space your program takes on a computer, use one of the other types of integers. Here are all the types of integers allowed in Java and their range of possible values:

    ◦   *byte*: numbers between -128 and 128

    ◦   *short*: numbers between -32,768 and 32,768

    ◦   *int*: numbers between -2,147,483,647 and 2,147,483,647

    ◦   *long*: numbers between -9,223,372,036,854,775,807 and 9,223,372,036,854,775,807

Lesson 8.2 – Convert a String to an Integer

The *input()* method reads user input as a string. You must change the entered string into an integer if you want to do integer addition.

Try It

Let the user enter any numbers.

1. Input the value of *a* from the user.

Listing 8-8, from Calculator.java

```
    . . .

  public Calculator() {
     int a = input();
     print("a is " + a);
     int b = 7;
     print("b is " + b);
     int c = a + b;
     print("c is " + c);
  }
     . . .
```

This results in a syntax error:

`Type mismatch: cannot convert from String to int`
input() returns a string. But you need to put the value from *input()* into an int variable.

To <u>convert</u> a string to an integer, use *Integer.parseInt()*. For example, to convert a string called *number* to an integer, use:

`Integer.parseInt(number);`

1. Add code to put the *input()* value into a string called *s*.

2. Convert *s* to an integer and put it in *a*. (Hint: use *Integer.parseInt()*.)

Listing 8-9, from Calculator.java

```
    . . .

  public Calculator() {
     String s = input();
     int a = Integer.parseInt(___);
     print("a is " + a);

     . . .
```

1. Run the program and enter a number.

The program should print the number you entered, print a 7, and then print their sum.

If you enter something other than a number, such as "Hello World", this program won't work. Ignore that for now. You'll fix that in one of the next lessons. First, make this program better for adding numbers.

1. Tell the user to enter a number.

Listing 8-10, from Calculator.java

```
    . . .

public Calculator() {
    print("_____");
    String s = input();
    int a = Integer.parseInt(s);
    print("a is " + a);

    . . .
```

1. What would you change to make the user to enter the second number?

Listing 8-11, from Calculator.java

```
    . . .

public Calculator() {
    print("Enter a number:");
    String s = input();
    int a = Integer.parseInt(s);
    print("a is " + a);
    print("_____");
    s = _____;
    int b = _____;
    print("b is " + b);
    int c = a + b;
    print("c is " + c);
}
    . . .
```

Change the program to print only the final equation.

1. Remove the code that prints the values of *a* and *b*.

2. Replace the code that prints *c* with code that prints *a*, a plus sign, *b*, an equal sign, and *c*, all joined together in one string.

Listing 8-12, from Calculator.java

```
    . . .

public Calculator() {
    print("Enter a number:");
    String s = input();
    int a = Integer.parseInt(s);

        (Code was removed from here.)

    print("Enter another number:");
    s = input();
    int b = Integer.parseInt(s);

        (Code was removed from here.)

    int c = a + b;
    print(_____ + " + " + _____ + " = " + _____);
}
    . . .
```

Does the user want to do more calculations?

1. Ask if the user wants to add a couple more numbers.

2. Put the answer in *s*.

Listing 8-13, from Calculator.java

```
    . . .

public Calculator() {

        . . .

    print(a + " + " + b + " = " + c);
    print("_____");
    s = _____;

        . . .
```

1. Repeat all the code in the constructor if the user enters "Y", "y", "Yes", or "yes". (Hint: use a *while* loop. Hint: check if the answer starts with "Y" or "y".)

Listing 8-14, from Calculator.java

```
    . . .
```

```
public Calculator() {
    while (s._____ || s._____) {
        print("Enter a number");
        String s = input();
        int a = Integer.parseInt(s);
        print("Enter another number:");
        s = input();
        int b = Integer.parseInt(s);
        int c = a + b;
        print(a + " + " + b + " = " + c);
        print("Do you want to do another?");
        s = input();
    }
}
    ...
```

This code results in a syntax error. The program doesn't know what *s* is in the *while* statement.

1. Declare *s* as a string and give it an initial value of "Y".

Listing 8-15, from Calculator.java

```
    ...

public Calculator() {
    String _____;
    while (s.startsWith("Y") || s.startsWith("y")) {
        print("Enter a number");
        String s = input();

        ...
```

That just made this line into a syntax error:

```
String s = input();
```

The syntax error says there's a duplicate local variable *s*. You're not allowed to declare the same variable more than once.

1. Remove "String" from the second time it declares *s* so it just assigns a value.

Listing 8-16, from Calculator.java

```
    ...

public Calculator() {
    String s = "Y";
    while (s.startsWith("Y") || s.startsWith("y")) {
        print("Enter a number");
        _____ = input();
```

Key Points and More

- To convert a string to an integer, use *Integer.parseInt()*.

- To convert an integer to a string, add it to an empty string. For example, if *num* is an integer, convert *num* to a string like this:

```
"" + num
```

Lesson 8.3 – Methods that Return a Value

A Method can return a value after it runs its code.

In this lesson, you'll write a method that converts a string to an integer, and returns that integer value.

Try It

Every time you told the user to enter a number, you did the same three steps:

- Print a message.

- Wait for the input.

- Turn the input into an integer.

If you put those three steps into a method, you can call that method whenever you want the user to enter an integer. This method would have to return a value.

1. First, add a method called *promptForInt()*. Type it exactly as shown.

Listing 8-17, from Calculator.java

```
   . . .

   private int promptForInt(String prompt) {
      int i = 0;

      return i;
   }
   . . .
```

int instead of *void* in front of the method name means it returns an integer. The *return* statement is how the method returns the integer. The method must first declare an integer and assign it a value before it can return the integer.

1. Add code between the declaration of *i* and the return of *i* to:

    1. Print *prompt*.

    2. Wait for input from the user.

    3. Convert that input into an integer and put it in *i*.

Listing 8-18, from Calculator.java

```
    . . .

private int promptForInt(String prompt) {
    int i = 0;
    print(_____);
    String s = _____;
    i = _____;
    return i;
}
    . . .
```

1. Replace the code in the constructor's loop that <u>prompts</u> for, inputs, and sets the value of *a*, with a call to *promptForInt()* to set the value of *a*. (Hint: pass the *input()* message as the parameter to *promptForInt()*.)

Listing 8-19, from Calculator.java

```
    . . .

public Calculator() {
    String s = "Y";
    while (s.startsWith("Y") || s.startsWith("y")) {
        int a = promptForInt("Enter a number");
        print("Enter another number:");

        . . .
```

1. What would you change to use *promptForInt()* to set *b* too?

Listing 8-20, from Calculator.java

```
    . . .

public Calculator() {
    String s = "Y";
    while (s.startsWith("Y") || s.startsWith("y")) {
        int a = promptForInt("Enter a number");
        int b = _____;
        int c = a + b;
```

. . .

1. Create a similar method called *promptForString()* that prompts for a string. It should:

   1. Take a string parameter called *prompt*.

   2. Print *prompt*.

   3. Wait for input from the user.

   4. Return that string.

Listing 8-21, from Calculator.java

```
. . .

private _____ promptForString(_____) {
   print(_____);
   String s = _____;
   return ____;
}
. . .
```

1. Now replace the constructor code that asks if the user wants to do another calculation, with a call to *promptForString()*.

Listing 8-22, from Calculator.java

```
. . .

public Calculator() {
   String s = "Y";
   while (s.startsWith("Y") || s.startsWith("y")) {
      int a = promptForInt("Enter a number");
      int b = promptForInt("Enter another number");
      int c = a + b;
      print(a + " + " + b + " = " + c);
      s = _____;
   }
}
. . .
```

Key Points and More

- Methods may return either zero or one value.

- Name a method's return type in the method's declaration. Return a value of that type using a *return* statement.

- Use *void* as the return type if the method returns no value. Such a method should have no *return* statement.

- When you write the code for a method that returns a value:

  ○ Declare a variable the same type as the return value.

  ○ Add a *return* statement to return that variable.

  ○ Then add the code between the two statements to set the variable to its desired value.

Lesson 8.4 – Try/Catch Blocks and Exceptions

If the user enters something other than a number for the Calculator program, the program stops immediately and cannot continue. It stops because something happens in the program that Java doesn't know how to handle. This is called an *unhandled exception*.

In this lesson, you'll learn how to write a *try/catch* block to handle exceptions. If the user enters an invalid number, your program will tell him/her to enter a valid number, then try to run the code again.

Try It

1. What happens if you run your Calculator program and enter something other than a number? For example, enter "abc".

You'll receive many red messages in the *Console* pane.

1. Look at the top red message:

```
Exception in thread "main" java.lang.NumberFormatException: For input
string: "abc"
```
This means it couldn't convert the string "abc" into an integer and threw a *NumberFormatException*.

- Scroll down to the first red message that names a class you created for your program:

```
at
annette.godtland.calculator.Calculator.promptForInt(Calculator.java:22)
```
This means the error is in my *Calculator* class, in *promptForInt()*, on line 22.

- Click the *Calculator.java:22* link to go to that line of code in the program.

So now we know it threw a *NumberFormatException* for input string "abc" when it tried to run this line of code:

```
i = Integer.parseInt(s);
```
Unexpected exceptions end programs. Your program ended when it hit the unexpected *NumberFormatException*. It was trying to convert the string into an integer.

The basic steps to make a program expect an exception are:

- Wrap the troublesome code in a *try* block.

- Place *catch* blocks at the end of the *try* block for each expected exception.

- Put code inside the *catch* block to run when that exception is caught.

What would you want your program to do if someone enters an invalid number like "abc"? Tell the user that "abc" isn't allowed, and tell him/her to try another number.

1. Add *try* and *catch* blocks to *promptForInt()* exactly as shown.

Listing 8-23, from Calculator.java

```
. . .

private int promptForInt(String prompt) {
   int i = 0;
   print(prompt);
   String s = input();
   try {
      i = Integer.parseInt(s);
   }
   catch(NumberFormatException e) {
      print(s + " is not a valid number. Try again.");
      i = promptForInt(prompt);
   }
   return i;
}

. . .
```

If you enter an invalid number now, it should ask you to try again. If you enter a valid number, it should continue the program without error.

Key Points and More

- Use a *try/catch* block if your code might throw an exception you would like to handle.

- If any line of code in a try block throws an expected exception, the program will:

   ◦ Skip the rest of the code in the *try* block,

   ◦ Run the code in the corresponding *catch* block,

   ◦ Then continue with the code after the *catch* blocks.

- If no code in the try block throws an exception, the program will:

   ◦ Complete the *try* block,

- Skip the *catch* blocks,

  - And continue with the code after the *catch* blocks.

- If a try block throws any other exception, the exception won't be "caught" and the program will end.

- The *try* block and *catch* block can have any number of lines of code.

- Include all the code in the *try* block you don't want run if the exception is thrown.

- Create one *catch* block for each exception you want to handle.

- Programs usually "handle" exceptions by printing a message to the user or by setting some default values so the code can run without the error.

- More exceptions will be covered in later lessons.

Lesson 8.5 – Integer Subtraction, Multiplication, and Division

You can add, subtract, multiply, and divide numbers in Java.

In this lesson, you'll add code to *Calculator* to let the user choose which operation to perform.

Try It

1. What do you think you should change to subtract *b* from *a*?

Listing 8-24, from Calculator.java

```
    . . .

  public Calculator() {
     String s = "Y";
     while (s.startsWith("Y") || s.startsWith("y")) {
        int a = promptForInt("Enter a number");
        int b = promptForInt("Enter another number");
        int c = a _____ b;
        print(a + " _____ " + b + " = " + c);
        s = promptForString("Do you want to do another?");
     }
  }
     . . .
```

Did 5 – 2 = 3? It should have.

Java uses the asterisk, *, for multiplication.

1. What would you change to multiply *a* and *b*?

Listing 8-25, from Calculator.java

```
    . . .

    public Calculator() {
        String s = "Y";
        while (s.startsWith("Y") || s.startsWith("y")) {
            int a = promptForInt("Enter a number");
            int b = promptForInt("Enter another number");
            int c = a _____ b;
            print(a + " _____ " + b + " = " + c);
            s = promptForString("Do you want to do another?");
        }
    }
    . . .
```

Did 5 * 2 = 10? It should have.

Java uses the forward slash, /, for division.

1. What would you change to divide *a* by *b*?

Listing 8-26, from Calculator.java

```
    . . .

    public Calculator() {
        String s = "Y";
        while (s.startsWith("Y") || s.startsWith("y")) {
            int a = promptForInt("Enter a number");
            int b = promptForInt("Enter another number");
            int c = a _____ b;
            print(a + " _____ " + b + " = " + c);
            s = promptForString("Do you want to do another?");
        }
    }
    . . .
```

Did 5 / 2 = 2.5? It should **not** have. It should say 5 / 2 = 2.

The numbers in this program are all integers, so all answers are integers. 2.5 isn't an integer. So 5 divided by 2 gives only the whole number part of the result. The next lesson shows how to use decimal numbers in Java so 5 divided by 2 would be 2.5. For now, you'll continue to use integers.

Let the user choose the operation:

1. Ask the user to enter +, -, *, or /, to set a string called *operation* .

2. Change the initial value of *c* to *0*.

3. Replace the print statement with a *switch* statement based on the value of *operation*.

4. Add a *case* for each value of *operation* to do the right calculation and print the right equation.

5. If the user enters anything else, tell him/her that an invalid operation operation was entered.

Listing 8-27, from Calculator.java

```
    . . .

public Calculator() {
    String s = "Y";
    while (s.startsWith("Y") || s.startsWith("y")) {
        int a = promptForInt("Enter a number");
        String operation = promptFor_____;
        int b = promptForInt("Enter another number");
        int c = 0;
        switch(_____) {
        case "___" :
            c = a ___ b;
            print(a + " ___ " + b + " = " + c);
            break;
        case "___" :
            c = a ___ b;
            print(a + " ___ " + b + " = " + c);
            break;
        case "___" :
            c = a ___ b;
            print(a + " ___ " + b + " = " + c);
            break;
        case "___" :
            c = a ___ b;
            print(a + " ___ " + b + " = " + c);
            break;
        default:
            print("_____");
        }
        s = promptForString("Do you want to do another?");
    }
    . . .
```

There's still another exception you should try to handle:

1. Try to divide a number by 0.

What happened? You should have an *ArithmeticException* for */ by zero* error in the *Console* pane.

Update the program to catch the exception:

1. Add a *try/catch* block around the code to be skipped if the exception is thrown. (Hint: it shouldn't divide the numbers or print the equation.)

2. Print an error message if it catches an *ArithmeticException*. (Hint: print the error message in the catch block right after the try block.)

Listing 8-28, from Calculator.java

```
    . . .

public Calculator() {

        . . .

    case "/" :
    _____  {
        c = a / b;
        print(a + " / " + b + " = " + c);
    }
    _____  (_____) {
        print("Division by zero is not allowed.");
    }
    break;

        . . .
```

Key Points and More

- Use + to add numbers, - to subtract numbers, * to multiply numbers, and / to divide numbers.

- Be aware that adding, subtracting, multiplying, and dividing integers returns the largest whole number less than or equal to the real answer. Decimal numbers will be covered in the next lesson.

- Division by zero isn't allowed and will throw an exception.

- If division by zero might happen and you don't want it to end the program, add code to catch an *ArithmeticException*.

Lesson 8.6 – Double Data Type

Declare decimal numbers in Java as <u>double</u> instead of int.

Try It

To declare a double variable called *temperature*, and assign it a value of 98.6, use:

```
double temperature = 98.6;
```

1. Declare *a*, *b*, and *c* to be double instead of int.

Listing 8-29, from Calculator.java

```
   . . .

   public Calculator() {
      String s = "Y";
      while (s.startsWith("Y") || s.startsWith("y")) {
   _____ a = promptForInt("Enter a number");
         String operation = promptForString("Enter +, - , *, or /");
   _____ b = promptForInt("Enter another number");
   _____ c = 0;
         switch(operation) {
            case "+" :


            . . .
```

1. Try to divide 5 by 2.

Did it print 2.5? It should have.

1. Try to multiply 2.5 and 2.

What happened? It should have printed:

```
2.5 is not a valid number. Try again.
```

Your code uses the *promptForInt()* method. *promptForInt()* was written to allow only integer numbers. You should create a different method to prompt for double.

To convert a string to double, use Double's *parseDouble()* method. For example, to convert a string called *number* to a double, use:

```
Double.parseDouble(number);
```

1. Create a new method called *promptForDouble()* by copying the *promptForInt()* method.

2. Can you guess what to change to make *promptForDouble()* work with double numbers?

Listing 8-30, from Calculator.java

```
   . . .

   private _____ promptFor_____(String prompt) {
   _____ d = 0;
      print(prompt);
      String s = input();
```

```
try {
    d = _____ (s);
}
catch (NumberFormatException e) {
    print(s + " is not a valid number.  Try again.");
    d = _____ (prompt);
}
return d;
}
    . . .
```

1. Now change the code in the constructor to call *promptForDouble()*.

Listing 8-31, from Calculator.java

```
    . . .

public Calculator() {
    String s = "Y";
    while (s.startsWith("Y") || s.startsWith("y")) {
        double a = _____ ("Enter a number");
        String operation = promptForString("Enter +, - , *, or /");
        double b = _____ ("Enter another number");
        double c = 0;
        switch(operation) {
            . . .
```

Your Calculator program should now work with decimal numbers.

Key Points and More

- Use the double data type for decimal numbers.

- Double data variables always print as a decimal number. For example, a double variable with a value of 2 will print as 2.0.

- Float is another type of decimal number in Java. Double is more precise (about 16 decimal places) than float (about 7 decimal places), so you have more accurate calculations using doubles. Both float and double allow much larger numbers than do int or long.

- If you type a number, such as 2, Java will think it as an integer. If you want Java to think two is a double, type it as a decimal number, like 2.0. If you want Java to think two is a float, type it ending with an *f*, like 2f or 2.0f.

Lesson 8.7 – Extend the DIYWindow Class

You now have three prompt methods: *promptForDouble()*, *promptForInt()*, and *promptForString()*. All three would be useful in many other programs. If you could put them in the *DIYWindow* class, then any class with DIYWindow as its superclass could also use these three prompt methods. However, you can't edit the *DIYWindow* file.

This lesson shows you how to add your own methods to an existing class by <u>extending</u> it.

Try It

Create the next class:

1. Create a new *Java project* called *My Window* and add *DIYJava.jar* to the project.

2. Create a new *package* called _____._____.mywindow in the project.

3. Create a new *class* called *MyWindow*, with superclass *DIYWindow*. It doesn't need a stub for *main()* or for its constructors.

Listing 8-32, from MyWindow.java

```
package annette.godtland.mywindow;

import com.godtsoft.diyjava.DIYWindow;

public class MyWindow extends DIYWindow {

}
```

1. Cut *promptForDouble()*, *promptForInt()*, and *promptForString()* from the *Calculator* class and paste them into the class block for the *MyWindow* class.

Listing 8-33, from MyWindow.java

```
    . . .

public class MyWindow extends DIYWindow {

  private double promptForDouble(String prompt) {
    double d = 0;
    print(prompt);
    String s = input();
    try {
      d = Double.parseDouble(s);
    }
    catch(NumberFormatException e) {
      print(s + " is not a valid number. Try again.");
```

```
       d = promptForDouble(prompt);
    }
    return d;
  }

  private int promptForInt(String prompt) {
    int i = 0;
    print(prompt);
    String s = input();
    try {
      i = Integer.parseInt(s);
    }
    catch(NumberFormatException e) {
      print(s + " is not a valid number. Try again.");
      i = promptForInt(prompt);
    }
    return i;
  }

  private String promptForString(String prompt) {
    print(prompt);
    String s = input();
    return s;
  }
}
}
```

The <u>build path</u> holds the location of the files, projects, and libraries needed for creating the Java project. You must put *MyWindow* in the build path for *Calculator* so *Calculator* knows where to find *MyWindow*. You can still add Java projects to the build path of an existing Java project.

1. Right-click on the *Calculator* project and select *Build Path / Configure Build Path....*

2. Click the *Projects* tab and click the *Add...* button.

3. Select your *My Window* project and click *OK*.

4. Click *OK* to close the *Java Build Path* window.

Now, go back to the *Calculator* class and make these changes:

1. Change the *import* statement to <u>import</u> _____._____.*mywindow.MyWindow* instead of *com.godtsoft.diyjava.DIYWindow.*

2. Change the class to extend *MyWindow* instead of *DIYWindow.*

```
Listing 8-34, from Calculator.java
```

```
package annette.godtland.calculator;

import _____;
```

```
public class Calculator extends _____ {
    . . .
```

There are still syntax errors:

```
The method promptForDouble(String) from MyWindow is not visible.
```
Have you wondered why some methods are defined as private and others as public? Private means only the class that defined it can see it and use it. Public means any class can see it and use it. Because *promptForDouble()* is declared as private and is not in the *Calculator* class, *Calculator* can't use it.

A third visibility option is to make a method <u>protected</u>. Protected means only classes that define it, and classes that extend the class that define it, can see it and use it. Since *Calculator* extends *MyWindow*, it could use the methods in *MyWindow* if they were protected.

1. Change all three methods in *MyWindow* to be protected.

Listing 8-35, from MyWindow.java

```
        . . .

_____ double promptForDouble(String prompt) {
        double d = 0;

            . . .

        return d;
    }

_____ int promptForInt(String prompt) {
        int i = 0;

            . . .

        return i;
    }

_____ String promptForString(String prompt) {
        print(prompt);
        String s = input();
        return s;
    }
        . . .
```

This is the end of the Calculator program.

1. Export your Calculator program if you want to run it without Eclipse.

Key Points and More

- A class that extends another class can use any of the others' methods if they are either public or protected.

  - Private means only the class it's defined in can use it.

  - Public means any class can use it.

  - Protected means only the class it's defined in, plus any classes which extends the class it's defined in, can use it.

- Until you have a reason a method should be used by other classes, declare it as private.

- Put a method into its class's superclass if the method might be used by other classes with the same superclass.

  - However, in this case, you couldn't edit the code for the superclass *DIYWindow*. Instead, you extended *DIYWindow* with your own class, *MyWindow*, and added the methods to *MyWindow*.

- Now all classes that extend *MyWindow* (classes with *MyWindow* as their superclass) have access to all the public and protected methods in *MyWindow* (*promptForInt()*, *promptForString()*, and *promptForDouble()*). And because *MyWindow* extends *DIYWindow*, all classes that extend *MyWindow* also have access to all the public and protected methods in *DIYWindow* (*print()* and *input()*).

Project 9 – Guess My Number

If the computer picks a <u>random</u> number between 0 and 100, how long would it take you to guess the number? Your next program will be a number guessing game.

Here's a screenshot of the Guess My Number program:

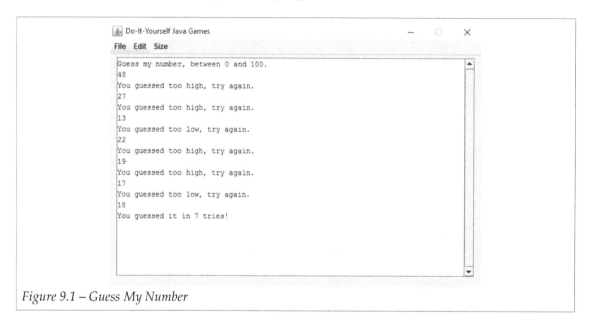

Figure 9.1 – Guess My Number

Lesson 9.1 – Comparing Numbers

In this lesson, you'll compare the value of the user's guess with a chosen number to see if he/she guessed it, guessed too high, or guessed too low.

Try It

Start writing the next program.

1. Create a new *Java project* called *Guess My Number* and add *My Window* and *DIYJava.jar* to the project. (Hint: *My Window* is a Java project, *DIYJava.jar* is an external JAR file. To add the *My Window* project, click the *Projects* tab, click *Add...*, and select *My Window*. To add the *DIYJava.jar* external JAR file, click the *Libraries* tab, and click *Add External Jar....*)

2. Create a new *package* called _____._____.guessmynumber in the project.

3. Create a new *class* called *GuessMyNumber,* with superclass *MyWindow* and with a stub for *main()* and its constructors.

4. Add code to *main()* to call the *GuessMyNumber* constructor.

Listing 9-1, from GuessMyNumber.java

```
package annette.godtland.guessmynumber;

import annette.godtland.mywindow.MyWindow;

public class GuessMyNumber extends MyWindow {

    public GuessMyNumber() {
    }

    public static void main(String[] args) {
        _____;

    }
}
```

1. Declare an integer called *myNumber* with a value of 56.

2. Declare another integer called *myGuess* and set its value by prompting the user to "Guess my number between 0 and 100".

Listing 9-2, from GuessMyNumber.java

```
    . . .

    public GuessMyNumber() {
        _____  _____ = 56;
        int _____ =
promptFor____ ("_____");
    }
    . . .
```

In Java, use a double equal sign, ==, to check if two numbers are equal. For example, to check if a variable named *score* is equal to 100, use:

```
if (score == 100)
```

1. Check if *myGuess* is equal to *myNumber.*

2. If it's equal, print the message "You guessed it!".

Listing 9-3, from GuessMyNumber.java

```
    . . .

    public GuessMyNumber() {
```

```
int myNumber = 56;
int myGuess = promptForInt("Guess my number, between 0 and 100.");
if(_____) {
    print("_____");
}
}
. . .
```

Use these operators to compare numbers:

- == returns true of they are equal.

- != returns true if they aren't equal.

- \> returns true if the first number is greater than the second number.

- \>= returns true if the first number is greater than or equal to the second number.

- < returns true if the first number is less than the second number.

- <= returns true if the first number is less than or equal to the second number.

1. What would you change to instead check if the numbers aren't equal?

2. Tell the user if the numbers aren't equal.

Listing 9-4, from GuessMyNumber.java

```
. . .

public GuessMyNumber() {
    int myNumber = 56;
    int myGuess = promptForInt("Guess my number, between 0 and 100.");
    if(myGuess _____ myNumber) {
        print("_____");
    }
}
. . .
```

1. If the numbers aren't equal, prompt the user to enter another number and put his/her answer into *myGuess*.

Listing 9-5, from GuessMyNumber.java

```
. . .

public GuessMyNumber() {
    int myNumber = 56;
    int myGuess = promptForInt("Guess my number, between 0 and 100.");
    if(myGuess != myNumber) {
        myGuess = _____("Sorry, that's not it. Try again.");
```

```
        }
    }
    . . .
```

1. How would you change the code to keep asking the user to try again while *myGuess* isn't equal to *myNumber*? (Hint: you learned about *while* loops when you wanted to repeat a block of code.)

Listing 9-6, from GuessMyNumber.java

```
    . . .

public GuessMyNumber() {
    int myNumber = 56;
    int myGuess = promptForInt("Guess my number, between 0 and 100.");
    _____(myGuess != myNumber) {
        myGuess = promptForInt("Sorry, that's not it. Try again.");
    }
}
    . . .
```

1. Run the program now. Enter some wrong guesses, then enter the correct number, 56. What happened?

2. Add code after the while block to tell the user he/she guessed the correct number.

Listing 9-7, from GuessMyNumber.java

```
    . . .

public GuessMyNumber() {
    int myNumber = 56;
    int myGuess = promptForInt("Guess my number, between 0 and 100.");
    while(myGuess != myNumber) {
        myGuess = promptForInt("Sorry, that's not it. Try again.");
    }
    print("_____");
}
    . . .
```

The program works a little better now, but it will take a long time for someone to really guess a number between 0 and 100. Give the user a clue.

1. What would you add to the program to tell the user if his/her guess is too low or too high?

Listing 9-8, from GuessMyNumber.java

```
    . . .
```

```
public GuessMyNumber() {

    . . .

    while(myGuess != myNumber) {
        if (myGuess ____ myNumber) {
            myGuess = promptForInt("You guessed too low, try again.");
        }
        else if (myGuess ____ myNumber) {
            myGuess = promptForInt("You guessed too high, try again.");
        }
    }
    print("You guessed it!");

        . . .
```

Key Points and More

- You can compare numbers in any statement that checks for true or false, such as in *if* statements or *while* loops.

- Use these operators to compare numbers:

    - == returns true of they are equal.

    - != returns true if they aren't equal.

    - > returns true if the first number is greater than the second number.

    - >= returns true if the first number is greater than or equal to the second number.

    - < returns true if the first number is less than the second number.

    - <= returns true if the first number is less than or equal to the second number.

- Make sure you don't mistakenly use the assignment operator, =, instead of the equal operator, ==, to compare two numbers. This doesn't give a syntax error. Instead, assignment is considered true or false, which has nothing to do with whether the numbers are equal. When this happens, it can be hard to figure out why your program doesn't work the way you want. Always use the double equal sign, ==, to check if two numbers are equal.

- Make sure you don't mistakenly use the double equal sign to compare strings. This will almost always return false, even if the two strings are made up of the same characters. Always use *equals()* to check if two strings are equal.

Lesson 9.2 – Generate Random Numbers

In this lesson, you'll change the program to pick a random number for the user to guess.

Try It

1. Create a new random number generator, a *Random,* called *rand* by adding code exactly as shown.

Listing 9-9, from GuessMyNumber.java

```
    . . .

public GuessMyNumber() {
    Random rand = new Random();
    int myNumber = 56;
    int myGuess = promptForInt("Guess my number, between 0 and 100.");
    while(myGuess != myNumber) {

        . . .
```

This will cause a syntax error:

```
Random cannot be resolved to a type.
```

1. Rest your cursor on the word marked as the syntax error to open *Quick Fix.*

2. Choose *Import 'Random' (java.util)* to fix the error.

Throughout the lessons, you'll often receive the syntax error that something couldn't be resolved to a type. When you receive that error, use Quick Fix to import the needed class. The class, along with its package name, will be added to the import statements at the beginning of the file.

Random's *nextInt()* method returns a random number between zero and one less than the number you give it. For example: to get 10 possible values from 0 through 9, use:

```
rand.nextInt(10);
```

If you want the values to start at 1 instead of 0, add 1 to the results. For example, to get 6 possible values from 1 through 6, use:

```
rand.nextInt(6) + 1;
```

1. Can you guess what parameter is needed for *nextInt()* to generate a random number from 0 through 100 for *myNumber*? (Hint: how many numbers are there if you include 0 and 100?)

Listing 9-10, from GuessMyNumber.java

```
    . . .
```

```
public GuessMyNumber() {
    Random rand = new Random();
    int myNumber = rand.nextInt(_____);
    int myGuess = promptForInt("Guess my number, between 0 and 100.");
    while(myGuess != myNumber) {

        . . .
```

Key Points and More

- Random, like String, is another type of data. New types of data are created as classes. Almost every new class used in your program will be marked as a syntax error. The error message will state that the class cannot be resolved to a type. Such classes must be imported. Import statements must include the full class name, including its package.

- Use *Quick Fix* to easily add import statements for classes new to the program.

- Open *Quick Fix* in one of several different ways:

    - Rest your mouse on the word in the code marked as a syntax error.

    - Right-click on the word in the code marked as a syntax error and choose *Quick Fix*.

    - Click on the syntax error mark in the left margin of the edit pane.

    - Right-click on the message in the *Problems* pane at the bottom of Eclipse and choose *Quick Fix*.

- Random's *nextInt()* returns a random number between zero and one less than the number you give it. For example:

    - To get 5 possible values from 0 through 4, use:

```
nextInt(5)
```
    - To get 5 possible values from 1 through 5, use:

```
nextInt(5)+1
```

Lesson 9.3 – Increment Integers

Programs often need to <u>increment</u> an integer, add a number to itself. In fact, it's so common that there are shortcut ways to do so. This lesson will cover two ways to increment an integer.

Try It

How many tries did it take you to guess the number? Let the program count the number of tries.

1. Declare an integer called *count* to hold the number of guesses. Start the count at 1 after

the user makes his/her first guess.

Listing 9-11, from GuessMyNumber.java

```
   . . .

public GuessMyNumber() {
   Random rand = new Random();
   int myNumber = rand.nextInt(101);
   int myGuess = promptForInt("Guess my number, between 0 and 100.");
   int _____ = _____;
   while(myGuess != myNumber) {

      . . .
```

1. Add 1 to the count after every guess.

Listing 9-12, from GuessMyNumber.java

```
   . . .

public GuessMyNumber() {

      . . .

   while(myGuess != myNumber) {
      if (myGuess < myNumber) {
         myGuess = promptForInt("You guessed too low, try again.");
      }
      else if (myGuess > myNumber) {
         myGuess = promptForInt("You guessed too high, try again.");
      }
      count = count + _____;
   }
      . . .
```

1. Then when the user finally guesses the number, print how many guesses he/she took.

Listing 9-13, from GuessMyNumber.java

```
   . . .

public GuessMyNumber() {

      . . .

   while(myGuess != myNumber) {
      if (myGuess < myNumber) {
         myGuess = promptForInt("You guessed too low, try again.");
```

```
          }
          else if (myGuess > myNumber) {
             myGuess = promptForInt("You guessed too high, try again.");
          }
          count = count + 1;
       }
       print("You guessed it in " + _____ + " tries!");
    }
       . . .
```

The Guess My Number program is now complete. But there are a couple Java shortcuts you could have used.

You can use the += assignment operator to increment a variable. For example, to increment variable *b* by 8 use:

b += 8;

    1.   How would you increment *count* by 1 using the += operator?

Listing 9-14, from GuessMyNumber.java

```
       . . .

    public GuessMyNumber() {

          . . .

          else if (myGuess > myNumber) {
             myGuess = promptForInt("You guessed too high, try again.");
          }
          count __ __;

          . . .
```

Similar assignment operators can be used to decrease, multiply, or divide a variable by a number: -=, *=, and /=.

Another often-used shortcut is when you want to increment or <u>decrement</u> a variable by 1. For example, to increment *b* by 1, use:

b++;

Similarly, to decrease *b* by 1, use:

b--;

    1.   Use the ++ operator to increment *count* by 1.

Listing 9-15, from GuessMyNumber.java

```
       . . .
```

```
public GuessMyNumber() {

    . . .

    else if (myGuess > myNumber) {
       myGuess = promptForInt("You guessed too high, try again.");
    }
    count _____;

    . . .
```

This is the end of the Guess My Number program.

1. Export your Guess My Number program if you want to run it without Eclipse.

Key Points and More

- Combined arithmetic assignment operators are quick ways for a variable to do an operation on itself.

  - a += b; adds *b* to *a* and puts the result in *a*.

  - a -= b; subtracts *b* from *a* and puts the result in *a*.

  - a *= b; multiplies *a* times *b* and puts the result in *a*.

  - a /= b; divides *a* by *b* and puts the result in *a*.

- Increment/decrement adds or subtracts one to/from itself:

  - a++; adds 1 to *a* and puts the result in *a*.

  - a--; subtracts 1 from *a* and puts the result in *a*.

Project 10 – Temperature Converter

Next, you'll write a program to convert Fahrenheit to Celsius and Celsius to Fahrenheit.

Here's a screenshot of the Temperature Converter program:

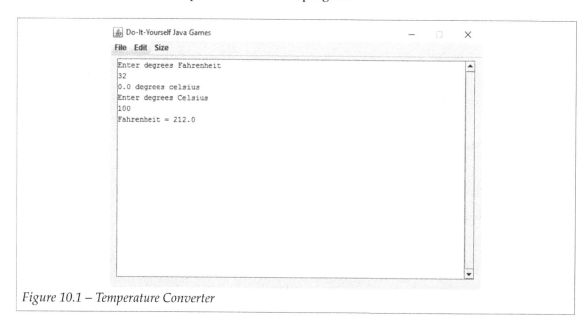

Figure 10.1 – Temperature Converter

Lesson 10.1 – Order of Operation

Java lets you add, subtract, multiply, divide, and call other methods, all in a single statement. Java performs those operations in a default order.

This lesson shows you how to control the order Java does the operations when more than one operation is in a statement.

Try It

Start writing the next program:

1. Create a new *Java project* called *Temperature Converter* and add *My Window* and *DIYJava.jar* to the project.

2. Create a new *package* called _____._____.*temperatureconverter* in the project.

3. Create a new *class* called *TemperatureConverter,* with superclass *MyWindow* and with a stub for *main()* and its constructors.

4. Add code to *main()* to call the *TemperatureConverter* constructor.

5. Add code to the constructor to print the value of 1 + 2 + 3.

Listing 10-1, from TemperatureConverter.java

```
package annette.godtland.temperatureconverter;

import annette.godtland.mywindow.MyWindow;

public class TemperatureConverter extends MyWindow {

    public TemperatureConverter() {
        print(__ + ___ + ___);
    }

    public static void main(String[] args) {
        _____;
    }
}
```

What did the program print? If you expected 6, you would have been right.

1. Change the program to print 1 + 2 * 3.

Listing 10-2, from TemperatureConverter.java

```
    . . .

    public TemperatureConverter() {
        print(1 + 2 __ 3);
    }
    . . .
```

What did the program print? If you expected 9, you would have been wrong. It prints 7.

Java does all multiplication and division first, then all addition and subtraction. To do these operations in a different order, put parentheses around the things you want done first.

Can you guess what these statements would print?

```
print((1+2)*3);
print(1+(2*3));
```
The first statement would print 9, the second would print 7.

To convert degrees Fahrenheit to degrees Celsius, subtract 32 from the degrees Fahrenheit, then multiply the difference by 5 and divide by 9.

1. Remove the current print statement from the constructor.

2. Prompt the user to enter degrees Fahrenheit. Put his/her answer in a double so you can have decimal numbers.

3. Convert degrees Fahrenheit to degrees Celsius and print the result. (Hint: add parentheses to the code to make sure it does the subtraction first.)

Listing 10-3, from TemperatureConverter.java

```
   . . .

public TemperatureConverter() {
   double f = _____("Enter degrees Fahrenheit.");
   print( f - 32 * 5 / 9);
}
   . . .
```

If you put the parentheses in the correct places, entering 32 degrees Fahrenheit should give you 0 degrees Celsius.

1. Add the text, " degrees Celsius" to the print statement so it's clear what the number represents.

Listing 10-4, from TemperatureConverter.java

```
   . . .

public TemperatureConverter() {
   double f = promptForDouble("Enter degrees Fahrenheit.");
   print((f - 32) * 5 / 9 + "_____");
}
   . . .
```

To convert Celsius to Fahrenheit, multiply the Celsius degrees by 1.8 then add 32. You don't need any additional parentheses to make this do the calculations in the right order.

1. Prompt the user to enter degrees Celsius and put his/her answer in a double called *c*.

2. To calculate the Fahrenheit value, multiply degrees Celsius by 1.8 then add 32. Print the Fahrenheit value.

Listing 10-5, from TemperatureConverter.java

```
   . . .

public TemperatureConverter() {
   double f = promptForDouble("Enter degrees Fahrenheit");
   print((f - 32) * 5 / 9 + " degrees Celsius");
```

```
    double c = _____("Enter degrees Celsius");
    print(1.8 * c + 32);
}
    . . .
```

32 degrees Fahrenheit should be converted to 0 degrees Celsius. 0 degrees Celsius should be converted to 32 degrees Fahrenheit.

But what if you add text in front of the equation that prints the results of 1.8 * c + 32? This is another common ordering mistake.

1. Add "Fahrenheit = " to the front of the second calculated temperature.

Listing 10-6, from TemperatureConverter.java

```
    . . .

public TemperatureConverter() {
    double f = promptForDouble("Enter degrees Fahrenheit");
    print((f - 32) * 5 / 9 + " degrees celsius");
    double c = promptForDouble("Enter degrees Celsius");
    print("Fahrenheit = " + 1.8 * c + 32);
}
    . . .
```

For 0 degrees Celsius, the program now prints:

```
Fahrenheit = 0.032
```

What happened? It knew the first plus sign meant to join strings, so it thought all plus signs were meant to join strings. So 1.8 times 0 was 0.0, then it joined 32 onto 0.0, to make it 0.032.

1. Add parentheses to calculate the temperature before it joins the result to the first string.

Listing 10-7, from TemperatureConverter.java

```
    . . .

public TemperatureConverter() {
    double f = promptForDouble("Enter degrees Fahrenheit");
    print((f - 32) * 5 / 9 + " degrees celsius");
    double c = promptForDouble("Enter degrees Celsius");
    print("Fahrenheit = " + (1.8 * c + 32));
}
    . . .
```

This is the end of the Temperature Converter program.

1. Export your Temperature Converter program if you want to run it without Eclipse.

Key Points and More

- Java normally does all multiplication and division in a statement before it does addition and subtraction.

- If Java sees the first plus sign is for joining strings, it assumes the next plus signs are also for joining strings.

- Use parentheses to change the usual order of operations when more than one operation is in a statement. The operations in the innermost parentheses will be done first.

Project 11 – Ten Little Chocolates

Ten Little Chocolates is a more socially acceptable version of an old children's song that teaches counting from one to ten, then backwards again, from ten to one. This project will write the words to the Ten Little Chocolates song using a very useful type of loop.

Here's a screenshot of the Ten Little Chocolates program:

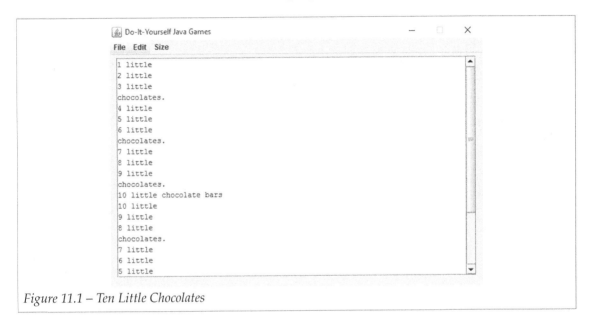

Figure 11.1 – Ten Little Chocolates

Lesson 11.1 – For Loops

A *for* loop allows you to easily repeat a block of code a set number of times.

Try It

Start writing the next program:

1. Create a new *Java project* called *Ten Little Chocolates* and add *My Window* and *DIYJava.jar* to the project.

2. Create a new *package* called _____._____.tenlittlechocolates in the project.

3. Create a new *class* called *TenLittleChocolates,* with superclass *MyWindow* and with a stub for *main()* and its constructors.

4. Add code to *main()* to call the *TenLittleChocolates* constructor.

Listing 11-1, from TenLittleChocolates.java

```
package annette.godtland.tenlittlechocolates;

import annette.godtland.mywindow.MyWindow;

public class TenLittleChocolates extends MyWindow {

    public TenLittleChocolates() {

    }

    public static void main(String[] args) {
        _____;
    }
}
```

1. Add code in the constructor exactly as shown.

Listing 11-2, from TenLittleChocolates.java

```
    . . .

    public TenLittleChocolates() {
        for(int i=1; i<4; i++) {
            print(i + " little");
        }
        print("chocolates.");
    }
    . . .
```

What did it print? Those are the first four lines of the Ten Little Chocolates song.

```
1 little
2 little
3 little
chocolates.
```

The next four lines of the song are supposed to be:

```
4 little
5 little
6 little
chocolates.
```

1. What do you think you should use in the *for* statement to print the next four lines of the song?

Listing 11-3, from TenLittleChocolates.java

```
      . . .

   public TenLittleChocolates() {
      for(int i=1; i<4; i++) {
         print(i + " little");
      }
      print("chocolates.");
      for(int i=____; i<____; i++) {
         print(i + " little");
      }
      print("chocolates.");
   }
      . . .
```

By now you can probably guess how to write the code to print the next five lines of the song:

```
7 little
8 little
9 little
chocolates.
10 little chocolate bars.
```
   1.   Print the next five lines of the song.

Listing 11-4, from TenLittleChocolates.java

```
      . . .

   public TenLittleChocolates() {

      . . .

      for(int i=4; i<7; i++) {
         print(i + " little");
      }
      print("chocolates.");
      for(_____) {
         print(_____);
      }
      print(_____);
      print(_____);
   }
      . . .
```

The song continues by counting down the number of chocolates. The next five lines should be

```
10 little
9 little
```

```
8 little
chocolates.
```

1. What do you think you need in the for loop to tell it to start counting at 10, stop before it reaches 7, and subtract one from the counting variable each time?

Listing 11-5, from TenLittleChocolates.java

```
    . . .

  public TenLittleChocolates() {

      . . .

     print("10 little chocolate bars");
     for(int i=_____; i___ _____; i___) {
        print(i + " little");
     }
     print("chocolates.");

      . . .
```

Did you get it right? The rest of the song goes like this:

```
7 little
6 little
5 little
chocolates.
4 little
3 little
2 little
chocolates.
1 little chocolate bar.
```

1. Add the rest of the code to finish the remaining nine lines of the song.

Listing 11-6, from TenLittleChocolates.java

```
    . . .

  public TenLittleChocolates() {

      . . .

     for(int i=10; i>7; i--) {
        print(i + " little");
     }
     print("chocolates.");
     _____ {
        _____;
     }
```

```
        _____;
        _____ {
            _____;
}
        _____;
        _____;

    . . .
```

This is the end of the Ten Little Chocolates program.

1. Export your Ten Little Chocolates program if you want to run it without Eclipse.

Key Points and More

- Use a *for* loop to repeat a block of code a set number of times.

- A *for* loop will repeat a block of code until a condition is met, much the same as a *while* loop repeats a block of code. *for* loops are different from *while* loops because you also declare an integer (an <u>index</u>) for the loop and how much to change that index each time through the loop.

- The index for the *for* loop can be used within the block of code.

- The index for the *for* loop can have any valid variable name. However, if the integer doesn't represent anything more than a counter, programmers usually name it *i. i* stands for index.

- The index of a *for* loop can start at any valid integer and be modified by any regular Java code. It is usually modified with the increment or decrement operator.

- The condition of a *for* loop can be any valid condition you would normally put in an *if* statement. It is usually compared with a <u>minimum</u> or <u>maximum</u> value.

Project 12 – Word Scramble

This next program creates a word <u>scramble</u> puzzle. The program will scramble the letters in a list of words for others to try to <u>unscramble</u>.

Here's a screenshot of the Word Scramble program:

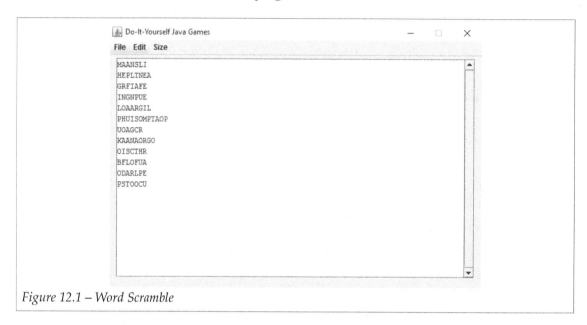

Figure 12.1 – Word Scramble

Lesson 12.1 – Comments

Comments are notes you can put in a program to remind yourself of what you wanted the code to do. Comments are ignored when the program runs, so you can type anything you want in the comments. Comments are also often used to label sections of code.

In this lesson, you'll use comments to plan the code to scramble a word.

Try It

Start writing the next program:

1. Create a new *Java project* called *Word Scramble* and add *My Window* and *DIYJava.jar* to the project.

2. Create a new *package* called _____._____.*wordscramble* in the project.

3. Create a new *class* called *WordScramble,* with superclass *MyWindow* and with a stub for *main()* and its constructors.

4. Add code to *main()* to call the *WordScramble* constructor.

Listing 12-1, from WordScramble.java

```
package annette.godtland.wordscramble;

import annette.godtland.mywindow.MyWindow;

public class WordScramble extends MyWindow {

    public WordScramble() {

    }

    public static void main(String[] args) {
        _____;
    }
}
```

Put the code to scramble a string in its own method so it can be used more than once.

1. Define a private method called *scramble()* that takes one parameter, a string called *word,* and returns a string.

2. In *scramble(),* declare a string called *scrambled,* assign it an initial value of an empty string, and return that string.

Listing 12-2, from WordScramble.java

```
    . . .

    private String scramble(String word) {
        String scrambled = "";

        return scrambled;
    }
    . . .
```

Add code to the constructor:

1. Create a string called *word* with a value of "ANIMALS".

2. Call the *scramble()* method with *word* as its parameter and assign the results of that call to a new string called *scrambled.*

3. Print that new string.

Listing 12-3, from WordScramble.java

```
    . . .

public WordScramble() {
    String word = "_____";
    String _____ = scramble(word);
    print(_____);
}
    . . .
```

Do you know how to scramble a word? It's easier if you make it into smaller steps. To scramble a word:

· Pick a random letter from the original word.

· Remove that letter from the original word.

· Add that letter to a new word.

· Repeat these steps until all letters have been removed from the original word.

To type comments into code, start the line with two forward slashes, //. Anything you type after the // on that line is a comment.

1. Type comments in *scramble()* to describe the steps to scramble a word.

Listing 12-4, from WordScramble.java

```
    . . .

private String scramble(String word) {
    String scrambled = "";

    // pick a random letter from the original word

    // remove that letter from the original word

    // _____

    // _____

    return scrambled;
}
    . . .
```

Key Points and More

· Difficult code is easier to write if you do it in smaller steps.

- Use comments to label what you want the code to do.

- It doesn't matter what you type in comment statements. Comments are ignored when the program runs. Comments are only there as notes to you, the programmer.

- To enter a comment, put a double forward slash, //, at the beginning of the comment line. I use this form of comment the most.

- The // comments can also be placed to the right of your code. For example:

```
int count = 0;   // count the number of guesses
```

- There is another type of comment that goes across more than one line. Mark the beginning of a comment that crosses lines with a forward slash followed by an asterisk, /*. Mark the end of the comment with an asterisk followed by a forward slash, */.

- The // form of comment always ends at the end of the line in which it started. The /* ... */ form of comment starts at the /* and continues across all lines to the */ .

  - I'll sometimes use the /* ... */ form of comment to "comment out" a section of code I want to temporarily remove from a program. Code in a comment is ignored when the program runs. It's easy to put the code "back in" later by just removing the /* and */ symbols.

Lesson 12.2 – String Length and Substring

Your program will need to know the length of a string, and be able to make a new string from part of a string. For that, you'll use String's *length()* and *substring()* methods.

Try It

1. Create a random number generator called *rand* in *scramble()*.

Listing 12-5, from WordScramble.java

```
    . . .

private String scramble(String word) {
    String scrambled = "";
    Random rand = _____ ;

    // pick a random letter from the original word

    . . .
```

Now write code for one step at a time, as stated in the comments. First, pick a random letter from the original word.

Do you remember how to generate a random number? Use Rand's *nextInt()* to pick a random number less than a given number. *scramble()* needs to pick a number less than the number of letters in *word*.

String has a method called *length()* that returns the number of characters in the string. For example, to find the length of a string called name, use:

```
name.length();
```
1. Add code to pick a random number less than the length of *word*.

Listing 12-6, from WordScramble.java

```
    . . .

    private String scramble(String word) {

        . . .

        // pick a random letter from the original word
        int length = word._____;
        int index = rand.nextInt(_____);

        . . .
```

A couple other string methods you'll use in this lesson are:

- *substring(beginIndex)* returns a string of the characters from *beginIndex* to the end of the string. *beginIndex* must be an integer less than the length of the string.

- *substring(beginIndex, endIndex)* returns a string of the characters from *beginIndex* to *endIndex*, but doesn't include the character at *endIndex*. *beginIndex* and *endIndex* must be integers less than the length of the string. *beginIndex* must be less than *endIndex*.

The characters in a string are numbered starting at 0. For example, the string "Hello World" has 11 characters, numbered 0 through 10, like this:

```
Hello World
01234567890
```
If your code had a variable called *greeting*, with a value of "Hello World", this code:

```
greeting.length()
```
would return 11.

This code:

```
greeting.substring(6)
```
would return "World".

This code:

```
greeting.substring(0, 7)
```

would return "Hello W".

And this code:

```
greeting.substring(4, 5)
```
would return just the letter "o".

In your code, *index* is a random number greater than or equal to zero and less than the length of *word*.

1. Use the *substring()* method to get the one letter at *index*. (Hint: follow the above example that returned only one letter.)

Listing 12-7, from WordScramble.java

```
    . . .

    private String scramble(String word) {

        . . .

        // pick a random letter from the original word
        int length = word.length();
        int index = rand.nextInt(length);
        String letter = word.substring(_____, _____);

        . . .
```

The comment for the next step says to remove that letter from the original word.

Unfortunately, there's no string method that removes a character from a given position. Instead, you'll:

- Create a string of the text before the character.

- Create another string of the text after the character.

- Join the two strings together.

1. Add code to do the above steps. (Hint: use both versions of *substring()* with the different number of parameters.)

Listing 12-8, from WordScramble.java

```
    . . .

    private String scramble(String word) {

        . . .

    // remove that letter from the original word
```

```
String firstString = word.substring(_____,_____);
String secondString = word.substring(_____);
word = _____ + _____;
```

   . . .

Key Points and More

- Use String's *length()* method to find the length of a string.

- Use String's *substring()* method to get part of a string.

  - The characters in a string are numbered starting at zero. Therefore, the last character of a string is numbered one less than the length of the string.

  - If you pass only one integer parameter into *substring()*, it will return the portion of the string starting at that index, through the end of the string.

  - If you pass two integer parameters into *substring()*, it will return the portion of the string from the first index to the second index, but it won't include the character at the second index.

Lesson 12.3 – Print to the Console

You can print to the *Console* pane of Eclipse without affecting what the user sees printed to the program window.

In this lesson, you'll print values of variables to the *Console* pane with code you will remove later.

Try It

When you run the Word Scramble program, it just opens an empty window. How can you tell if it scrambled the word correctly?

Java has a method, *System.out.println()*, that prints to the *Console* pane of Eclipse instead of to the program window. Use *System.out.println()* the way you used *print()*. For example, to print the value of a variable called *name* to the *Console* pane, use:

```
System.out.println("name = " + name);
```
   1. Use *System.out.println()* to print the value of *index*, *letter*, and *word* to the *Console* pane.

Listing 12-9, from WordScramble.java

   . . .

```
   private String scramble(String word) {
```

```
    . . .

    // pick a random letter from the original word
    int length = word.length();
    int index = rand.nextInt(length);
    System.out.println("index = " + _____);
    String letter = word.substring(index, index+1);
    System.out.println("letter = " + _____);

    // remove that letter from the original word
    String firstString = word.substring(0,index);
    String secondString = word.substring(index+1);
    word = firstString + secondString;
    System.out.println("word = " + _____);

    . . .
```

When you run the program, it should print to the *Console* pane of Eclipse.

Based on the value it generated for *index*, did it remove the correct letter?

1. Run the program a few times.

It should remove a different letter each time.

The next step of the program is to add that letter to the new word.

1. Add the picked letter to *scrambled* and print *scrambled* to the *Console* pane.

Listing 12-10, from WordScramble.java

```
    . . .

    private String scramble(String word) {

        . . .

        // add that letter to a new word
        scrambled += _____;
        System.out.println("scrambled = " + _____);

    . . .
```

The next comment says to repeat these steps. In other words, wrap the steps in a loop that repeats until all the letters have been removed from the original word.

How will you know when all the letters have been removed? (Hint: what will the length of the word be after all the letters have been removed?)

Make these changes to the code:

1. Repeat the code that picks the random letter, removes it from the original word, and adds it to the new word, until all the letters have been removed from the original word. (Hint: use a *while* loop.)

2. Move the comment about repeating these steps to the top of the loop.

Listing 12-11, from WordScramble.java

```
   . . .

   private String scramble(String word) {

      . . .

      // repeat these steps until all the letters have been removed from
the original word
      while (word.length()>____) {
         // pick a random letter from the original word
         int length = word.length();

         . . .

         // add that letter to a new word
         scrambled += letter;
         System.out.println("scrambled = " + scrambled);

      }
      return scrambled;

      . . .
```

Key Points and More

- Print to the *Console* pane of Eclipse using *System.out.println()*.

- Use any string as the parameter for *System.out.println()*.

- Add *System.out.println()* statements to your program to see what the program is doing without printing to the program window.

- Remove all *System.out.println()* statements once your program works as planned. You'll remove the *System.out.println()* statements from this program in a later lesson.

Lesson 12.4 – Arrays

An <u>array</u> is a list of data of all the same type. In this lesson you'll put a list of words to scramble in an array of strings.

Try It

Arrays hold lists of data. Data in arrays must all be of the same type, such as all string data or all int data. To declare an array variable, put square brackets, [ ], after its name. For example, to declare an array of strings called *myFamily*, use:

```
String myFamily[]
```

One way to put data in an array is to assign a list to the array when you declare it. To type a list of data, put the data in curly brackets with a comma between each item. To assign a list of three strings to the array *myFamily*, use:

```
String myFamily[] = {"Annette", "Paul", "Leah"};
```

Make the following changes to the constructor:

1. Replace the string called *word* with an array of strings called *words*.

2. Add your own animals to this list of words so there are 12 words.

3. Add a comment above the array to describe that you are creating a list of words

Listing 12-12, from WordScramble.java

```
    . . .

    public WordScramble() {

        // create a list of words
        String words[] = {"ANIMALS", "ELEPHANT", "GIRAFFE", "PENGUIN",
            "GORIALLA","_____", "_____", "_____",
            "_____", "_____", "_____","_____"};

        String scrambled = scramble(word);
        print(scrambled);

        . . .
```

There will now be syntax errors in the program. You will fix those errors with the next code change.

To use an item in an array, put the item's index in square brackets. Like string indexes, array indexes start at 0. So an array with 12 items would have index values of 0 through 11. For example, to refer to the first item in the list called *myFamily*, use:

```
myFamily[0]
```

To refer to the third item in the list, use:

```
myFamily[2]
```

To find out how many items are in the list, use:

```
myFamily.length
```

Note, there are no parentheses after *length*.

1. Change the code so it scrambles the first word in the list. (Hint: pass the first item in *words* to *scramble()*.)

Listing 12-13, from WordScramble.java

```
    . . .

public WordScramble() {

    String words[] = {"ANIMALS", "ELEPHANT", "GIRAFFE", "PENGUIN",
        "GORIALLA", "HIPPOPOTAMUS", "COUGAR", "KANAGAROO", "OSTRICH",
        "BUFFALO", "LEOPARD", "OCTOPUS"};

    String scrambled = scramble(_____);
    print(scrambled);

        . . .
```

1. Run the program and see if it scrambles the first word in the list.

For practice, change the program so it scrambles the last word in the list:

1. Before it scrambles the word, create an integer called *numberOfWords*, whose value is the number of words in the list. (Hint: use array's *length*.)

2. Change the code to scramble the last word in the list. (Hint: use *numberOfWords*. Hint: is the index of the last word the same as *numberOfWords*?)

Listing 12-14, from WordScramble.java

```
    . . .

public WordScramble() {

    . . .

    int numberOfWords = words._____;
    String scrambled = scramble(_____);
    print(scrambled);

        . . .
```

Run the program and see if it scrambles the last word in the list.

So now you know how to use the first word in the list, the last word in the list, and how many words are in the list. That's all the information you need to create a *for* loop.

1. Put the scramble and print statements into a *for* loop to scramble and print each word in

the list.

Listing 12-15, from WordScramble.java

```
    . . .

  public WordScramble() {

      . . .

    int numberOfWords = words.length;

    // for each word in the list, scramble the word and print it
    for (int i=_____; i<_____; i___) {
       String scrambled = scramble(words[_____]);
       print(scrambled);
    }
      . . .
```

When you run the program, it should produce a list of twelve scrambled words. If you don't like how it scrambled some of the words, run the program again.

You can copy the list of words from the window and paste it into your own document, e-mail, or other program.

1.   Delete the *System.out.println()* statements from the program.

There's no need for the *System.out.println()* statements anymore, but leave the comments in. Comments are nice to always remind you of what you wanted the code to do.

Key Points and More

- Arrays are lists of data. Once an array is declared, its size cannot be changed.

- Arrays can only hold one type of data, such as strings, ints, doubles, or even types you define yourself. You declare the type of data the array will hold when you declare the array.

- One way to put data in an array is to assign to it a comma-separated list of items in curly brackets. Another way to put data into an array will be covered in a later lesson.

- To use to an item in an array, put its index number in square brackets, [ ].

- Array items index numbers start at 0. Therefore, the index of the last item is one less than the size of the array.

- To get the size of an array, use its *length,* like the following code. Note: there are no parentheses after *length.*

```
names.length
```

Lesson 12.5 – Static Methods

A static method only uses the data passed in as its parameters. Static methods are easy to call from any other class.

In this lesson, you'll make the *scramble()* method a static method so you can easily scramble words for other programs too.

Try It

First, move the scramble method to a different class.

Start creating another class:

1. Create a new *Java project* called *My String Methods*. Nothing else needs to be added to the project.

2. Create a new *package* called _____._____.*mystringmethods* in the project.

3. Create a new *class* called *MyStringMethods,* with *Object* as the default superclass and no stub for *main()* nor constructors.

Listing 12-16, from MyStringMethods.java

```
package annette.godtland.mystringmethods;

public class MyStringMethods {

}
```

1. Cut the entire *scramble()* method from the *WordScramble* class and paste it into the *MyStringMethods* class.

Listing 12-17, from MyStringMethods.java

```
. . .

public class MyStringMethods {

  private String scramble(String word) {
    String scrambled = "";
    Random rand = new Random();
    // repeat these steps until all the letters have been removed from
the original word
    while (word.length()>0) {
      // pick a random letter from the original word
```

```
        int length = word.length();
        int index = rand.nextInt(length);
        String letter = word.substring(index, index+1);

        // remove that letter from the original word
        String firstString = word.substring(0,index);
        String secondString = word.substring(index+1);
        word = firstString + secondString;

        // add that letter to a new word
        scrambled += letter;
    }
    return scrambled;
    }
}
```

The *scramble()* method in *MyStringMethods* is declared as private. If you leave it as private, no other classes can use it.

1. Make *scramble()* public by replacing *private* with *public*.

Listing 12-18, from MyStringMethods.java

```
    . . .

_____ String scramble(String word) {
    String scrambled = "";
    Random rand = new Random();

    . . .
```

The *scramble()* method doesn't use any variables other than those declared within it and passed in as its parameters. Nor does the *scramble()* method use any methods that don't come with Java. That means you can declare *scramble()* as static.

1. Make *scramble()* static by adding *static* after *public*.

Listing 12-19, from MyStringMethods.java

```
    . . .

public _____ String scramble(String word) {
    String scrambled = "";
    Random rand = new Random();

    . . .
```

Because *scramble()* is both public and static, other classes can call it using MyStringMethod's class name. For example, to scramble a variable called *name* from another class, the other class would use:

```
MyStringMethods.scramble(name)
```

This is similar to how you used *Integer.parseInt()* in previous lessons. *parseInt()* is a public static method in the Integer class.

In order for another class to use *scramble()*, it must first have the *My String Methods* project in its build path.

1. Go back to the *Word Scramble* project and add the *My String Methods* project to its build path. (Hint: right-click on the project and choose *Build Path / Configure Build Path....*)

2. Next, go to the *WordScramble* class and replace the call to *scramble()* to now call the *scramble()* method in *MyStringMethods*. (Hint: you can use Quick Fix to import the *MyStringMethods* class.)

Listing 12-20, from WordScramble.java

```
    . . .

    public WordScramble() {

        . . .

        // for each word in the list, scramble the word and print it
        for (int i=0; i<numberOfWords; i++) {
            scrambled = _____.scramble(words[i]);

        . . .
```

WordScramble no longer needs to import java.util.Random since it no longer uses the Random class.

1. Delete *import java.util.Random* from WordScramble.

Listing 12-21, from WordScramble.java

```
package annette.godtland.wordscramble;

    (Code was removed from here.)

import annette.godtland.mystringmethods.MyStringMethods;
import annette.godtland.mywindow.MyWindow;

    . . .
```

This is the end of the Word Scramble program.

1. Export your Word Scramble program if you want to run it without Eclipse.

Key Points and More

- Put methods you might want other classes to use into a separate class.

- Methods can be private, protected, or public.

  - A private method can be used only by the class in which it is defined.

  - A protected method can be used in the class in which it is defined and in any class that extends its class.

  - A public method may be be used in any class, even in unrelated classes.

- Make all methods private unless you have a reason for them to be protected or public.

- A static method must be self contained. It can only use the data passed in as parameters or declared in the method itself. And it can only use the methods that come with Java or are also static.

- To declare a method as static, add the word static after the word private, protected, or public.

- Public static methods are easy to call from any class by adding the class name to the front of the method. For example *scramble()* is a public static method of *MyStringMethods*. To call it, use:

```
newWord = MyStringMethods.scramble(word);
```

- Public methods that aren't static require you to first declare a new variable of that type, then call the method from that variable. For example, *nextInt()* is a public method of Random(), but it isn't static. To call it, use:

```
Random rand = new Random();
index = rand.nextInt(10);
```

- In an earlier lesson, *MyWindow* extended *DIYWindow* (the superclass) to share the *promptForInt()* method. Why shouldn't *MyStringMethods* extend *DIYWindow* too? Extend a superclass when the method should be used by classes of the same type (superclass). *scramble()* won't only be used by *DIYWindow* classes or *MyWindow* classes. Therefore *scramble()* should not be in a class that extends those classes.

- Both *scramble()* and *parseInt()* are static methods. Why did you have to add the *My String Methods* project to the build path to use *scramble()*, but you didn't have to add the Integer project to use *parseInt()*? The Integer class is part of the Java Development Kit. So Integer is already included in the build path of every class. *MyStringMethods* isn't part of the Java Development Kit, and so you must add *My String Methods* to the build path yourself.

Project 13 – Secret Code

The Secret Code program lets you to create secret messages to share with your friends.

Here's a screenshot of the Secret Code program:

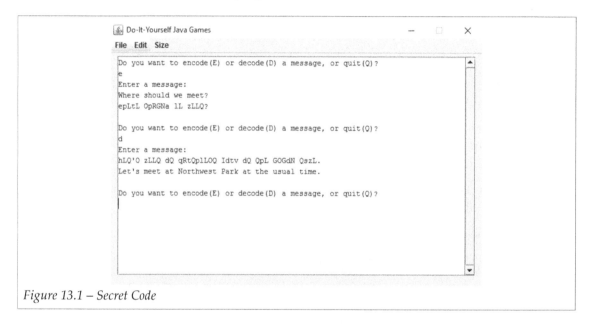

Figure 13.1 – Secret Code

Lesson 13.1 – Write to a File

Write data to a file so the data can be used again by the same program or by another program.

In this lesson, you'll create a key to code and decode messages, then write that key to a file.

Try It

Start writing the next program:

1. Create a new *Java project* called *Secret Code Key* and add *My Window, My String Methods,* and *DIYJava.jar* to the project.

2. Create a new *package* called _____._____.*secretcodekey* in the project.

3. Create a new *class* called *SecretCodeKey*, with superclass *MyWindow* and with a stub for *main()* and its constructors.

4. Add code to *main()* to call the *SecretCodeKey* constructor.

Listing 13-1, from SecretCodeKey.java

```
package annette.godtland.secretcodekey;

import annette.godtland.mywindow.MyWindow;

public class SecretCodeKey extends MyWindow {

   public SecretCodeKey() {

   }

   public static void main(String[] args) {
   _____;
   }
}
```

First, you'll scramble the alphabet. The scrambled alphabet will be the key used to code and decode secret messages.

1. Declare a string called *alphabet* with all the upper and lowercase letters of the alphabet.

Listing 13-2, from SecretCodeKey.java

```
   . . .

   public SecretCodeKey() {
      String alphabet = "_____";
   }
   . . .
```

1. Next, scramble the *alphabet* string and put it in a new string called *scrambled*. (Hint: use *scramble()* in the *MyStringMethods* class.)

Listing 13-3, from SecretCodeKey.java

```
   . . .

   public SecretCodeKey() {
      String alphabet =
"ABCDEFGHIJKLMNOPQRSTUVWXYZabcdefghijklmnopqrstuvwxyz";
      String scrambled = _____.scramble(_____);
   }
   . . .
```

1. Finally, print both the alphabet and the scrambled alphabet.

Listing 13-4, from SecretCodeKey.java

```
    . . .

    public SecretCodeKey() {
       String alphabet =
"ABCDEFGHIJKLMNOPQRSTUVWXYZabcdefghijklmnopqrstuvwxyz";
       String scrambled = MyStringMethods.scramble(alphabet);
       print(_____);
       print(_____);
    }
    . . .
```

When you run the program, you should see both the alphabet and the scrambled alphabet.

Next, you'll save the alphabet and key in a file. Writing to a file involves these steps:

- Open the file by creating a *BufferedWriter* variable.

- Write to the file by calling the BufferedWriter's *write()* method.

  ◦ Repeat calls to *write()* until you've written all the strings to the file.

  ◦ Use BufferedWriter's *newLine()* method if you want the next string to be on a new line of the file.

- Close the file by calling the BufferedWriter's *close()* method.

For example, to write *Hello* and *World* to a file called "myFile.txt", with each word on a separate line of the file, use this code:

```
String fileName = "myFile.txt";
BufferedWriter out = new BufferedWriter(new FileWriter(new
File(fileName)));
out.write("Hello");
out.newLine();
out.write("World");
out.close();
```

1. How would you write *alphabet* and *scrambled* to a file called "key.txt", with each string on a different line of the file?

2. Close the file after you write the two strings to the file.

Listing 13-5, from SecretCodeKey.java

```
    . . .

    public SecretCodeKey() {

       . . .
```

```
print(alphabet);
print(scrambled);

String fileName = "_____";
BufferedWriter out = new BufferedWriter(new FileWriter(new
File(fileName)));
    out.write(_____);
    out._____;
    out.write(_____);
    out._____;

    . . .
```

1. Use Quick Fix to add the needed import statements if you receive messages that something couldn't be resolved to a type.

You'll also receive a syntax error for Unhandled exception, _IOException_.

1. Add a _try/catch_ block around the _BufferedWriter, write()_, and _close()_ statements.

2. If it catches the _IOException_, print a message that the file couldn't be opened.

Listing 13-6, from SecretCodeKey.java

```
    . . .

public SecretCodeKey() {

    . . .

    String fileName = "key.txt";
    try {
        BufferedWriter out = new BufferedWriter(new FileWriter(new
File(fileName)));
        out.write(alphabet);
        out.newLine();
        out.write(scrambled);
        out.close();
    }
    catch (_____) {
        print("Could not open file " + fileName);
    }
    . . .
```

When you run the program, it should still print both the alphabet and the scrambled alphabet in the window. But it should now also print both alphabets into a file called _key.txt_.

1. If you want to see what is in the file your program just created, go to the _Secret Code Key_ folder in your Java work folder and open the _key.txt_ file.

1. If you double-click *key.txt* and it doesn't open the file, right-click on the file and choose *Open with / Notepad* or or any other basic text editor to see what was written to the file.

Key Points and More

- To write to a file, create a *BufferedWriter* variable, call its *write()* method as many times as needed, then close the file using *close()*.

  ◦ Only strings can be written to a file. Therefore, you must convert data into a string before you write it to a file.

  ◦ Call the *newLine()* method to make the next *write()* write to a new line in the file.

  ◦ Write each variable on a new line if each variable will later be read from the file and put into separate variables.

- Writing to a file can cause an *IOException*. Wrap the create, write, and close steps, and any other code you don't want it to run if it can't open the file, in a *try/catch* block.

- Writing to a file will create a new file if it doesn't exist.

- Writing to a file will replace what is in the file if the file already exists.

- Writing to a file without a path name will put the file in your class's Java project folder.

- Include the path name with the file name if you want to save the file in a different location. The path name is the full folder name starting with the drive letter. However, keep in mind that the path must already exist on any computer on which you run the program. For example, to save *key.txt* in *c:\users\Annette*, use the following code. (Hint: use the escape character in front of each backslash in Java strings.)

```
fileName = "c:\\users\\Annette\\key.txt";
```

- Use Notepad or any other basic text editor to see what was written to the file.

- What characters do you want encoded in your secret message? Just the alphabet? Upper and lowercase letters? How about numbers, spaces, or punctuation marks? Put all the characters you want encoded into *alphabet* and run the program again. The more characters you include in the original *alphabet*, the more difficult it will be for someone to try to figure out your encoded message.

Lesson 13.2 – Read from a File, Catch Multiple Exceptions

In this lesson, you'll use another program to read the data written to the file in the last program. More than one exception can occur when you read from a file.

Try It

Start writing the next program:

1. Create a new *Java project* called *Secret Code* and add *My Window* and *DIYJava.jar* to the project.

2. Create a new *package* called _____._____.secretcode in the project.

3. Create a new *class* called *SecretCode*, with superclass *MyWindow* and with a stub for *main()* and its constructors.

4. Add code to *main()* to call the *SecretCode* constructor.

Listing 13-7, from SecretCode.java

```
package annette.godtland.secretcode;

import annette.godtland.mywindow.MyWindow;

public class SecretCode extends MyWindow {

    public SecretCode() {

    }

    public static void main(String[] args) {
        _____;
    }
}
```

The Secret Code program should use the same *key.txt* file you created with the *Secret Code Key* program.

1. Go to the *Secret Code Key* folder in your Java work folder. Copy *key.txt* from that folder and paste it into the *Secret Code* folder in your Java work folder.

To read from a file, you'll do these steps:

- Open the file by creating a *BufferedReader* variable.

- Read a line from the file by calling the BufferedReader's *readLine()* method.

    ◦ Repeat calls to *readLine()* until you've read all the strings you want from the file.

- Close the file by calling the BufferedReader's *close()* method.

For example, to read two lines from a file called "myFile.txt", use this code:

```
String fileName = "myFile.txt";
BufferedReader in = new BufferedReader(new FileReader(new
File(fileName)));
```

```
String line1 = in.readLine();
String line2 = in.readLine();
in.close();
```

1. Read the alphabet and key from a file called "key.txt" and put them in strings called *alphabet* and *key*.

Listing 13-8, from SecretCode.java

```
    . . .

    public SecretCode() {
        String fileName = "_____";
        // read the alphabet and key from the file
        BufferedReader in = new BufferedReader(new FileReader(new
File(fileName)));
        String alphabet = in._____;
        String key = in._____;
        in._____;
    }
    . . .
```

---

1. Use Quick Fix to add the needed import statements if you receive messages that something couldn't be resolved to a type.

You'll also receive syntax errors for unhandled exceptions *FileNotFoundException* and *IOException*.

1. Add a *try* block with two *catch* blocks.

    1. If it catches *FileNotFoundException*, print a message that the file couldn't be found.

    2. If it catches *IOException*, print a message that the file couldn't be opened.

Listing 13-9, from SecretCode.java

```
    . . .

    public SecretCode() {
        String fileName = "key.txt";
        try {
            // read the alphabet and key from the file
            BufferedReader in = new BufferedReader(new FileReader(new
File(fileName)));
            String alphabet = in.readLine();
            String key = in.readLine();
            in.close();
        }
        catch (_____ e) {
            print("Could not find file " + fileName + ".");
        }
        catch (_____ e) {
```

```
        print("Could not open file " + fileName + ".");
    }
}
    . . .
```

1. Now, print *alphabet* and *key* so you can see that it read from the file correctly. (Hint: it should only print the alphabet and key if it successfully read from the file. So should the print statements be in the *try* block or after the *catch* block?)

Listing 13-10, from SecretCode.java

```
    . . .

public SecretCode() {

        . . .

    in.close();

    print(_____);
    print(_____);
}
    . . .
```

If you run the program, it should print both the alphabet and key from the file.

Key Points and More

- To read from a file, create a *BufferedReader* variable, call its *readLine()* method as many times as needed, then close the file using *close()*.

- Reading from a file can cause a *FileNotFoundException* or an *IOException*. Wrap the entire process of open, read, and close, and any other code you don't want it to run if it can't find or open the file, in a *try/catch* block.

- Reading from a file without a path name will look for the file in your class's project folder.

- If you want to read from a file in a different location, include the path name with the file name. The path name is the full folder name starting with the drive letter. For example, to read from *key.txt* in *c:\users\Annette*, use the following code. (Hint: remember to use the escape character in front of each backslash in Java strings.)

```
fileName = "c:\\users\\Annette\\key.txt";
```

Lesson 13.3 – Methods with Multiple Parameters

So far, you created methods with zero or one parameter. In this lesson, you'll create a method with more than one parameter.

Try It

1. Create a private method called *encode()* to encode and decode messages.

2. *encode()* should accept three strings parameters: *message*, *fromAlphabet*, and *toAlphabet*; and should return a string.

3. Declare a string called *newMessage*, initially empty, and return it.

Listing 13-11, from SecretCode.java

```
    . . .

private ____ encode(____ message, ____ fromAlphabet, ___ toAlphabet) {
    String newMessage = "_____";

    return _____;
}
    . . .
```

Make these changes to the code in the constructor:

1. Remove the code that prints *alphabet* and *key*.

2. Declare a string called *messageToEncode* and initialize it by prompting the user to enter a message to encode.

3. Declare a string called *encodedMessage* and initialize it with a call to *encode()*. Pass *encode()* the message, the alphabet, and the key.

4. Print the *encodedMessage..*

Listing 13-12, from SecretCode.java

```
    . . .

public SecretCode() {

        . . .

    String key = in.readLine();
    in.close();

    (Code was removed from here.)
```

```
     String messageToEncode = _____ (_____ );
     String encodedMessage = encode (_____ , _____ , _____ );
     print (_____ );
}
  . . .
```

The program will print an empty string no matter what you enter. You'll add code to scramble the message in the next lesson.

Key Points and More

- A method can be defined with any number of parameters.

- If a method defines more than one parameter, the call to the method must pass the same number of parameters in the same order.

Lesson 13.4 – Index of Characters in a String

Your Secret Code program will need to find each character of the message in the alphabet string and find which character is in the same position of the key string. To do this, it will have to find the index of a character in a string.

Try It

String's *indexOf()* method returns the position of the first occurrence of a search string in a string. For example, if a variable called *text* has the value of "Hello World", and you wanted to know the position of the blank in the string, you would use:

```
text.indexOf(" ");
```
The above code would return a value of 5 because indexes in strings start with 0.

If the search string is in the string more than once, *indexOf()* returns the position of its first occurrence. For example,

```
text.indexOf("l");
```
would return a value of 2.

If the search string isn't in the string, it returns a value of -1. For example,

```
text.indexOf("a");
```
would return a value of -1.

The method, *indexOf()* is case-sensitive. For example,

```
text.indexOf("h");
```
would return a value of -1 because there's no lowercase *h* in "Hello World".

To replace every letter in a message with its corresponding letter in the key, you'll do these steps:

- Take the first letter of the message.
- Find the index of that letter in the "from alphabet".
- If the letter is in the "from alphabet", get the letter in the same position of the "to alphabet" and add that new letter to the new message.
- If that letter isn't in the "from alphabet", add that letter to the new message.
- Repeat these steps using the next letter in the message.

1. Add comments to *encode()* for the above steps.

Listing 13-13, from SecretCode.java

```
    . . .

    private String encode(String message, String fromAlphabet, String
toAlphabet) {
        String newMessage = "";

        // _____

        // _____

        // _____

        // _____

        // _____

        return newMessage;
    }
    . . .
```

---

1. Get the first letter of *message* and put it in a string called *letter*. (Hint: use *substring()*.)

2. Get the position of that letter in *fromAlphabet* and put it in an integer called *letterPos*. (Hint: use *indexOf()*.)

Listing 13-14, from SecretCode.java

```
    . . .

    private String encode(String message, String fromAlphabet, String
toAlphabet) {

        . . .
```

```
// take the first letter of the message
String letter = message._____(_____, _____);

// find the index of that letter in the "from alphabet"
int letterPos = fromAlphabet._____(_____);

    . . .
```

1. If that letter is in *fromAlphabet* do the following. (Hint: what would *indexOf()* return if the letter isn't found?)

    1. Find the letter in the same position of the *toAlphabet* and put it in a string called *newLetter*. (Hint: use *substring()*.)

    2. Add that new letter to the new message.

Listing 13-15, from SecretCode.java

```
    . . .

  private String encode(String message, String fromAlphabet, String
toAlphabet) {

      . . .

    // if it is in the "from alphabet", find the letter in the same
position
    // in the "to alphabet" and add that new letter to the new message.
    if (letterPos ____ _____) {
      String newLetter = toAlphabet.substring(_____, _____);
      newMessage += _____;
    }
    . . .
```

1. If the letter isn't in *fromAlphabet*, add the letter to *newMessage*.

Listing 13-16, from SecretCode.java

```
    . . .

  private String encode(String message, String fromAlphabet, String
toAlphabet) {

      . . .

    // if it is not in the "from alphabet", add that letter to the new
message.
    else {
      newMessage _____ _____;
```

```
      }
         . . .
```

1. Put the code into a loop. Include everything from taking the first letter of the message through adding the letter to the message. (Hint: use a *for* loop.)

2. Make the *for* loop loop through each letter in the message.

3. Replace the code which took the first letter of the message to now take the letter at *i*.

4. Move the comment to repeat these steps to the top of the loop.

Listing 13-17, from SecretCode.java

```
         . . .

   private String encode(String message, String fromAlphabet, String
toAlphabet) {

         . . .

      // repeat these steps with each letter in the message.
      for (int i=____; i<message._____; i____) {
         // take the next letter of the message
         String letter = message.substring(_____, _____);

           . . .

      // if it is not in the "from alphabet", add that letter to the
new message.
         else {
            newMessage += letter;
         }
      }
         . . .
```

If you run the program and enter a message, it should print the message in the secret code.

Key Points and More

- Use String's *indexOf()* method to find the position of a search string in a string.

- The first character in a string is considered to be in position 0.

- *indexOf()* will return the position of only the first occurrence of a search string.

- *indexOf()* will return -1 if the search string isn't in the string.

- *indexOf()* is case-sensitive. A search for a lowercase letter won't return the index of the same uppercase letter.

Lesson 13.5 – Boolean Data Type

So far, you've used string, integer, and double data in your programs. In this lesson, you'll use boolean data. Boolean data can only have two possible values: true or false.

Try It

Decoding a message is very similar to encoding a message. The only difference is that to decode a message you use the key as the *fromAlphabet* and the alphabet as the *toAlphabet*.

Add code to the constructor:

1. Decode *encodedMessage* using *encode()* and put the result in a new string called *decodedMessage*. (Hint: pass in the encoded message, the key, and the alphabet in the correct order to decode a message as described above.)

2. Print the decoded message.

Listing 13-18, from SecretCode.java

```
    . . .

public SecretCode() {

    . . .

    String messageToEncode = promptForString("Enter a message:");
    String encodedMessage = encode(messageToEncode, alphabet, key);

    print(encodedMessage);
    String decodedMessage = encode(_____, _____, _____);
    print(_____);


    . . .
```

When you run the program, it should print the encoded message, then decode it back to the original message.

Next, let the user choose between encoding or decoding a message.

Another data type that would work well in this program is called a boolean. Booleans can only be true or false.

Boolean variables are declared as *boolean*. To assign true or false to a boolean, type true or false without quotes. For example, to declare a boolean called *done* with the value of true, use:

```
boolean done = true;
```

You don't need comparison operators to test if a boolean variable is true or false. For example, to test if *done* is true, use:

```
if (done)
```

To test if *done* is false, use the not operator:

```
if (!done)
```

Make these changes to the program:

1. Remove the five lines of code in the constructor that prompt the user to enter a string, through the line that prints the decoded message.

2. Declare a boolean called *quit*, initially false.

3. Add a while loop to continue while *quit* isn't true.

4. Inside that loop, declare a string called *option* that asks if the user wants to encode a message, decode a message, or quit.

Listing 13-19, from SecretCode.java

```
    . . .

  public SecretCode() {

        . . .

      String key = in.readLine();
      in.close();

        (Code was removed from here.)

_____ quit = _____;
  while (_____) {
      String option = _____;
  }
}
    . . .
```

1. Add a *switch* statement based on the value of *option*.

2. Add a *case* to the switch statement so if the user enters a "Q", set *quit* to true.

Listing 13-20, from SecretCode.java

```
    . . .

  public SecretCode() {

        . . .
```

```
        String option = promptForString("Do you want to encode(E) or
decode(D) a message, or quit(Q)?");

        switch(_____) {
            // quit
            case "___" :
                quit = _____;
                break;
        }
        . . .
```

1. Add a *case* to the *switch* statement so if the user enters an "E", prompt for a message, encode it, and print it. (Hint: use *encode()* with *alphabet* as the *fromAlphabet* and *key* as the *toAlphabet*.)

Listing 13-21, from SecretCode.java

```
    . . .

  public SecretCode() {

        . . .

        case "Q" :
            quit = true;
            break;
        // encode a message
        case "___" :
            String messageToEncode = _____;
            String encodedMessage = encode(_____,_____,_____);
            print(_____);
            break;
        }
        . . .
```

1. Add a *case* to the *switch* statement so if the user enters a "D", prompt for a message, decode it, and print it. (Hint: use *encode()* with *key* as the *fromAlphabet* and *alphabet* as the *toAlphabet*.)

Listing 13-22, from SecretCode.java

```
    . . .

  public SecretCode() {

        . . .

        print(encodedMessage);
```

```
        break;
    // decode a message
    case "D" :
        String messageToDecode = _____;
        String decodedMessage = encode(_____,_____,_____);
        print(_____);
        break;

            . . .
```

If you run the program now, use copy and paste to more easily enter the encoded message to decode it.

The program should also handle other things the user might enter.

1.   Add a *default* case to tell the user it is an invalid entry if he/she enters anything else.

Listing 13-23, from SecretCode.java

```
      . . .

   public SecretCode() {

            . . .

        print(decodedMessage);
        break;
    // anything else
    _____ :
        print(option + " is not a valid option.");

            . . .
```

Key Points and More

- Declare boolean variables as *boolean*.

- Booleans must have a value of only true or false.

- To assign a value to a boolean variable, set it to true or false (type true or false without quotes) or set it to a condition which returns true or false. For example:

```
boolean done = i==10;
```

- Use booleans where conditions can be used, such as in *if* statements and *while* loops.

- To test for the opposite value of a boolean, use the not operator. For example:

```
if (!done)
```

Lesson 13.6 – Case without Break

A typical *switch* statement has a *break* statement at the end of each *case*. However, the *break* statement is optional. Some code is easier to write if you leave out the *break* statement.

Try It

The program works pretty well, but you could make it a little nicer to use.

1. Add a blank line after it prints *encodedMessage* and *decodedMessage*. (Hint: what do you add to a string to tell it to split a string into a second line?)

Listing 13-24, from SecretCode.java

```
    . . .

  public SecretCode() {

        . . .

      case "E" :
          String messageToEncode = promptForString("Enter a message:");
          String encodedMessage = encode(messageToEncode, alphabet,
key);
          print(encodedMessage + "_____");
          break;
      // decode a message
      case "D" :
          String messageToDecode = promptForString("Enter a message:");
          String decodedMessage = encode(messageToDecode, key,
alphabet);
          print(decodedMessage + "_____");
          break;

        . . .
```

Let the user enter either upper or lowercase letters for E, D, or Q. This is easy to do using *case* statements.

If you have a *case* statement without a *break* statement, the program continues to run the code in the next *case*. For example, if you want either "Y" or "y" to set repeat to true, you could use:

```
case "Y" :
case "y" :
  repeat = true;
  break;
```

1. Can you guess what to add to the program so both "Q" and "q" run the same code, so "E" and "e" run the same code, and so "D" and "d" run the same code?

Listing 13-25, from SecretCode.java

```
    . . .

  public SecretCode() {

      . . .

    switch(option) {
      // quit
      case "Q" :
      _____ :
        quit = true;
        break;
      // encode a message
      case "E" :
      _____ :
        String messageToEncode = promptForString("Enter a message:");
        String encodedMessage = encode(messageToEncode, alphabet,
key);
        print(encodedMessage + "\n");
        break;
      // decode a message
      case "D" :
      _____ :
        String messageToDecode = promptForString("Enter a message:");
        String decodedMessage = encode(messageToDecode, key,
alphabet);
        print(decodedMessage + "\n");
        break;
      // anything else
      default :
        print(option + " is not a valid option.");
    }
      . . .
```

Key Points and More

- *Case* statements typically end with *break* statements.

- If a *case* doesn't have a *break* statement, the program continues to run the code in the next *case*. Use this technique when two *cases* should execute the same code or when one *case* does a small amount of code before it runs the same code in another *case*.

Lesson 13.7 – System Exit

In this lesson, you'll add a system exit to your program. A system exit closes the window and ends the program.

Try It

One more thing that would be nice to add to this program would be to exit the program when the user chooses to quit. To exit a program, use:

```
System.exit(0);
```

If you exit the program, it will also close the window.

1. Add code to exit the program after the end of the *while* loop. That way, when the user decides to quit, the loop exits, the window closes, and the program exits.

Listing 13-26, from SecretCode.java

```
    . . .

public SecretCode() {

        . . .

    boolean quit = false;
    while (!quit) {

        . . .

    }
    _____;
    }
    catch (FileNotFoundException e) {

        . . .
```

Key Points and More

- Use *System.exit(0)* to close the window and end the program.

Lesson 13.8 – Data File with the Jar File

Exported JAR files contain only the program files, not the data files. This lesson explains how a program can use the data file when you run the program outside of Eclipse as a JAR file.

Try It

This is the end of the Secret Code program. If you want to run it without Eclipse:

1.   Export your Secret Code program.

2.   Copy the *key.txt* file to the same folder as the *SecretCode.jar* file.

If you want an icon on your desktop to start the Secret Code program, put a shortcut to *SecretCode.jar* on your desktop:

1.   Right-click on *SecretCode.jar* and choose *Copy*.

2.   Right-click on your desktop and choose *Paste shortcut*.

3.   As long as what you created on the desktop was a shortcut, not a copy, you don't need to copy *key.txt* to the desktop. The *key.txt* file must be in the same folder as the actual *SecretCode.jar* file.

Give copies of both *SecretCode.jar* and *key.txt* to anyone with whom you want to share secret messages. Both of you must use the same *SecretCode.jar* and *key.txt* files. Copy and paste messages to and from the Secret Code program window to encode and decode messages you send each other.

Key Points and More

*   Give both *SecretCode.jar* and *key.txt* to anyone with whom you want to share your Secret Code program.

*   If you wrote the program using the file without a path, for example, "key.txt", the *key.txt* file must be placed in the same folder as the *SecretCode.jar* file.

    ◦   If you create a shortcut to the *SecretCode.jar* file, the *key.txt* file still must remain in the same folder as the *SecretCode.jar* file. The *key.txt* file shouldn't be moved to the same folder as the shortcut.

*   If you wrote the program using the file with a path, for example, "c:\Users\Annette\key.txt", the *key.txt* file must be placed in that location on all users' computers. The *SecretCode.jar* file could then be in any folder.

Project 14 – Word Mastermind

The goal in the Word Mastermind game is to guess a four letter word. A clue will contain an "O" for each correct letter you guessed in the correct position and an "X" for each correct letter you guessed in the wrong position.

Here's a screenshot of the Word Mastermind program:

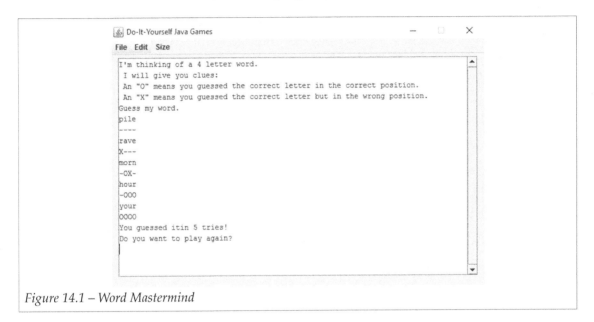

Figure 14.1 – Word Mastermind

Lesson 14.1 – Prompt for Yes or No

A prompt for Yes or No could be useful in many programs. It should display a prompt and make sure the user enters Y, y, N, or n.

Try It

Add a method to *MyWindow* to prompt for Yes or No. Do you know what visibility the method should have so any class which extends *MyWindow* can use it?

1. Add a protected method to the *MyWindow* class called *promptForYesNo()*. It should take a string parameter called *prompt* and return a *boolean*.

2. Declare a boolean called *yes*, initially true.

3. Return the value of *yes*.

Listing 14-1, from MyWindow.java

```
        . . .

_____ promptForYesNo(_____) {
_____ yes = _____;
    return _____;
}
        . . .
```

Now you need code to call *promptForYesNo()*.

Start writing the next program:

1. Create a new *Java project* called *Word Mastermind* and add *My Window, My String Methods,* and *DIYJava.jar* to the project.

2. Create a new *package* called _____._____.wordmastermind in the project.

3. Create a new *class* called *WordMastermind,* with superclass *MyWindow* and with a stub for *main()* and its constructors.

4. Add code to *main()* to call the *WordMastermind* constructor.

Listing 14-2, from WordMastermind.java

```
package annette.godtland.wordmastermind;

import annette.godtland.mywindow.MyWindow;

public class WordMastermind extends MyWindow {

    public WordMastermind() {

    }

    public static void main(String[] args) {
        _____;
    }
}
```

Add code to the constructor:

1. Declare a boolean called *repeat,* initially true.

2. Add a *while* loop that continues while repeat is true.

3. Inside the loop, print the word "Hello".

Listing 14-3, from WordMastermind.java

```
    . . .

    public WordMastermind() {
    _____ repeat = _____ ;
      while (_____) {
        print(_____);
      }
    }
    . . .
```

Because repeat is always true, it will keep printing "Hello" forever or until you close the window.

1. Close the window to end the program. If you're unable to close the window, click the *Terminate* button in the *Console* pane.

Add code inside the while loop:

1. To set *repeat*, call *promptForYesNo()* to ask the user if he/she wants to repeat this.

Listing 14-4, from WordMastermind.java

```
    . . .

    public WordMastermind() {
      boolean repeat = true;
      while(repeat) {
        print("Hello");
    _____ = promptForYesNo(_____);
      }
    }
    . . .
```

Because *promptForYesNo()* always returns true without ever waiting for input, the program still just keeps printing Hello.

1. Add a *while* loop to the *promptForYesNo()* method in *MyWindow*. Continue the loop until the user enters a valid answer. (Hint: create a boolean called *valid*, initially false.)

   1. Prompt the user for a string. (Hint: use the prompt from the parameter.)

   2. Use a *switch* statement based on the user's response to the prompt to determine if he/she answered "Y", "y", "N", "n", or an invalid answer. Set *yes* and *valid* according to the user's response.

Listing 14-5, from MyWindow.java

```
    . . .

    protected boolean promptForYesNo(String prompt) {
```

```
    boolean yes = true;
    boolean valid = _____;
    while(!valid) {
       String YorN = promptForString(_____);
       switch (YorN) {
          case "Y" :
          case "y" :
             yes = _____;
             valid = _____;
             break;
          case "N" :
          case "n" :
             yes = _____;
             valid = _____;
             break;
          default :
             print("Enter Y for yes, or N for no.");
             valid = _____;
       }
    }
    return yes;
}
    . . .
```

Now when you run the program, it should print Hello then ask if you want to repeat it. (Hint: make sure you have the *WordMastermind* class selected in Eclipse when you click the *run* button.)

- If you enter "Y" or "y", it should repeat "Hello".

- If you enter anything other than "Y", "y", "N", or "n", it should ask you to enter "Y" or "N".

- If you enter "N" or "n", it shouldn't repeat "Hello" anymore.

Key Points and More

- You now have a handy method to ask the user a yes or no question and put the answer in a boolean variable.

- You can use *promptForYesNo()* in any class that extends *MyWindow*.

- *promptForYesNo()* will only recognize "Y", "y", "N", or "n". It won't accept "Yes" or "No".

- Make sure your prompt string tells the user to respond with "Y" or "N".

Lesson 14.2 – Replace Characters in a String

The Word Mastermind program has to replace characters in a string at a given position. There's no string method to do that. So in this lesson, you'll write your own *replaceStringAt()* method.

Try It

Any class should be able to use the new *replaceStringAt()* method, not just those classes that extend *MyWindow*. So you'll put *replaceStringAt()* in *MyStringMethods* instead of in *MyWindow*.

replaceStringAt() will be self-contained. It doesn't use any methods or variables other than those that come with Java or are passed in as parameters. So it can be a static method.

1. Add a public static method called *replaceStringAt()* to the *MyStringMethods* class. It should take three parameters: a string called *originalString*, an integer called *index*, and another string called *replaceString*. It should also return a string.

2. Declare a string variable called *newString*, assign it an initial value of *originalString*, and return *newString*.

Listing 14-6, from MyStringMethods.java

```
. . .

public _____    replaceStringAt(_____) {
    String _____ = originalString;
    return _____;
}

. . .
```

How can you replace characters in a string starting at a given position, using methods you've learned so far?

- Break the string into two strings: the text before the index and the text after the positions the replacement string would fill.

- Join the first string, the replacement string, and the second string together.

How do you calculate where to start the second string? (Hint: if you put a three character replacement string at index 5, it would take up positions 5, 6, and 7. In other words, the second string would start at index 8. Index 8 happens to be the start index, 5, plus the length of the replacement string, 3.)

Add code to the *replaceStringAt()* method:

1. Create a string of all the characters before the index.

2. Create another string of all the characters that should be after the replacement string.

3. Join the strings together, with the replacement string in the middle.

Listing 14-7, from MyStringMethods.java

```
    . . .

  public static String replaceStringAt(String originalString, int
index, String replaceString) {
      String newString = originalString;
      String firstString = originalString.substring(_____, _____);
      String secondString = originalString.substring(_____ + _____);
      newString = _____ + _____ + _____;
      return newString;
  }
    . . .
```

Change the code in *WordMastermind* to test this new *replaceStringAt()* method:

1. Remove all the code in the constructor of *WordMastermind*.

2. Create a string with an initial value of "book".

3. Starting in position 3, replace the letters with "t". (Hint: use *replaceStringAt()*.)

4. Print the new word.

Listing 14-8, from WordMastermind.java

```
    . . .

  public WordMastermind() {
      String word = _____;
      word = _____.replaceStringAt(_____, _____, _____);
      print(_____);
  }
    . . .
```

It should have printed "boot".

1. Change the code to replace the letters starting in position 1 with "an".

Listing 14-9, from WordMastermind.java

```
    . . .

  public WordMastermind() {
      String word = "book";
      word = MyStringMethods.replaceStringAt(word, _____, _____);
      print(word);
  }
    . . .
```

It should have printed "bank".

It seems to work well, but there are a couple problems with this code. What if you enter an index past the end of the word?

1. Change the code to add an "s" at the end of the word, starting in position 4.

Listing 14-10, from WordMastermind.java

```
    . . .

  public WordMastermind() {
    String word = "book";
    word = MyStringMethods.replaceStringAt(word, _____, "_____");
    print(word);
  }
    . . .
```

If you use an index past the end of the string, it causes an error when you run the program.

The Word Mastermind program should only replace characters, not add characters.

1. Add code to *replaceStringAt()* to only replace characters if the index is before the end of the string. (Hint: if the index is less than the length of the string.)

Listing 14-11, from MyStringMethods.java

```
    . . .

  public static String replaceStringAt(String originalString, int
index, String replaceString) {
    String newString = originalString;
    // only replace the string if the index is inside the original
string
    if (index < _____) {
      String firstString = originalString.substring(0,index);
      String secondString = originalString.substring(index +
replaceString.length());
      newString = firstString + replaceString + secondString;
    }
    return newString;
  }
    . . .
```

If you use *replaceStringAt()* to add an "s" to the end of the word, it shouldn't replace anything. The program should now print "book" and cause no errors.

There's another problem with this code. What if you enter an index before the end of the string but the replacement string goes beyond the end of the string?

1. Change the code in the *WordMastermind* constructor to replace letters starting at position 2 with "ating".

Listing 14-12, from WordMastermind.java

```
    . . .

public WordMastermind() {
    String word = "book";
    word = MyStringMethods.replaceStringAt(word, _____, "_____");
    print(word);
}
    . . .
```

This program gives an error when it's run.

If the replacement string is too long, *replaceStringAt()* should replace only the characters that fit before the end of the original string.

1. Add code to *replaceStringAt()* to find out how much room is available in the original string after the index. (Hint: use *length()* of the original string and the *index*.)

2. Check if the replacement string is too long to fit. (Hint: if its *length()* is greater than the room available.)

3. If the replacement string is too long, take only as many characters as will fit. (Hint: use *substring()* based on the room available.)

Listing 14-13, from MyStringMethods.java

```
    . . .

public static String replaceStringAt(String originalString, int
index, String replaceString) {
    String newString = originalString;
    // only replace the string if the index is inside the original
string
    if (index <= originalString.length()) {
        // if replaceString is too long to fit, truncate it.
        int roomAvailable = originalString._____ - _____;
        if(replaceString._____ > _____) {
            replaceString = replaceString.substring(0, _____);
        }
        String firstString = originalString.substring(0,index);

    . . .
```

Now when you run *WordMastermind*, it should print boat.

Key Points and More

- You now have a handy method to replace characters at a position in a string.

- Because *replaceStringAt()* is a static method, you can use it in any class by including the class name, like this:

```
MyStringMethods.replaceStringAt(originalString, index, replaceString);
```

- *replaceStringAt()* will only replace characters in the original string. It won't add characters to the string. If the replace string is too long to fit, or if the index is beyond the end of the string, only the characters within the original string will be replaced.

Lesson 14.3 – Instance Variables

A variable declared at the beginning of the class definition can be used by all the class's methods. It doesn't need to be passed to the methods as a parameter. Such a variable is called an instance variable.

Try It

You are now done testing the new methods. Next, start rewriting the code for the *Word Mastermind* game.

1. Remove all the code from the *WordMastermind* constructor.

First, you'll just print the clue. If the word the user is supposed to guess is "quit", and his/her guess is "lint", the program should give a clue of "-X-O". The "X" means the second letter of the guess is in the word but in the wrong position. The "O" means the fourth letter of the guess is in the word and in the right position.

1. Add strings to the constructor:

    1. *word*, with initial value of "quit".

    2. *guess*, with initial value of "lint".

    3. *clue*, with initial value of "----".

Listing 14-14, from WordMastermind.java

```
    . . .

public WordMastermind() {
    String word = "_____";
    String guess = "_____";
    String clue = "_____";
}
    . . .
```

1. Create two private methods: *findRightPlaceLetters()* and *findWrongPlaceLetters()*. Each should take one parameter of a string called *guess*, and return nothing.

Listing 14-15, from WordMastermind.java

```
    . . .

    private _____  findRightPlaceLetters(_____)  {

    }

    private _____  findWrongPlaceLetters(_____)  {

    }
    . . .
```

1. Add code to the constructor to call these two new methods, then print the value of clue.

Listing 14-16, from WordMastermind.java

```
    . . .

public WordMastermind() {
    String word = "quit";
    String guess = "lint";
    String clue = "----";

    findRightPlaceLetters(guess);
    findWrongPlaceLetters(guess);

    print(clue);
}
    . . .
```

Right now, the two methods don't do anything so the program just prints this:

Steps to set the clue for the letters in the right position are:

- Loop through all the letters of the guess.
- If the guess letter is the same as the letter in that position of word:
  - Set the letter in that position of the clue to "O".
  - Set the letter in that position of the word to "-".

The last step removes the letter from the word so *findWrongPlaceLetters()* can't use that letter again.

1. Add code to do the above steps. (Hint: use *substring()* to find the letters. Hint: use *replaceStringAt()* to put the "O" in *clue* and the "-" in *word*.)

Listing 14-17, from WordMastermind.java

```
    . . .

  private void findRightPlaceLetters(String guess) {
      // loop through all the letters of the guess
      for(int i=____; i<_____; i_____) {
          // get the letter in that position of the guess and word
          String guessLetter = guess.substring(____, _____);
          String wordLetter = word.substring(____, _____);
          // if guess letter is same as word letter, set clue to O and
word to -
          if (_____.equals(_____)) {
              clue = MyStringMethods.replaceStringAt(clue, ___, "____");
              word = MyStringMethods.replaceStringAt(word, ___, "____");
          }
      }
  }

    . . .
```

There will be some syntax errors even if you filled in the blanks correctly.

Look at the structure of the blocks of code in the class.

Listing 14-18, from WordMastermind.java

```
  . . .

public class WordMastermind extends MyWindow {

    . . .

  public WordMastermind() {
      String word = "quit";
      String guess = "lint";
      String clue = "----";

      . . .

  }

  private void findRightPlaceLetters(String guess) {

      . . .

  }
```

```
        . . .
}
```

Where are *word* and *clue* and *findRightPlaceLetters* compared to the curly brackets that mark each block of code?

- • *word* and *clue* are declared within the curly brackets of the constructor.

- • *findRightPlaceLetters()* isn't within the curly brackets of the constructor.

So *findRightPlaceLetters()* can't see or use *word* or *clue*. However:

- • *findRightPlaceLetters()* is within the curly brackets of the *WordMastermind* class.

Instead, you should declare *word* and *clue* within the *WordMastermind* class definition, not in the constructor. Then both the constructor and *findRightPlaceLetters()* can see and use those variables.

Variables declared in the class block are called instance variables. Just like methods in a class, instance variables should be declared as public, private, or protected.

Make these changes:

1. Add *word* and *clue* as private string instance variables for the class.

2. Remove the string declaration from *word* and *clue* in the constructor.

Listing 14-19, from WordMastermind.java

```
    . . .

public class WordMastermind extends MyWindow {
_____ String word;
_____ String clue;

    . . .

  public WordMastermind() {
    word = "quit";
    String guess = "lint";
    clue = "----";

      . . .

  }
    . . .
```

That should fix the syntax errors.

When you run the program now, it should print

```
---O
```

since the last letter of the guess, "lint", matches the letter in the same position of the original word, "quit".

Next, write the code for *findWrongPlaceLetters()*. To determine which letters are correct but in the wrong place:

- Loop through all the letters of *guess*.

- If the letter is in the word: (Hint: if *indexOf()* the letter is greater than -1.)

   ◦ Replace the letter where it was found in *word* with "-".

   ◦ If the character in *clue* at the loop index position is still "-", set it to "X" .

1. Add code to do the above steps.(Hint: use *substring()* to find the letters. Hint: use *indexOf()* to get the index of a letter and to find out if it's in *word*. Hint: use *replaceStringAt()* to put the "X" in *clue* and the "-" in *word*.)

Listing 14-20, from WordMastermind.java

```
    . . .

private void findWrongPlaceLetters(String guess) {
    // loop through all the letters of the guess
    for(_____) {
        // get the guess letter at position i
        String letter = guess._____;
        // if letter is in word (indexOf > -1)
        int letterLoc = _____;
        if (letterLoc_____ _____) {
            // replace letter in word with -
            word = _____(word, _____, "____");
            // set clue at the loop index to X if it is still -
            String clueLetter = clue._____;
            if (_____.equals("-")) {
                clue = _____(clue, ___, "____");
            }
        }
    }
}
    . . .
```

If you run the program now, it should give the correct clue:

-X-O

Key Points and More

- Variables declared in the class block are called instance variables.

- Instance variables can be seen and used by all non-static methods in the class in which it was declared. Because static methods must be self-contained, they cannot use instance variables that aren't static. Static instance variables are covered in a later lesson.

- Like methods in a class, instance variables must be declared as private, protected, or public. Choose the least visible option you need.

- Why didn't you just pass *word* and *clue* as parameters to these methods? As mentioned in an earlier lesson, parameters only send a copy of the variable. If a method changes a variable declared as a parameter, it only changes the copy, not the original value. You needed these methods to change the value of the original variables. Therefore, you can't just pass them as parameters.

Lesson 14.4 – Convert a String to Uppercase

A program is easier to use if the user can enter input with either uppercase (capitalized) or lowercase letters. However, Java strings are case-sensitive. For example: "Quit" isn't equal to "quit" in Java.

You can write your program so input is not case-sensitive by changing all user input, and the text you plan to compare it with, to uppercase. Then the user may enter either uppercase or lowercase text.

Try It

Your program now prints the correct clue if the word is "quit" and the guess is "lint". Next, let the user enter his/her own guess.

1. Change the code to ask the user to guess a word instead of setting guess to "lint".

2. Make a copy of *word* and put it in a new string called *originalWord*.

3. Create a boolean called *solved*, initially set to false.

4. Repeat these steps while not *solved*:

   1. Reset *word* and *clue* to their original values.

   2. Set *clue* by calling *findRightPlaceLetters()* and *findWrongPlaceLetters()*.

   3. If *guess* is equal to *originalWord*, the puzzle is solved. Otherwise, prompt the user for another guess. (Hint: use just the *clue* as the prompt.)

5. Congratulate the user.

Listing 14-21, from WordMastermind.java

. . .

```
public WordMastermind() {
   word = "quit";

   // Prompt user for a guess
   String guess = _____;
   _____ originalWord = _____;
   _____ solved = _____;

   // Repeat while not solved
   while (_____) {
      // reset word and clue for each guess
      word = _____;
      clue = _____;

      // set the clue
      findRightPlaceLetters(guess);
      findWrongPlaceLetters(guess);

      // did he guess it?
      if(_____) {
         solved = _____;
      }
      else {
         guess = _____;
      }
   }

   // congratulate the user
   print("OOOO");
   print(_____);
}
   ...
```

This program doesn't work very well if the user enters a word with more than four letters. If his/her guess isn't four letters, he/she should guess again.

1. Wrap all the code in the *while* loop into an *if* statement that runs only if the guess is four letters.

2. If the guess isn't four letters, ask the user to guess again.

Listing 14-22, from WordMastermind.java

```
   ...

public WordMastermind() {

      ...
```

```
while (!solved) {
    if (_____) {
        // reset word and clue for each guess
        word = originalWord;
        clue = "----";

        . . .

        else {
            guess = promptForString(clue);
        }
    }
    else {
        guess = _____;
    }
}

    . . .
```

This program doesn't work very well if the word is lowercase and the user's guess has some uppercase letters.

You can use String's *toUpperCase()* method to convert a string to all uppercase. For example, to convert a string called *name* to uppercase, use:

```
name = name.toUpperCase();
```

1. Convert both *word* and *guess* to uppercase.

Listing 14-23, from WordMastermind.java

```
    . . .

public WordMastermind() {
    word = "quit";
    word = word._____;

    // Prompt user for a guess
    String guess = promptForString("Guess my word");
    guess = guess._____;
    String originalWord = word;

        . . .

        else {
            guess = promptForString(clue);
            guess = guess._____;
        }
    }
    else {
```

```
      guess = promptForString("Your guess must contain 4 letters.");
      guess = guess._____;
   }
}
      . . .
```

This program would also be easier to use if you first give the user instructions for how to play.

```
I'm thinking of a 4 letter word.
  I will give you clues:
  An "O" means you guessed the correct letter in the correct position.
  An "X" means you guessed the correct letter but in the wrong position.
```

1. Add code to print the above instructions at the start of the game. (Hint: use the escape character for quotes within strings.)

Listing 14-24, from WordMastermind.java

```
   . . .


public WordMastermind() {

      . . .

      // prompt the user for a guess
      print("_____");
      print("_____");
      print("_____");
      print("_____");
      String guess = promptForString("Guess my word");
      guess = guess.toUpperCase();


      . . .
```

Another way to improve this program would be to tell the user how many tries he/she took to guess the word.

1. Declare a new integer called *count*, initially 1, after the user's first guess.

2. Increment *count* by 1 with each next guess.

3. Tell the user how many guesses it took him/her to solve the puzzle.

Listing 14-25, from WordMastermind.java

```
   . . .


public WordMastermind() {

      . . .
```

```
String guess = promptForString("Guess my word");
guess = guess.toUpperCase();
int count = _____;

      . . .

    // did he guess it?
    if(guess.equals(originalWord)) {
      solved = true;
    }
    else {
      guess = promptForString(clue);
      guess = guess.toUpperCase();
      count____;
    }

      . . .

  // congratulate the user
  print("OOOO");
  print("You guessed it in " + _____ + " tries!");
}
  . . .
```

Key Points and More

- String's *equals()* method is case-sensitive. If the strings you compare don't use the same capitalization for all of their letters, *equals()* will return false.

- Don't force the user to enter a value in uppercase or lowercase. Instead, allow him/her to enter either. Then convert both the input value, and the value you compare it against, to uppercase.

- To convert a string to uppercase, use String's *toUpperCase()* method.

Lesson 14.5 – Empty Array

In this lesson, you'll declare an array before you're ready to put the data into it. You can declare an empty array as long as you know the number of items that will eventually be put into the array.

Try It

In this lesson, your program will pick a random word from the file of 342 common four-letter words. But first, your program must declare the array to hold 342 words.

To declare an array of strings by its size, initialize it as a new string array with its size in square brackets. For example, to initialize a string called *names* to hold 10 items, use:

```
String names[] = new String[10];
```

1. Add a variable called *numberOfWords* whose initial value is the number of words in the file: 342.

2. Add an empty string array called *words* whose size is the number of words in the file. (Hint: use the *numberOfWords* variable.)

Listing 14-26, from WordMastermind.java

```
    . . .

public WordMastermind() {
    int numberOfWords = _____;
    String words[] = new String[_____];

    word = "quit";

    . . .
```

One of the files you should have downloaded was a file called *wordMastermind.txt*. You'll use it for this program.

1. Copy the *wordMastermind.txt* file from your Java work folder and put it in the *Word Mastermind* folder in your Java work folder.

Do you remember how to read from a file?

1. Put the name of the file, "wordMastermind.txt" into a string called *fileName*.

2. Open the file by that name.

3. Loop through all the words in the file. (Hint: use a *for* loop and *numberOfWords*.)

    1. Read one line at a time and put its value in the next index of the *words* array.

4. Close the file.

Listing 14-27, from WordMastermind.java

```
    . . .

public WordMastermind() {

    . . .

    String words[] = new String[numberOfWords];
    String fileName = _____;
```

```
    // read a list of words from the file
    BufferedReader in = new BufferedReader(new FileReader(new
File(_____)));
    for (int i=____ ; i<_____; i__ ) {
        words[___] = in._____;
    }
    in._____;

    . . .
```

1. Add code to handle the exceptions *FileNotFoundException* and *IOException*. If the program is unable to read from the file, it shouldn't run any of the rest of the program. (Hint: the entire rest of the constructor should be in the *try* block.)

Listing 14-28, from WordMastermind.java

```
    . . .

public WordMastermind() {

    . . .

    String fileName = "wordMastermind";

    try {
        // read a list of words from the file

        . . .

        print("You guessed it in " + count + " tries!");
    }
    catch(_____) {
        print("Could not find file " + _____);
    }
    catch(_____) {
        print("Could not read from file " + _____);
    }
}
    . . .
```

You now have a list of four-letter words in an array called *words*.

1. Add code to pick a random word from that list and assign it to *word*. (Hint: use Random's *nextInt()* to pick a number between 0 and the number of words in *words*.)

Listing 14-29, from WordMastermind.java

```
    . . .
```

```java
public WordMastermind() {

    . . .

    String fileName = "wordMastermind.txt";
    Random rand = new _____;

    try {
        // read a list of words from the file
        BufferedReader in = new BufferedReader(new FileReader(new
File(fileName)));
        for (int i=0; i<numberOfWords; i++) {
            words[i] = in.readLine();
        }
        in.close();

        int pick = rand._____;
        word = words[_____];
        word = word.toUpperCase();

        // Prompt user for a guess

        . . .
```

Remember, you can add *System.out.println()* statements to print the word in the *Console* pane. It will be easier to test the program when you can see the random word it chose. Don't forget to remove all *System.out.println()* statements when you're done with the program.

Next, add code to ask the user if he/she wants to play again:

1. After the words are read from the file, create a boolean called *repeat*, initially true.

2. Loop through the rest of the code in the *try* block while *repeat* is true.

3. Print a blank line after you congratulate the user.

4. After a game, ask the user if he/she wants to play again. (Hint: use *promptForYesNo()* and put the response in *repeat*.)

5. Print a blank line between games.

6. Close the window if the user doesn't want to play again. (Hint: use *System.exit(0)*.)

Listing 14-30, from WordMastermind.java

```java
    . . .

public WordMastermind() {
```

```
        . . .

      in.close();

_____ repeat = _____ ;
while(_____) {
    int pick = rand.nextInt(numberOfWords);

       . . .

    print("You guessed it in " + count + " tries!_____");

    repeat = _____ ;
    print();
}
System._____ ;

    . . .
```

Key Points and More

· You don't have to initialize the contents of an array when you declare it. However, you must assign values into each item of the array before you try to use the items in the array.

· To declare an empty array, put the expected number of items for the array in square brackets.

· The *wordMastermind.txt* file was created from Dr. Edward Fry's Instant Word List (High Frequency Words). The Fry word list is claimed to contain the most used words in reading and writing for young readers.

Lesson 14.6 – Static Final Variables

If you know a variable will hold data that will never change, you can declare it as static and <u>final</u>.

Try It

A previous lesson covered instance variables. This lesson will cover static final variables.

· Instance variables might be different every time the program is run, for each <u>instance</u> of the class. For example, the instance variable *word* will be different each time the program is run. Instances of a class will be covered more in a later lesson.

· Static variables are variables shared by every instance of the class. If one instance of the class updates the value of a static variable, all instances of that class see the same new value for that variable.

- Final variables are variables whose value is never changed by the program. For example, the name of the word list file for the *Word Mastermind* game will never be changed by the program.

To declare a static variable, declare it within the class definition like you did with the instance variables and add *static* to its declaration. For example, if the string variable called *name* were to be declared as private and static, use:

```
private static String name = "Annette";
```

If that variable were never to be changed by the program, you could also declare it as final like this:

```
private static final String name = "Annette";
```

You have two variables whose values should be the same for all instances of the *WordMastermind* class and are never changed by the program.

1. Move the declaration of *numberOfWords* and *fileName* to the class definition, and make them private, static, and final.

Listing 14-31, from WordMastermind.java

```
        . . .


public class WordMastermind extends MyWindow {
    private String clue;
    private String word;
    _____  _____  _____   int numberOfWords = 342;
    _____  _____  _____   String fileName = "wordMastermind.txt";

    public WordMastermind() {

        (Code was removed from here.)

    String words[] = new String[numberOfWords];

        (Code was removed from here.)

    Random rand = new Random();


        . . .
```

Now, if you ever change the name or contents of the *wordMastermind.txt* file, you can easily find and change its declaration at the top of your program as well.

Another change not required, but usually done, is to name all final variables with all uppercase letters. It's just one more clue to you as the programmer that these variables cannot be changed by the program:

1. Rename numberOfWords to NUMBEROFWORDS.

2. Rename fileName to FILENAME.

Listing 14-32, from WordMastermind.java

```
    . . .

  private String word;
  private String clue;
  private static final int _____ = 342;
  private static final String _____ = "wordMastermind.txt";

  public WordMastermind() {
    String words[] = new String[_____];
    Random rand = new Random();

    try {
       // read a list of words from the file
       BufferedReader in = new BufferedReader(new FileReader(new
File(_____))));
         for (int i=0; i<_____; i++) {
           words[i] = in.readLine();
         }
         in.close();

         boolean repeat = true;
         while(repeat) {
           int pick = rand.nextInt(_____);

             . . .

    }
    catch(FileNotFoundException e) {
      print("Could not find the file " + _____);
    }
    catch(IOException e) {
      print("Could not read from file " + _____);
    }
      . . .
```

This is the end of the Word Mastermind program. If you want to run it without Eclipse:

1. Export your Word Mastermind program.

2. Copy the *wordMastermind.txt* file to the same folder as the *WordMastermind.jar* file.

Key Points and More

- Declare a variable as static if it should be shared with every instance of the class and they should all use the same value.

- Static methods cannot access regular instance variables but they can access *static* instance variables.

- Declare a variable final if its value will never be changed by the program. For example, the program might change the value of *word*, but will never change the value of *fileName*. Therefore, *fileName* could be declared as final.

- Might a variable ever be static but not final? Yes, if two instances of a class share one variable they both update, they would have to use a static but not final instance variable. Instances of classes will be covered in more detail in a later lesson.

- Moving variables to instance variables makes it easy to find and change the variables at the top of the program.

Project 15 – Hangman

Next, you'll create a Hangman program. Hangman is another guessing game. In this game, you have to guess a phrase. You'll be given a puzzle that shows how many words are in the phrase and how many letters are in each word. If you guess a correct letter, the puzzle will show every place it's used in the phrase. If you guess an incorrect letter, that letter will be added to the list of wrong guesses, and another part of a stick man will be added to the hangman gallows. You must guess the phrase before all ten parts of the stick man are drawn.

Here's a screenshot of the Hangman program:

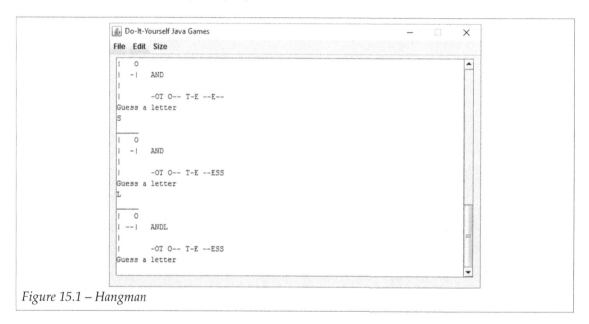

Figure 15.1 – Hangman

Lesson 15.1 – Switch Statement with Integers

So far, all your *switch* statements have been based on strings. In this lesson, you'll use a *switch* statement based on integers.

Try It

Start writing the next program:

1. Create a new *Java project* called *Hangman* and add *My Window, My String Methods,* and *DIYJava.jar* to the project.

2. Create a new *package* called _____._____.*hangman* in the project.

3. Create a new *class* called *Hangman,* with superclass *MyWindow* and with a stub for *main()* and its constructors.

4. Add code to *main()* to call the *Hangman* constructor.

Listing 15-1, from Hangman.java

```
package annette.godtland.hangman;

import annette.godtland.mywindow.MyWindow;

public class Hangman extends MyWindow {

   public Hangman() {

   }

   public static void main(String[] args) {
      _____;
   }
}
```

1. Add three private string instance variables to this program named *phrase, clue,* and *wrongLetters.* They don't need initial values.

Listing 15-2, from Hangman.java

```
package annette.godtland.hangman;

import annette.godtland.mywindow.MyWindow;

public class Hangman extends MyWindow {
   private String phrase;
   private String clue;
   private String wrongLetters;

   public Hangman() {

   }
      . . .
```

1. Create a new private method called *printPuzzle().* It should take no parameters and return nothing.

2. Call *printPuzzle()* from the constructor.

3. Add code to *printPuzzle()* to draw a stick man on the gallows to look like the following

images. (Hint: use the escape character to print a backslash.)

```
_____
|   O
|  --|--
|  _/ \_
|
```

Listing 15-3, from Hangman.java

```
    . . .

 public Hangman() {
     _____;
 }

 private void printPuzzle() {
     print("_____");
     print("_____");
     print("_____");
     print("_____");
     print("_____");
 }
     . . .
```

1. In the constructor, assign "ABC" to *wrongLetters* before you print the puzzle.

2. Change *printPuzzle()* to print *wrongLetters* four spaces past the stick figure's arm.

Listing 15-4, from Hangman.java

```
    . . .

 public Hangman() {
     wrongLetters = _____;
     printPuzzle();
 }

 private void printPuzzle() {
     print("_____");
     print("|     O");
     print("|  --|--    " + _____);
     print("|  _/ \\_");
     print("|");
 }
     . . .
```

There are ten parts to the stick figure. The game should print only the head if the user guesses one wrong letter, the head and torso if the user guesses a second wrong letter, etc. If ten wrong letters are guessed, the game should print the entire stick figure.

1. Write just the structure of a *switch* statement in *printPuzzle()*, based on how many letters are in *wrongLetters*. (Hint: use the length of *wrongLetters*.)

   1. Write *case* statements for values 0 through 10. You'll add code for the *cases* later. (Hint: the *case* values are integers instead of strings, so these *case* values shouldn't have quotes.)

Listing 15-5, from Hangman.java

```
. . .

private void printPuzzle() {
    switch (_____) {
        case 0:
            break;
        case 1:
            break;
        case 2:
            break;
        case ___:
            break;
        case ___:
                _____;
        case ___:
                _____;
        case ___:
                _____;
        case ___:
                _____;
                _____:
                _____;
                _____:
                _____;
                _____:
                _____;
    }
    print("_____");
    print("|     O");
    print("|  --|--     " + wrongLetters);
    print("|  _/ \\_");
    print("|");
}

. . .
```

The ten *cases* should draw these images:

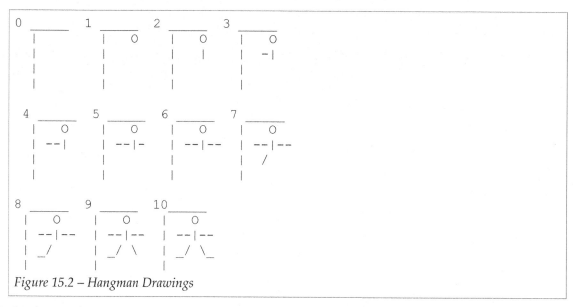

```
0  _____     1  _____     2  _____     3  _____
   |         |     O      |     O      |     O
   |         |           |     |      |    -|
   |         |           |           |
   |         |           |           |

4  _____     5  _____     6  _____     7  _____
   |    O     |    O      |    O       |    O
   | --|      | --|-      | --|--      | --|--
   |         |           |            |   /
   |         |           |            |

8  _____     9  _____    10 _____
   |   O      |   O       |   O
   | --|--    | --|--     | --|--
   | _/       | _/ \      | _/ \_
   |         |           |
```

Figure 15.2 – Hangman Drawings

The first and last line printed will be the same for all 10 images, so those two lines don't need to be part of the *case* code.

1. Move the first *print()* statement above the *switch* statement.

2. Move the next three *print()* statements to *case* 10.

3. Leave the last *print()* statement after the end of the *switch* statement.

Listing 15-6, from Hangman.java

```
    . . .

private void printPuzzle() {
    _____;
    switch (wrongLetters.length()) {
       case 0:
          break;
       case 1:
          break;
       case 2:
          break;
       case 3:
          break;
       case 4:
          break;
       case 5:
          break;
       case 6:
```

```
        break;
      case 7:
         break;
      case 8:
         break;
      case 9:
         break;
      case 10:

         _____;
         _____;
         _____;
         break;
   }
   print("|");
}
   . . .
```

Add code to the rest of the *case* statements:

1. Copy the *print()* statements from *case* 10 and paste them in *cases* 0 through 9.

2. Modify the code you pasted in *case* 0 so none of the stick man is printed.

3. Modify the code you pasted in *case* 1 so only the head is printed.

4. Modify the code you pasted in *case* 2 so only the head and torso are printed.

5. Modify the code in *cases* 3-9 so only the parts shown in the earlier diagram are printed.

Listing 15-7, from Hangman.java

```
   . . .

private void printPuzzle() {
   print("_____");
   switch (wrongLetters.length()) {
   case 0:
      print("|");
      print("|            " + wrongLetters);
      print("|");
      break;
   case 1:
      print("|    O");
      print("|            " + wrongLetters);
      print("|");
      break;
   case 2:

      _____;
      _____;
      _____;
```

```
            break;
        case 3:
            _____;
            _____;
            _____;
            break;
        case 4:
            _____;
            _____;
            _____;
            break;
        case 5:
            _____;
            _____;
            _____;
            break;
        case 6:
            _____;
            _____;
            _____;
            break;
        case 7:
            _____;
            _____;
            _____;
            break;
        case 8:
            _____;
            _____;
            _____;
            break;
        case 9:
            _____;
            _____;
            _____;
            break;
        case 10:
            print("|    O");
            print("| --|--     " + wrongLetters);
            print("| _/ \\_");
            break;
        }
        print("|");
    }
    ...
```

When you run the program, it should print the stick figure's head, torso, and part of an arm, since *wrongLetters* has three letters in it.

1. Change *wrongLetters* to have anywhere from zero through ten letters and make sure it prints the correct stick figure.

Listing 15-8, from Hangman.java

```
   . . .

 public Hangman() {
    wrongLetters = _____;
    printPuzzle();
 }
    . . .
```

Key Points and More

- This lesson introduced the use of integer values instead of strings for the *switch* statements. Byte, short, and character types are also allowed. See the next lesson to learn about character data types.

- You can also use *Enum* data types in *switch* statements, but the *Enum* data type isn't covered this book.

Lesson 15.2 – Character Data Type

Character data is another data type. It's always a single character.

In this lesson, you'll use character data as you examine each individual letter in the hangman phrase.

Try It

Character data might at first look similar to string data, but it's quite different:

- Character data can only be a single character.

- Characters are declared as <u>char</u>.

- Use single-quotes instead of double-quotes around character data.

- Compare character data like you compare integers: use the double equal sign (==), less than sign (<), greater sign (>), etc., instead of calling methods like *equals()* as you do with strings.

There's a String a method, *charAt()*, to get a character at an index in the string. For example, if the string *greeting* is "Hello World", you can check if the letter in position 1 is an "e" by using this code:

```
String greeting = "Hello World"
char c = greeting.charAt(1);
if (c=='e') {
  print("found e in position 1");
}
```

1. Create a new private method called *blankOutClue()*. It should take no parameters and return nothing.

2. At the start of the constructor, set the phrase to "HELLO WORLD" and call *blankOutClue()*.

Listing 15-9, from Hangman.java

```
    . . .

public Hangman() {
    phrase = "_____";
    blankOutClue();

    wrongLetters = "ABC";
    printPuzzle();
}

_____ blankOutClue(_____) {

}
    . . .
```

To blank out the clue, you need to do these steps:

· Start with an empty clue.

· For each letter in the phrase:

   ◦ If the letter is a blank, add a blank to the clue.

   ◦ If the letter is anything else, add a dash to the clue.

1. Add comments to *blankOutClue()* for each of the above steps.

Listing 15-10, from Hangman.java

```
    . . .

private void blankOutClue() {
    // _____
    // _____
    // _____
    // _____
}
```

. . .

1. Write the code to do each of the steps in the comments.

Listing 15-11, from Hangman.java

. . .

```
private void blankOutClue() {
    // start with an empty clue
    clue = _____;
    // for each letter in the phrase
    for(int i=___; i<_____; i____) {
        char letter = phrase.charAt(____);
        // if the letter is a blank, add a blank to the clue
        if (letter ____'____') {
            clue += _____;
        }
        // if it is anything else, add a dash to the clue
        else {
            clue += _____;
        }
    }
}
```

. . .

1. Finally, add code to the last print statement in *printPuzzle()* to print ten spaces and the clue.

Listing 15-12, from Hangman.java

. . .

```
private void printPuzzle() {

    . . .

    }
    print("|            " + _____);
}
```

. . .

Does it now print the appropriate clue of dashes for each letter in "HELLO WORLD" and a space between each word? Is the clue lined up below the wrong letters? If the clue isn't printing correctly, fix the code.

Key Points and More

- Character values are always a single character.

- Declare character data as *char*.

- Type character values with single quotes, like this:

```
char initial = 'A'.
```
- Characters are case-sensitive.

- Get a character from a string using String's *charAt()* method, giving the index of the character.

- Use the double equal sign (==), greater than sign (>), or less than sign (<) to check a character's value.

Lesson 15.3 – Index of Next Character

You'll need to find all indexes of a letter in the phrase. The *indexOf()* method you've used so far only found the first index of the letter. In this lesson, you'll use a second version of String's *indexOf()* method, which lets you specify where to start looking for the next index of the letter.

Try It

To replace letters in the clue if the user guessed a correct letter:

- Find the first index of the guessed letter.

- As long as it finds the guessed letter,

  - Replace the dash in the same position of the clue with the letter.

  - Find the next occurrence of the guessed letter.

- Print the puzzle again.

1. Add comments to the constructor, after the puzzle is printed, for each of the above steps.

Listing 15-13, from Hangman.java

```
. . .

public Hangman() {
   phrase = "HELLO WORLD";
   blankOutClue();

   wrongLetters = "ABC";
   printPuzzle();
```

```
//  _____
//  _____
//  _____
//  _____
//  _____
}
   . . .
```

How do you find the first index of a letter? Use String's *indexOf()* method. If the index is -1, it wasn't found.

How do you replace a string within a string? Use *replaceStringAt()*, which you created in the *MyStringMethods* class.

How do you find the next index of a letter in a string? Use String's *indexOf()* method, starting after the index where the previous one was found. Note, this is the version of *indexOf()* that takes two parameters. Use the search string and the search start index as the parameters.

1. Declare a string called *guess*, with an initial value of "*L*".

2. Can you figure out the code needed to do each of the steps in the comments? (Hint: see the above notes about *indexOf()* and *replaceStringAt()*.)

Listing 15-14, from Hangman.java

```
   . . .

public Hangman() {

      . . .

   String guess = "___";
   // find the first occurrence of the guessed letter in the phrase
   int index = _____;
   // as long as it finds the guessed letter
   while(_____) {
      // replace the dash in the same position of the clue with the
letter
      clue = _____.replaceStringAt(_____, _____, _____;
      // find the next occurrence of the guessed letter
      index = phrase.indexOf(_____,_____);
   }
   // print the puzzle again
   _____;

      . . .
```

It should print the puzzle twice: once with the puzzle all dashes, and a second time with the puzzle filled in with "L" shown in the correct locations:

```
_____
|   O
|  -|      ABC
|
|          _____ _____

_____
|   O
|  -|      ABC
|
|          --LL- ---L-
```

1. Try the puzzle a few times, using different phrases and different letters. Make sure it finds every place the guessed letter is in the phrase.

Next, update *wrongLetters* with the letters tried but not found:

1. Change the initial value of *wrongLetters* to be an empty string.

2. Declare a boolean variable, called *found*, initially false, because the letter was not yet found.

3. If the guessed letter was found, set *found* to true.

4. Once the program doesn't find the letter, check the value of *found*. If the letter was never found, add the guessed letter to the string of *wrongLetters*.

Listing 15-15, from Hangman.java

```
    . . .

public Hangman() {

      . . .

    wrongLetters = "___";
    printPuzzle();

    String guess = "L";
    boolean found = _____;
    // find the first occurrence of the guessed letter in the phrase
    int index = phrase.indexOf(guess);
    // as long as it finds the guessed letter
    while(index>-1) {
        found = _____;
        // replace the dash in the same position of the clue with the
letter
        clue = MyStringMethods.replaceStringAt(clue, index, guess);
        // find the next occurrence of the guessed letter
        index = phrase.indexOf(guess,index+1);
```

```
}
if (_____) {
    wrongLetters += _____;
}
// print the puzzle again
printPuzzle();

    . . .
```

1. Run the program a few times. Use different values for the guess.

If the guessed letter is in the phrase, the puzzle should show that letter everywhere it occurs in the phrase. Otherwise, the program should add the guess to the list of wrong letters.

Key Points and More

· String's *indexOf()* returns the first index of either a string or a character in the string.

· Use *indexOf()*'s optional second parameter to indicate where to start the search.

· To search for the next index of a string, start the search after the previous index of the string.

Lesson 15.4 – Check User Input

You should try to write programs so users can't enter invalid input. In this lesson, you'll handle several cases of bad data the user might try to enter.

Try It

It's time to let the user guess the letters. In fact, you should let the user keep guessing letters until the game is done.

When is the game done? When the puzzle is solved or when the stick man is complete.

How can you tell when the puzzle is solved? When there are no more dashes in the clue. (Hint: use String's *contains()* method to check if the string contains a dash.)

How can you tell when the stick man is complete? When the user made ten wrong guesses. (Hint: when the *length()* of *wrongLetters* is ten.)

1. Put a *while* loop around all the code from the declaration of *guess* through the second time it prints the puzzle.

2. Continue the loop while there are dashes in *clue* and the stick man isn't complete. (Hint: see the above notes about *contains()* and *length()*.)

3. Change *guess* to now prompt the user to guess a letter.

Listing 15-16, from Hangman.java

```
    . . .

public Hangman() {

    . . .

    // repeat until phrase solved or hangman complete (10 tries)
    while(clue._____ && wrongLetters._____) {
        String guess = _____;
        boolean found = false;

        . . .

        // print the puzzle again
        printPuzzle();
    }
}
    . . .
```

If you play the game, it probably won't take you very long to see it doesn't handle bad input very well.

At least three things should be fixed in this program:

- Always convert the user's guess to uppercase.

- Make sure the user never enters more than one letter. If he/she enters more than one letter, print an error message and ask him/her to try again. Don't add the invalid guess to *wrongLetters*.

- If the user already guessed the letter, ask him/her to try again. Don't add the same guess to *clue*, nor add it to *wrongLetters*. How can you tell if the user guessed the letter before? All previously guessed letters are in *clue* or in *wrongLetters*.

Add code to do this:

1. Convert *guess* to uppercase.

2. Make sure the user never enters more than one letter at a time.

3. Tell the user if the letter has already been guessed.

Listing 15-17, from Hangman.java

```
    . . .
```

```
public Hangman() {

    ...

    String guess = promptForString("Guess a letter");
    guess = _____;
    // must be one letter
    if (guess._____) {
      print("Your guess must contain only 1 letter. Guess again.");
    }
    // guess must not have been tried before
    else if (clue._____ || wrongLetters._____) {
      print("You already guessed " + guess + ". Guess again.");
    }
    else {
      boolean found = false;
      // find the first occurrence of the guessed letter

        ...

      // print the puzzle again
      printPuzzle();
    }
    ...
```

The loop ended because the user either solved the puzzle or made ten wrong guesses. Now you should congratulate the user only if he/she solved the puzzle. How do you know if the puzzle was solved? If there are no dashes left in the clue.

1. After the while loop:

    1. Congratulate the user if he/she solved the puzzle.

    2. Tell the user what the phrase was if he/she didn't solve the puzzle.

Listing 15-18, from Hangman.java

```
    ...

  public Hangman() {

    ...

    // repeat until phrase solved or hangman complete (10 tries)
    while(clue.contains("-") && wrongLetters.length() < 10) {

      ...

    }
```

```
    if (!clue._____) {
       print ("Congratulations! You guessed it before you were
hanged!");
    }
    else {
       print ("Sorry, you lose. The phrase was " + _____);
    }
  }
    ...
```

Key Points and More

- When you write programs that require user input, make sure he/she enters valid data.

Lesson 15.5 – Read All Lines of a File, Null Values

In previous programs, you knew how many lines were in a file. You wrote code to read that many lines from the file. In this lesson you will read all the lines of a file no matter how many lines are in the file.

Reading from a file will return _null_ when nothing is left to read. You must stop reading from the file when a null value is returned.

Try It

One of the files you should have downloaded was a file called *phrases.txt*. You'll use it for this program.

1. Copy the *phrases.txt* file from your Java work folder to the *Hangman* folder in your Java work folder.

A variable with no value is said to have a *null* value. Check for *null* value by comparing a variable with *null*. For example, to check if a String called *answer* has a value, check if it is not equal to *null*:

```
if (answer!=null)
```

Always check for *null* using the equal sign, not the *equal()* method, even for strings.

To read all the lines from a file when you don't know how many lines there are, do these steps:

- Open the file by creating a *BufferedReader* variable.

- Read a line from the file by calling the BufferedReader's *readLine()* method.

- While what is read is not *null*:

  - Do what you want with the line just read.

- Read another line from the file.

- Close the file by calling the BufferedReader's *close()* method.

For example, to read and print all the lines from a file called "myFile.txt", use this code:

```
BufferedReader in = new BufferedReader(new FileReader(new
File("myFile.txt")));
String line = in.readLine();
while (line!=null) {
  print(line);
  line = in.readLine();
}
in.close();
```

1. Create a private static final string instance variable called *FILENAME*, set to "phrases.txt".

2. Put the entire contents of the constructor into a *try* block.

3. Add code to the start of the *try* block to read all the lines from the file. Close the file when you're done. (Hint: read while what was read in is not null.)

4. Add catch blocks to catch *FileNotFoundException* and *IOException* and print messages when those exceptions are thrown.

Listing 15-19, from Hangman.java

```
    . . .

  private String phrase;
  private String clue;
  private String wrongLetters;

  private static final String FILENAME = "_____";

  public Hangman() {

    try {
      BufferedReader in = _____;
      String s = in._____;
      while (_____) {
        s = in._____;
      }
      in._____;

      phrase = "HELLO WORLD";
      blankOutClue();

      . . .
```

```
        else {
            print ("Sorry, you lose. The phrase was " + phrase);
        }
    }
    catch(FileNotFoundException e) {
        print(_____);
    }
    catch(IOException e) {
        print(_____);
    }
        . . .
```

This program won't do anything different when you run it. It reads in all the lines of the file, but it doesn't do anything with them yet.

Key Points and More

- A *null* variable is a variable that has no value.

- To check if a variable equals *null*, use the equal sign, not the *equals()* method, even when checking strings.

- To read all the lines of a file, read a line, then while what was read is not *null*:

  - Do something with what was read

  - Read the next line.

- *Hangman* always reads all the lines of the file. You can change what is in *phrases.txt* at any time and you won't have to change the Hangman program.

Lesson 15.6 – Array Lists

The arrays you've used so far had to hold a set number of items. In this lesson, you'll instead use an <u>ArrayList</u>. The number of items in an ArrayList can be changed at any time by the program.

Try It

You'll use an ArrayList instead of an array so you can delete some phrases from that file or add others of your own. The size of an ArrayList isn't set in the program code, so you can change what is in the *prhases.txt* file at any time without changing the Hangman program.

To declare an ArrayList, put its type of data in angle brackets, < >. For example, to declare an ArrayList of strings named *cities*, use:

```
ArrayList<String> cities = new ArrayList<String>();
```

Items must be added to an ArrayList one at a time. To add a string value to the end of an

ArrayList, use *add()*. For example, to add "Minneapolis" to the end of *cities*, use:

```
cities.add("Minneapolis");
```

In fact, you can insert a value anywhere in the list when you specify the index. For example, to add "Boston" to the beginning of *cities*, use:

```
cities.add(0, "Boston");
```

When you insert a value before the end of the list, all values after it are pushed out one more index.

To get a value from an ArrayList, use *get()* with the index. For example, to get the second value (index 1) from *cities*, use:

```
cities.get(1);
```

To get the number of items in an ArrayList, use *size()*. For example, to get the number of items in *cities*, use:

```
cities.size();
```

1. In the constructor, declare an ArrayList of type String named *phrases*. Initialize the ArrayList by calling its constructor.

2. While the line read is not null, add the line to *phrases*.

Listing 15-20, from Hangman.java

```
    . . .

  public Hangman() {
     ArrayList<_____> _____ = new ArrayList<_____>();

     try {
        BufferedReader in = new BufferedReader(new FileReader(new
File(FILENAME)));
        String s = in.readLine();
        while (s != null) {
           phrases._____(____);
           s = in.readLine();
        }
        . . .
```

Next, pick a random phrase from the ArrayList.

1. Declare a Random called *rand* at the start of the constructor and initialize it by calling its constructor.

2. Get a random phrase from *phrases* and assign it to *phrase*. (Hint: use ArrayList's *size()* and Random's *nextInt()*.)

3. Convert *phrase* to uppercase.

Listing 15-21, from Hangman.java

```
    . . .

public Hangman() {
    ArrayList<String> phrases = new ArrayList<String>();
    Random rand = _____;

    try {

        . . .

        in.close();
        int numberOfPhrases = phrases._____;

        int pick = rand.nextInt(_____);
        phrase = phrases._____(_____);
        phrase = phrase._____;
        blankOutClue();

        . . .
```

The program should now use a random phrase from the *phrases.txt* file.

One last way to make this program better would be to ask the user if he/she wants to play again after the puzzle is solved.

1. Declare a boolean called *again*, initially true.

2. Move everything, from picking the next random integer through printing the sorry message at the end of the puzzle, into a *while* loop that continues while *again* is true.

3. Before the end of the *while* loop, ask the user if he/she wants to play again and put his/her answer in *again*. (Hint: use *promptForYesNo().*)

4. Close the window after the loop. (Hint: use *System.exit(0).*)

Listing 15-22, from Hangman.java

```
    . . .

public Hangman() {

    . . .

    int numberOfPhrases = phrases.size();

    boolean again = _____;
    while (_____) {
        int pick = rand.nextInt(numberOfPhrases);
```

```
    phrase = phrases.get(pick);

    . . .

      print("Sorry, you lose. The phrase was " + phrase);
    }
    again = _____;
  }
  System._____;

} catch (FileNotFoundException e) {

    . . .
```

This is the end of the Hangman program. If you want to run it without Eclipse:

1. Export your Hangman program.

2. Copy the *phrases.txt* file to the same folder as the *Hangman.jar* file.

Key Points and More

- An ArrayList can hold a list of an unknown number of items or a list whose number of items might change.

- An ArrayList must hold data of all the same type.

- ArrayLists can only hold items that are Java <u>objects</u>. In other words, they must have class definitions and usually have methods.

  - Strings are Java objects; they have a class definition and methods. So strings can be put into an ArrayList.

  - Java int, double, char, boolean, byte, short, long, and float aren't Java objects. These types are called Java <u>primitives</u>. They can be put in arrays but not in ArrayLists.

  - If you need to put primitive values into an ArrayList, make them into Java objects by using their <u>wrappers</u>. For example, to create an Integer object from an int called *num*, use:

```
Integer obj = new Integer(num);
```

  - You can get the primitive value back out of the object wrapper if you call its value method. For example, to get the int value back out of the above integer variable, use:

```
int num = obj.intValue();
```

  - Objects will be explained in further detail in the next lesson.

- To declare an ArrayList, use:

```
ArrayList<type> = new ArrayList<type>()
```
where type is the type of data the ArrayList will hold.

- To add an item to the end of the ArrayList, use *add()* with the item as the parameter.

- To add an item to the middle of the ArrayList, use *add()* with the index as the first parameter.

  - You'll receive an error if you try to add an item to an index past the end of the ArrayList. So make sure your index is valid before you use it.

- To get the value of an item in the ArrayList, use *get()* with the index as the parameter.

  - You'll receive an error if you try to get an item from an index past the end of the ArrayList. So make sure your index is valid before you use it.

- Because *Hangman* uses an ArrayList, you can change what is in *phrases.txt* and you won't have to change the Hangman program.

Project 16 – Crazy Eights

In the Crazy Eights card game, you take turns with your opponent, trying to be first to get rid of all your cards. Normally, you must play a card that matches the discard's suit or rank. However, you can play any eight at any time, regardless of its suit and the discard's suit. When you play an eight, you name the suit that must be played next. If you cannot play a card, you must pick up another card.

Here's a screenshot of the Crazy Eights program:

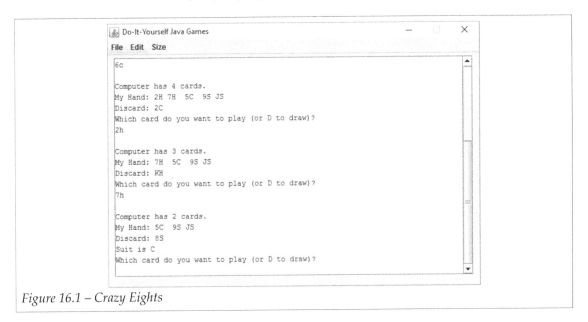

Figure 16.1 – Crazy Eights

Lesson 16.1 – Objects, Card

One of the most powerful features of Java is its use of objects, called Object Oriented Programming. You've used objects in all of the programs so far. But until the tips in the last lesson, objects haven't been mentioned.

You've created many classes. Classes declare the data used by the class and define the methods used to manipulate that data. In the main method of every program, you created a new instance of the class. The instance is also called the object.

In this lesson, you'll create a Card class. You'll create many instances of a Card to play a card game. In other words, you'll create many Card objects.

Card won't be a program. Card will be a class definition for Card objects used in the program.

Try It

What are some of the objects you use to play a real card game? Individual cards, a deck of cards, and a hand of cards. In this project, you'll create one Card class, one Deck class, and one Hand class. The Crazy Eights program will create one Deck object, two Hand objects, and many Card objects as instances of those classes.

You'll put the card-related classes in their own *Cards* project, separate from the *Crazy Eights* project, in case you want to use them to create other card games.

1. Create a new *Java project* called *Cards*, and add *My String Methods* to the project.

2. Create a new *package* called _____._____.cards in the project.

3. Create a new *class* called *Card*, using the default *Object* as its superclass. Don't create a stub for *main()* nor for its constructors.

Listing 16-1, from Card.java

```
package annette.godtland.cards;

public class Card {

}
```

Each card will have one character for its rank and another character for its suit.

The rank will be A, 2, 3, 4, 5, 6, 7, 8, 9, T, J, Q, or K. A is for ace, T is for 10, J is for jack, Q is for queen, and K is for king.

The suit will be H, D, C, or S. H is for hearts, D is for diamonds, C is for clubs, and S is for spades.

Each instance of a card has a different suit and rank. Therefore, suit and rank should be instance variables.

1. Add private character instance variables called *rank* and *suit* with initial values of '8' and 'H'. (Hint: characters are typed with single quotes around them.)

Listing 16-2, from Card.java

```
package annette.godtland.cards;

public class Card {
    _____;
    _____;
}
```

1. Add a public *toString()* method that takes no parameters and returns a string.

2. *toString()* should join rank and suit together to create a string, and return that string. (Hint: the easiest way to convert characters to a string is to add them to an empty string.)

Listing 16-3, from Card.java

```
    . . .

    public _____ toString(_____) {
        String rs = "" + _____ + _____;
        return _____;
    }
}
```

Next, you need a program that uses the Card class:

Start writing the next program:

1. Create a new *Java project* called *Crazy Eights* and add *My Window, Cards,* and *DIYJava.jar* to the project.

2. Create a new *package* called _____._____.*crazyeights* in the project.

3. Create a new *class* in the *crazyeights* package called *CrazyEights,* with superclass *MyWindow* and with a stub for *main()* and its constructors.

4. Add code to *main()* to call the *CrazyEights* constructor.

Listing 16-4, from CrazyEights.java

```
package annette.godtland.crazyeights;

import annette.godtland.mywindow.MyWindow;

public class CrazyEights extends MyWindow {

    public CrazyEights() {

    }

    public static void main(String[] args) {
        _____;
    }
}
```

In previous lessons, you created a new *Random* object using:

```
Random rand = new Random();
```

1. Create a new Card object called *card* in the constructor for CrazyEights the same way.

2. Convert *card* to a string and print the card's value. (Hint: use your new *toString()* method.)

Listing 16-5, from CrazyEights.java

```
. . .

public class CrazyEights extends MyWindow {

    public CrazyEights() {
        Card card = _____;
        print(card._____);
    }

    public static void main(String[] args) {
        new CrazyEights();
    }
}
```

When you run the program, it should print

8H

because that's the initial value of card, as defined in your Card class.

Key Points and More

- Classes define objects. When you create a new variable of a type of a class, you create an instance of the class. The instance can also be called an object.

- Objects have instance variables and methods. Instance variables exist for each instance of the object. For example, each Card will have its own values for its instance variables: *rank* and *suit*.

- To create an instance of an object, declare a variable of that type object, then call its constructor. For example:

```
Card card = new Card();
```

- Java provides a default constructor with no parameters if you didn't create a constructor for the class. So you can still call *new Card()* to create a Card object, even if Card doesn't have a constructor.

- You should write a *toString()* method for all your object classes. Java looks for a *toString()* method if you join the object to a string. For example, if you write this code:

```
print("My card is " + card);
```

Java will call the *toString()* method to convert *card* to a string.

Lesson 16.2 – Constructors

Every program had a constructor. The constructor was called when a new instance of the program was created in *main()*.

So far, all your constructors took no parameters. But like other methods, constructors can have any number of parameters. In this lesson, you'll create a Card constructor to create a card from a string.

Try It

Rules to create your own constructor are:

- The constructor name must be exactly the same as the name of the class, including the same capitalization.
- Constructors must be public.
- Constructors have no return type.
- Constructors can have parameters.

For example, a constructor for the *CrazyEights* class with an integer parameter for the number of players would look like this:

```
public CrazyEights(int numberOfPlayers) {
}
```

Rather than have your Card class's value always be "8H", you should let your constructor create a card from a value.

1. Change the initial values for *rank* and *suit* in the Card class to each be blank.

2. Create a Card constructor with one string parameter called *rs*.

3. The constructor should assign the first character of *rs* to rank and the second character to *suit*. (Hint: use *charAt()*.)

Listing 16-6, from Card.java

```
    . . .

    private char rank = ___;
    private char suit = ___;

    public Card(String rs) {
        rank = rs._____;
        suit = rs._____;
    }
    . . .
```

1.   Now, change the *CrazyEights* program to pass "7S" to the constructor for *card*.

Listing 16-7, from CrazyEights.java

```
    . . .

  public CrazyEights() {
     Card card = new Card(_____);
     print(card.toString());
  }
     . . .
```

When you run the program, it should print

7S

Key Points and More

· Constructors look like methods, but their name must be identical to the class name, with the same capitalization.

· Constructors are always public and don't have a return type as part of their definition since they never return a value.

· You can have more than one constructor for a class. Each constructor must have a different number of parameters or different types of parameters.

· Constructors are called when other code creates a new instance of a class. For example, to call the Card constructor with one string parameter, you could use:

```
new Card("QH");
```

· If you don't write a constructor for a class, Java provides a default constructor with no parameters. That default constructor does nothing other than create the class's instance variables. So if your class doesn't need to run any code when an object is created, you don't need to provide a constructor for that class.

Lesson 16.3 – Modulo

Modulo lets you convert any integer into an integer between a range of values. For example, you'll need to convert an integer to a number between 0 and 12 to represent the 13 cards in each suit.

In this lesson, you'll create a second Card constructor to create a Card object from an integer.

Try It

You'll need to create string variables of all the possible ranks and suits. The possible ranks or suits should never change, so they should be final. All cards should use the same possible ranks or suits, so they should be static.

1. Add a private, static, final string instance variable called *RANKS*, initially a string of all the possible rank values: "A23456789TJQK".

2. Add a private, static, final string instance variable called *SUITS*, initially a string of all the possible suit values: "HDCS".

Listing 16-8, from Card.java

```
   . . .

private char rank = ' ';
private char suit = ' ';

_____    RANKS = _____;
_____    SUITS = _____;

public Card(String rs) {

   . . .
```

Currently, you can create a card from a string. It would also be very useful to create a card from an integer between 0 and 52. That would require another constructor.

1. Add a second constructor with one parameter, an integer called *id*.

Listing 16-9, from Card.java

```
   . . .

public Card(_____) {

}

public Card(String rs) {

   . . .
```

A deck of 52 cards will need values of "AH", "2H", "3H, ..., "KS". In other words, the first 12 numbers in 0 to 51 should be converted to 0 through 11 for an index into RANK, and 0 for an index into SUIT. The next 12 numbers should be converted to 0 through 11 again for the index into RANK, but 1 for the index into SUIT, etc.

Remember when you first looked at integer division? When you divided 5 by 2, the Calculator program said the answer was 2. It dropped the remainder. You can now make good use of how that works.

If you divide numbers 0 through 51 by 13, the first 12 numbers would give a result of 0, the next 12 numbers would give a result of 1. etc. So to calculate the suit index, divide the number by 13.

Modulo is another Java operation, similar to division. Instead of giving the whole number and dropping the remainder, modulo drops the whole number and gives the remainder. The modulo symbol is %. So 5 modulo 2 would be coded as 5 % 2 and would give a result of 1 because 5 divided by 2 is 2 with a remainder of 1.

If you use modulo 13 on numbers 0 through 51, the first 12 numbers would give results of 0 through 11, the next 12 numbers would give results of 0 through 11 again, etc. So to calculate the rank index, use modulo 13 on the number.

You are now ready to add code to the Card constructor that accepts an integer as a parameter.

1. Convert *id* into a number between 0 and 12. Then get the character at that position in *RANKS* and put it in *rank*. (Hint: according to the above notes, do you divide or modulo by 13? Hint: use *charAt()* to get a character from a position in a string.)

2. Convert *id* into a number between 0 and 3. Then get the character at that position in *SUITS* and put it in *suit*. (Hint: according to the above notes, do you divide or modulo by 13?)

Listing 16-10, from Card.java

```
    . . .

public Card(int id) {
    rank = RANKS.charAt(id __ 13);
    suit = SUITS.charAt(id __ 13);
}
    . . .
```

There are a couple problems with this new Card constructor. If you give it an integer larger than 52, the suit index will be greater than the number of possible ranks. Or if you give it a negative integer, the suit and rank index will be invalid.

But how do you make sure the initial number is always between 0 and 51? Use modulo 52. If the number is negative, multiply it by -1.

At the start of the constructor that takes an integer:

1. Convert *id* into a number from 0 to 51. (Hint: according to the above notes, do you divide or modulo by 52?)

2. If *id* is less than 0, multiply it by -1.

Listing 16-11, from Card.java

```
    . . .

public Card(int id) {
    id = id ____ 52;
    if(id ____ ____) {
        id = id ____ ____;
    }
    rank = RANKS.charAt(id%13);
    suit = SUITS.charAt(id/13);
}
    . . .
```

The Card constructor that takes an integer should work fine now. But the Card constructor that takes a String has problems if the string isn't two characters or has characters not in *RANKS* or *SUITS*.

In the Card constructor with the string parameter:

1. Check if *rs* is two characters. (Hint: use *length()*.)

2. If *rs* is two characters:

    1. Assign the first and second characters of *rs* to new char variables, called *r* and *s*, instead of *rank* and *suit*.

    2. If *r* and *s* are in RANKS and SUITS, then set *rank* and *suit* to *r* and *s*. (Hint: use *indexOf()* to find out if a character is in a string.)

Listing 16-12, from Card.java

```
    . . .

public Card(String rs) {
    if(rs._____) {
        char ____ = rs.charAt(0);
        char ____ = rs.charAt(1);
        int ri = RANKS.indexOf(____);
        int si = SUITS.indexOf(____);
        if (ri>____ && si>____) {
            rank = ____;
            suit = ____;
        }
    }
}
    . . .
```

Now, if anyone tries to create a Card using an invalid string, *rank* and *suit* will be blank.

Change *CrazyEights* to see these two constructors work.

1. Try to create a new Card using different integers. Try numbers between 0 and 51. Try larger numbers.

2. Try to create a new Card using different strings. Try valid card strings. Try strings too long or too short. Try strings of characters not in SUIT or RANK.

Listing 16-13, from CrazyEights.java

```
   . . .

public CrazyEights() {
   Card card = new Card(_____);
   print(card.toString());
}
   . . .
```

Key Points and More

·   Modulo is similar to division but returns the remainder of the division result instead of the whole number of the result. For example, 14 modulo 4 would be 2.

·   The modulo symbol is the percent sign, %. For example, 14 modulo 4 would be coded as 14 % 4.

·   Modulo can be used to turn any integer to a specific range, such as four suits in a deck of cards, 6 dots on a die, etc.

Lesson 16.4 – Other Card Methods

In this lesson, you'll create methods to get the card's rank or suit, check if it's a valid card, check if the card is equal to or greater than another card, and check if a character is a valid suit.

Try It

Most classes need a public way to get the values of the private instance variables.

1. Add public methods called *getRank()* and *getSuit()*. Neither method should take parameters. *getRank()* should return this card's rank. *getSuit()* should return this card's suit.

Listing 16-14, from Card.java

```
   . . .
```

```
public char getRank() {
    return _____;
}

public char getSuit() {
    return _____;
}
    . . .
```

The game will also need to know if the instance of the card is valid.

1. Add a public method called *isValid()*. It should take no parameters and return a boolean.

2. *isValid()* should return true if this card is valid. (Hint: a card is **invalid** if *suit* is blank.)

Listing 16-15, from Card.java

```
    . . .

public _____ isValid() {
    boolean valid = false;
    if (_____) {
        valid = true;
    }
    return _____;
}
    . . .
```

Next, add a method to check if this card is equal to another card.

1. Add a public method called *equals()*. It should take one parameter, a Card called *card*, and return a boolean.

2. *equals()* should return true if the *card* in the parameter is equal to this card. (Hint: cards are equal if they both have the same rank and suit. Hint: use *getSuit()* and *getRank()* to get the suit and rank of the *card* in the parameter. Use *suit* and *rank* to get the suit and rank of this card.)

Listing 16-16, from Card.java

```
    . . .

public boolean equals(Card card) {
    boolean equals = _____;
    if ((card._____ == suit) && (card._____ == rank)) {
        equals = _____;
    }
    return _____;
}
```

. . .

Add a method to check if this card is greater than another card.

1. Add a public method called *isGreaterThan()*. It should take one parameter, a Card called *card*, and return a boolean.

2. Get the suit and rank of the *card* in the parameter and put them in characters called *cardSuit* and *cardRank*.

3. Check if the index of *suit* in SUITS is greater than the index of *cardSuit* in SUITS. If so, this card as greater than *card*. (Hint: use *indexOf()*.)

4. Otherwise, check if *suit* of this card is equal to *cardSuit*. If it is equal, then compare their ranks:

    1. If the index of *rank* in RANKS is greater than the index of *cardRank* in RANKS, then this card is greater than *card*.

Listing 16-17, from Card.java

```
    . . .

_____ isGreaterThan(_____) {
    boolean greaterThan = _____;
    _____ cardSuit = card._____;
    _____ cardRank = _card._____;
    if (_____) {
       greaterThan = _____;
    }
    else if (_____) {
       if (_____) {
          greaterThan = _____;
       }
    }
    return _____;
}
    . . .
```

One more method should be added to check if a character is a valid suit. This method can be static because the only thing it uses from this class is the static string *SUITS*.

1. Add a public static method called *isValidSuit()*. It should take one parameter, a character, and return a boolean.

2. *isValidSuit()* should return true if the character is in *SUITS*. (Hint: use String's *indexOf()* method.)

Listing 16-18, from Card.java

```
    . . .

public _____ isValidSuit(_____) {
   boolean valid = false;
   if (_____) {
      valid = true;
   }
   return _____;
}
    . . .
```

Make changes to *CrazyEights* to test the new methods.

1. Create two cards and print them.

2. If either card isn't valid, print a message.

3. If the cards are equal, print a message.

4. If the first card is greater than the second card, print a message.

5. Create a character called *c* and assign it any character value. Print one message if *c* is a valid suit and a different message if it isn't. (Hint: use Card's *isValidSuit()* method. Hint: use the *Card* class name when you call its static *isValidSuit()* method.)

Listing 16-19, from CrazyEights.java

```
    . . .

public CrazyEights() {
   Card card1 = _____;
   print(card1._____);
   Card card2 = _____;
   print(card2._____);
   if (_____) {
      print("The first card is not valid");
   }
   if (_____) {
      print("The second card is not valid");
   }
   if (_____) {
      print("The cards are equal.");
   }
   else {
      print("The cards are not equal.");
   }
   if (_____) {
      print("The first card is greater.");
```

```
   }
   else {
     print("The first card is not greater.");
   }
   char c = ____;
   if (_____) {
     print(__ + "is a valid suit");
   }
   else {
     print(__ + "is not a valid suit");
   }
 }
   . . .
```

1. Try different values for *card1, card2,* and *c* to make sure all methods work as they should.

Key Points and More

- *isGreaterThan()* checks which card is greater based on the order the characters appear in the *SUITS* and *RANKS* strings. If you want the cards arranged in a different order, change the order of the characters in *SUITS* and *RANKS*. For example, if you want Ace to be after King, use:

```
RANKS = "23456789TJQKA";
```

- This Card class could be used for other card games. Consider adding other methods and/or instance variables you might want for other card games. For example, if you wanted to keep score, you might add an array instance variable of integers called *value*, to hold point values for each card.

Lesson 16.5 – Deck

The Crazy Eights game will need a deck of 52 cards.

In this lesson, you'll create a Deck class and add methods to deal cards from the deck, shuffle the deck, reuse the deck, and tell the program how many cards are left in the deck.

Try It

1. Create a new *class* in the *cards* package called *Deck*, using the default *Object* as its superclass. Create a stub its constructor, but not for *main()*.

Listing 16-20, from Deck.java

```
package annette.godtland.cards;
```

```
public class Deck {

   public Deck() {

   }

}
```

Each deck should have a stack of cards (a list) and a random number generator to shuffle the deck.

1. Add a private ArrayList instance variable of type Card called *cards*, initialized by calling its constructor.

2. Add a private Random() instance variable called *rand*, initialized by calling its constructor.

Listing 16-21, from Deck.java

```
   . . .

public class Deck {
   _____  cards = _____;
   _____  rand = _____;

   public Deck() {

      . . .
```

The Deck's constructor should create 52 card objects and put them in the list of cards.

1. Loop through the numbers 0 through 51 to create 52 cards and add them to *cards*. (Hint: use the Card constructor that takes an integer as its parameter.)

Listing 16-22, from Deck.java

```
      . . .

   public Deck() {
      for(_____) {
         Card card = new _____;
         cards.add(_____);
      }
   }
      . . .
```

1. Add a public *toString()* method that takes no parameters and returns a string.

2. Loop through all the cards in *cards*, add them to a string, placing a space between each

card in the string. (Hint: use ArrayList's *size()* to find out how many cards are in the list, and therefore, how many times to repeat the loop.)

3. Return the string.

Listing 16-23, from Deck.java

```
    . . .

  public _____ toString(____) {
     String deckString = _____;
     for(_____) {
        Card card = cards._____;
        deckString += _____;
     }
     return _____;
  }
    . . .
```

Now you need your program to make use of a deck.

Change the constructor in CrazyEights:

1. Remove all the code currently in the constructor.

2. Create a Deck called *deck*.

3. Print the *deck*. (Hint: use Deck's *toString()*.)

Listing 16-24, from CrazyEights.java

```
    . . .

  public CrazyEights() {
     _____ deck = new _____;
     print(_____);
  }
    . . .
```

It should print all the cards of the deck, with a space between each card.

Next, you need to add code to shuffle a deck.

1. Create a new public method in Deck called *shuffle()*. It should take no parameters and return no value.

2. Create a new ArrayList of type Card, called *shuffled*.

3. Loop through all the *cards* in the deck. (Hint: use ArrayList's *size()* to determine how many times.)

4. For each card in *deck*, get the current size of the deck, remove a random card from *cards*, and add it to *shuffled*. (Hint: *cards* changes size as each card is removed, so pick a random card based on the current size of *cards*. Hint: remove a card using ArrayList's *remove()*. Hint: add a card using ArrayList's *add()*.)

5. Set *cards* to the value of *shuffled*.

Listing 16-25, from Deck.java

```
. . .

_____ shuffle(_____) {
        _____ shuffled = new _____;
    int numberOfTimes = _____;
    for(_____){
        int deckSize = _____;
        int pick = rand._____;
        Card card = cards.remove(_____);
        shuffled._____;
    }
    cards = _____;
}
    . . .
```

1. Now, call *shuffle()* at the end of the Deck constructor so it always shuffles a new deck.

Listing 16-26, from Deck.java

```
. . .

public Deck() {
    for(int i=0; i<52; i++){
        Card card = new Card(i);
        cards.add(card);
    }
    _____;
}
    . . .
```

Run the Crazy Eights program again. It should now print a shuffled deck.

Next, add code to deal one card at a time.

1. Add a pubic method to *Deck* called *deal()*. It should take no parameters and return a Card.

2. Remove the first card of *deck* and return it. (Hint: use ArrayList's *remove()*.)

Listing 16-27, from Deck.java

```
. . .
```

```
_____ deal (_____) {
    Card card = _____;
    return _____;
}
    . . .
```

Your program will need a way to reuse the discard pile and make it into a deck.

1. Create a public method for Deck called *reuse()*. It should take one parameter, an ArrayList of type Card called *newCards*, and return nothing.

2. Set *cards* to the value of *newCards*.

Listing 16-28, from Deck.java

```
    . . .

_____ reuse (_____) {
    cards = _____;
}
    . . .
```

You'll also need a way to find out how many cards are in the deck.

1. Create a public method for Deck called *size()*. It should take no parameters and return an integer.

2. Return the size of *cards*. (Hint: use ArrayList's *size()*.)

Listing 16-29, from Deck.java

```
    . . .

_____ size(___) {
    return cards._____;
}
    . . .
```

Add to the Crazy Eights constructor to see if the new methods work.

1. Print the size of the deck.

2. Create an ArrayList of type Card called *discardPile*, initialized by calling its constructor.

3. Create a loop to repeat 10 times: deal a card from the *deck*, print it, and put it in the *discardPile*.

4. Print the *deck* size, replace the *deck* by reusing the *discardPile*, print the *deck* again, then print the *deck* size.

Listing 16-30, from CrazyEights.java

```
   . . .

public CrazyEights() {
   Deck deck = new Deck();
   print(deck.toString());
   print(deck._____);
   ArrayList<Card> discardPile = _____;
   for(_____) {
      Card card = deck._____;
      print(_____);
      discardPile._____;
   }
   print(deck._____);
   deck.reuse(_____);
   print(deck._____);
   print(deck._____);

}
   . . .
```

Run the program again. It should print the full deck, then 52, then the first ten cards taken from the deck, then 42, then the same ten cards printed as a deck, then 10.

Key Points and More

· You should be able to use this Deck class to create other card games.

· Consider adding instance variables and methods you might need for other card games. For example, you might want another constructor that takes an integer parameter for how many decks to use for the game.

Lesson 16.6 – Hand

A Hand is similar to a deck. It also is a list of cards. However, a hand is used differently than a deck, so it needs different methods.

In this lesson, you'll create a Hand class and add a method to print the hand. You'll also add methods to add or remove cards from the hand, find what card is at an index of the hand, check if the hand contains a given card, and get the number of cards in the hand.

Try It

1. Create a new *class* in the *cards* package called *Hand*, using the default *Object* as its *superclass*. Don't create a stub for *main()* nor for its constructors.

2. Add a private ArrayList instance variable of type Card called *cards*, initialized by calling its constructor.

Listing 16-31, from Hand.java

```
package annette.godtland.cards;

public class Hand {
    _____ cards = _____;
}
```

No code needs to run when a Hand is created, so Hand doesn't need a constructor.

Add a method to add a card to a hand. It should arrange the cards in order from smallest to largest.

How do you put cards in order when you use real cards? One way is to pick up a card and compare it to the first card in your hand. If it's greater than the first card, compare it to the next card. Continue this until you reach a card it isn't greater than, and insert it before that card. Write code to do the same thing.

1. Add a public method called *add()* to Hand. It should take one parameter, a Card called *card*, and return no value.

2. Create an integer called *index*, initially 0, for where to insert *card* in *hand*.

3. Create a boolean called *done*, initially false, for when it has found where to insert *card* in *hand*.

4. Repeat while *done* is still false, and you haven't yet gone through all the cards in the hand:

    1. Get the card at *index* and put it in a Card called *cardInHand*. (Hint: use ArrayList's the *get()* method.)

    2. If *card* is greater than *cardInHand*, increment *index*. Otherwise set *done* to true. (Hint: use Card's *isGreaterThan()* method.)

5. Add *card* to *cards* at *index*. (Hint: use ArrayList's *add()* method that takes 2 parameters.)

Listing 16-32, from Hand.java

```
    . . .

    public void add(Card card) {
```

```
_____  index = _____;
_____  done = _____;
while(!_____ && index < _____) {
   Card cardInHand = _____;
   if (card._____) {
      _____;
   }
   else {
      _____;
   }
}
cards.add(_____);
   }
}
```

Next, add a *toString()* method to Hand. *toString()* should add each card to a string with a space between each card.

1. Add a public method called *toString()* to Hand. It should take no parameters and return a string.

2. Create an empty string called *string*.

3. Loop through all the *cards*:

   1. Get each card and add it and a space to *string*.

4. Return *string*.

Listing 16-33, from Hand.java

```
   . . .

_____ String toString(____) {
   String string = ____;
   for (_____) {
      Card card = _____;
      string += _____;
   }
   return _____;
   }
}
```

Add code to the *toString()* method to insert a couple extra spaces between each suit. Extra spaces between suits will make it easier to see how many cards are in each suit.

1. If this isn't the first card, get the suit of the previous card and the suit of the current card. If they are different suits, add a couple extra spaces to *string*. (Hint: to determine if this is the first card, look at the value of the *for* loop index variable.)

Listing 16-34, from Hand.java

```
    . . .

public String toString() {
    String string = "";
    for (int i=0; i<cards.size(); i++) {
        Card card = cards.get(i);
        // if this is not the first card, compare it with the
        // previous card.  If the suits are different add a
        // couple extra spaces
        if (_____) {
            Card priorCard = _____;
            char priorSuit = _____;
            char currentSuit = _____;
            if (_____) {
                string += _____;
            }
        }
    }
    string += card.toString() + " ";

    . . .
```

Go back to *CrazyEights* and try out some of the new code. You'll create a Deck, deal 7 cards to a hand, then print the hand.

1. Remove all the code from the constructor.

2. Add code to create a new Hand called *hand*.

3. Create three cards called *card1*, *card2*, and *card3*: a King of Clubs, 7 of Hearts, and Jack of Clubs. (Hint: use the Card constructor that takes a string.)

4. Add the cards to the *hand*.

5. Print the *hand*. (Hint: use *toString()*.)

Listing 16-35, from CrazyEights.java

```
    . . .

public CrazyEights() {
    Hand hand = _____;
    Card card1 = _____;
    Card card2 = _____;
    Card card3 = _____;
    hand.add(_____);
    hand.add(_____);
    hand.add(_____);
```

```
      print(_____);
    }
      . . .
```

Run the program again. It should print the cards, in order, with extra space between suits:

7H   JC KC

To play a card from the hand, you have to remove a card from the hand.

1. Add a public method to Hand called *remove()*. It should take one parameter, a Card called *card*, and return nothing.

2. Create an integer called *index*, initially 0, for where it finds *card* in the hand.

3. Create a boolean called *found*, initially false, for when it finds *card* in the hand.

4. Repeat while not *found* and haven't yet gone through all the cards in the hand:

    1. If the card at *index* is equal to *card*, remove it from *cards*, and set *found* to true. (Hint: use ArrayList's *remove()* method for removing an item at an index.)

    2. Otherwise, increment *index*.

Listing 16-36, from Hand.java

```
      . . .

   public void remove(Card card) {
   _____ index = _____;
   _____ found = _____;
      while(_____ && _____) {
         Card compareCard = _____;
         if(compareCard._____) {
            cards._____;
            found = _____;
         }
         else {
                    _____
         }
      }
   }
}
```

You'll also need a way to check if a hand contains a given card.

1. Add a public method to Hand called *contains()*. It should take one parameter, a Card called *card*, and return a boolean.

2. Create an integer called *index*, initially 0, for where it finds *card* in the hand.

3. Create a boolean called *contains*, initially false, for when it finds *card* in the hand.

4. Repeat while not *contains* and haven't yet gone through all the cards in the hand:

    1. If the card at *index* is equal to *card* set *contains* to true.

5. Return *contains.*

Listing 16-37, from Hand.java

```
    . . .

_____ contains(_____) {
    _____ index = _____;
    _____ contains = _____;
    while(_____ && _____) {
      Card compareCard = _____;
      if(compareCard._____) {
        contains = _____;
      }
      else {
        _____
      }
    }
    return contains;
  }
}
```

Next you'll add a method to get the card at a particular position in the hand.

- Add a public method to Hand called *cardAt()*. It should take one parameter, an integer called *index*, and return a Card.

- *cardAt()* should return the card in *cards* at *index*. Hint: use ArrayList's *get()*.

Listing 16-38, from Hand.java

```
    . . .

_____ cardAt(_____) {
    return cards._____;
  }
}
```

And one last method you'll need is to find out how many cards are in the Hand.

1. Add a public method to Hand called *size()*. It should take no parameters and return an integer.

2. Return the size of *cards.*

Listing 16-39, from Hand.java

```
    . . .

_____ size(____) {
    return _____;
}
}
```

Go back to *CrazyEights* and try out the new methods.

1. Create a fourth card, called *card4*; a 2 of Diamonds.

2. Print the size of the hand.

3. If *card3* is in the hand, print a message.

4. If *card4* is in the hand, print a message.

5. Remove *card2* and *card4* from the hand.

6. Print the hand.

7. Print the size of the hand.

Listing 16-40, from CrazyEights.java

```
    . . .

public CrazyEights() {
    Hand hand = new Hand();
    Card card1 = new Card("KC");
    Card card2 = new Card("7H");
    Card card3 = new Card("JC");
    Card card4 = _____;
    hand.add(card1);
    hand.add(card2);
    hand.add(card3);
    print(hand.toString());
    print(_____);
    if (_____) {
       print("Found Jack of Clubs");
    }
    if (_____) {
       print("Found 2 of Diamonds");
    }
    hand.remove(_____);
    hand.remove(_____);
    print(_____);
    print(_____);
```

```
    }
    . . .
```

It should have printed:

```
7H    JC KC
3
Found Jack of Clubs
JC KC
2
```

Key Points and More

- You should be able to use this Hand class to create other card games.

- Consider adding instance variables and methods you might need for other card games.

Lesson 16.7 – Crazy Eights: Setup

To set up the *Crazy Eights* game, the program should deal seven cards to each player, turn up a discard, and show the status of the game.

Try It

1. Remove all the code currently in the constructor of the *CrazyEights* class.

2. Add these instance variables:

   1. *deck* should be a private Deck, initialized by calling its constructor.

   2. *myHand* should be a private Hand, initialized by calling its constructor.

   3. *computerHand* should be a private Hand, initialized by calling its constructor.

   4. *discard* should be a private Card.

   5. *discardPile* should be a private ArrayList of type Card, initialized by calling its constructor.

   6. *rand* should be a private Random, initialized by calling its constructor.

   7. *activeSuit* should be a private character, initialized as a space character.

Listing 16-41, from CrazyEights.java

```
    . . .

public class CrazyEights extends MyWindow {

_____ deck = _____;
```

```
_____        myHand = _____;
_____        computerHand = _____;
_____        discard;
_____        discardPile = _____;
_____        rand = _____;
_____        activeSuit = _____;

public CrazyEights() {

        (Code was removed from here.)


}
    . . .
```

Next, you need to deal cards to each player. But since you'll deal cards from more than one place in the program, you should put the deal code in a method that can be called many times.

1. Add a private method to *CrazyEights* called *deal()*. It should take no parameters and return a Card.

2. If there aren't any cards in *deck*, reuse the *discardPile*, shuffle the *deck*, empty the *discardPile*, and print a blank line and a message telling the user you reshuffled the discard pile. (Hint: use Deck's *reuse()* to reuse *discardPile*. Hint: use ArrayList's *clear()* to empty the *discardPile*.)

3. Deal a Card from *deck* and return it. (Hint: use Deck's *deal()*.)

Listing 16-42, from CrazyEights.java

```
    . . .

    private Card deal() {
        // if end of deck, reuse the discard pile and shuffle it.
        if (_____) {
            deck._____;
            deck._____;
            discardPile._____;
            print();
            print("_____");
        }

        // deal a card from the deck
        Card card = _____;
        return _____;
    }
}
```

Next, deal seven cards to each player and turn up the discard card. Also, set the active suit if the initial discard is an 8.

1. In the constructor, repeat seven times: deal a card and add it to *myHand*, then deal another card and add it to *computerHand*. (Hint: use CrazyEights's *deal()*.)

2. Deal one more card and make that the *discard*.

3. If *discard* is an 8, set *activeSuit* to the suit of the discard.

4. Otherwise, set *activeSuit* to a blank character.

Listing 16-43, from CrazyEights.java

```
    . . .

public CrazyEights()
    // deal 7 cards to each of us
    for (_____) {
        Card card1 = _____;
        myHand._____;
        Card card2 = _____;
        computerHand._____;
    }

    // turn up the discard
    discard = _____;

    // if discard is an 8, set the active suit
    if (_____) {
        activeSuit = _____;
    }
    else {
        activeSuit = _____;
    }

}
    . . .
```

Next, show the status of the game.

1. Add a private method called *showStatus()*. It should take no parameters and return nothing.

2. Print a blank line, the number of cards in *computerHand*, the cards in *myHand*, and the *discard*.

3. If the discard is an 8, also print the *activeSuit*.

Listing 16-44, from CrazyEights.java

```
. . .
_____ showStatus(_____) {
   print();
   print("Computer has " + _____ + " cards.");
   print("My Hand: " + _____);
   print("Discard: " + _____);
   if(discard.getRank()_____) {
      print("Suit is " + _____);
   }

}
. . .
```

Now, show the status of the cards.

1. Call *showStatus()* from the constructor:

Listing 16-45, from CrazyEights.java

```
   . . .

public CrazyEights() {

   . . .

   else {
      activeSuit = ' ';
   }

   _____;
}
   . . .
```

Run the program. It should show that there are seven cards in the computer hand, the seven cards that are in your hand, and the discard. If the discard is an 8, it should show the active suit.

Lesson 16.8 – Crazy Eights: Your Turn

When it's your turn in *Crazy Eights*, you need to either play a valid card or draw a card. Drawing a card means taking an additional card from the deck and putting it in your hand. Playing a card means removing a card from your hand and putting it on the discard pile.

For now, consider a card as a valid play if it has a valid rank and suit, is in your hand, and matches the suit or rank of the discard. Allowing an eight will be added in a later lesson.

Try It

A couple of methods to help make writing the rest of the code a little easier are for drawing the user's card and for playing the user's card.

First, create a method to draw the user's card.

1. Add a private method called *drawMyCard()*. It should take no parameters and return nothing.

2. Deal a new card. (Hint: use CrazyEight's *deal()*.)

3. Print a blank line and a message to tell the user the card he/she drew.

4. Add the drawn card to *myHand*.

Listing 16-46, from CrazyEights.java

```
    . . .

_____ drawMyCard(_____) {
_____ drewCard = _____;
    print();
    print("You drew " + _____);
    myHand._____;
}
    . . .
```

Next, create a method to discard the user's card.

1. Add a private method called *discardMyCard()*. It should take one parameter, a Card called *myCard*, and return nothing.

2. Remove *myCard* from *myHand*.

3. Add the current *discard* to the *discardPile*.

4. Assign *myCard* to be the new *discard*.

Listing 16-47, from CrazyEights.java

```
    . . .

_____ discardMyCard(_____) {
    myHand._____;
    discardPile._____;
    discard = _____;
}
    . . .
```

To help organize the code, put the code for the user's turn into its own method called *playMyCard().*

1. Add a private method called *playMyCard()*. It should take no parameters and return nothing.

2. Show the status.

3. Ask the user which card he/she wants to play, or press D to draw. Put his/her answer in a string called *rankSuit*. (Hint: use *promptForString().*)

4. Convert *rankSuit* to uppercase.

5. If *rankSuit* is a D, draw a card. (Hint: use *drawMyCard().*)

6. If *rankSuit* is not a D, play the card: create a Card from *rankSuit*, call it *selectedCard*, and discard it. (Hint: use *discardMyCard().*)

Listing 16-48, from CrazyEights.java

```
    . . .

_____ playMyCard(_____) {
_____;
String rankSuit = _____;
rankSuit = rankSuit._____;
// if draw, draw a card
if (_____) {
    _____;
}
// else play the card
else {
    Card selectedCard = _____;
    _____;
}
}
    . . .
```

1. In the constructor, play the user's card before showing the status. (Hint: use *playMyCard().*)

Listing 16-49, from CrazyEights.java

```
    . . .

public CrazyEights() {

    . . .

    else {
        activeSuit = ' ';
```

```
        }

        _____;
        showStatus();
    }
        . . .
```

Run the program.

If the you enter a card in your hand, the next status should show that the card was removed from your hand and should now be the discard.

If you enter a D, the next status should show one more card in your hand.

But there are several other things that could happen that the program doesn't handle well: What if you enter something that isn't a valid card, such as "123"? What if you enter a valid card, but it isn't in your hand? What if you enter a card that's valid, is in your hand, but doesn't match the suit or rank of the discard?

1. Add a private method called *isValidPlay()*. It should take a string parameter called *rankSuit* and return a boolean.

2. Create a boolean called *validPlay* set to true.

3. Create a Card called *card* from the *rankSuit*.

4. If *card* isn't valid, print a message that *rankSuit* isn't a valid card and set *validPlay* to false. (Hint: use Card's *isValid()* method.)

5. Otherwise, if *card* isn't in *myHand*, tell the user it isn't in his/her hand and set *validPlay* to false. (Hint: use Hand's *contains()* method.)

6. Otherwise, if *card*'s suit doesn't match *discard*'s suit and *card*'s rank doesn't match *discard*'s rank, print a message saying *card* can't be played on *discard* and set *validPlay* to false. (Hint: use Card's *getSuit()* and *getRank()* methods. Hint: compare the characters with ==.)

7. Return *validPlay*.

Listing 16-50, from CrazyEights.java

```
        . . .

    _____ isValidPlay(_____) {
        boolean validPlay = _____;
        Card card = _____;

        // is it a valid card?
        if (_____) {
            print(_____);
```

```
      validPlay = _____;
   }

   // is that card in my hand?
   else if(_____) {
      print(_____);
      validPlay = _____;
   }

   // does the discard match the rank or suit?
   else if ((_____)
         && (_____)) {
      print(_____);
      validPlay = _____;
   }

   return _____;
}
   . . .
```

Next, if the user enters an invalid card, it should prompt him/her to try again.

1. Add a boolean to *playMyCard()* called *validPlay*, initially false.

2. Move the code, starting where it prompts the user through the end of the method, into a loop that continues while *validPlay* is false.

3. Set *validPlay* to true when *rankSuit* is 'D':

4. Add the additional condition when the *rankSuit* isn't 'D' to now only run that code if *rankSuit* is a valid play. (Hint: use *isValidPlay()*.)

5. Set *validPlay* to true after the user discards the card.

Listing 16-51, from CrazyEights.java

```
      . . .

   private void playMyCard() {
      showStatus();
      boolean validPlay = _____;
      // repeat until a valid play has been entered
      while (_____) {
         String rankSuit = promptForString("Which card do you want to
play (or D to draw)?");
         rankSuit = rankSuit.toUpperCase();
         // if draw, draw a card
         if (rankSuit.equals("D")) {
            drawMyCard();
            validPlay = _____;
```

```
      }
      // if valid play, play the card
      else if (_____) {
         Card selectedCard = new Card(rankSuit);
         discardMyCard();
         validPlay = _____;
      }
   }
}
   . . .
```

Finally, if the user drew a valid card, discard it.

1. In the *drawMyCard()* method, if *drewCard* is a valid play, tell the user he/she played it, then discard it. (Hint: convert *drewCard* to a String to check if it's a valid play. Hint: use the *discardMyCard()* method to discard the card.)

Listing 16-52, from CrazyEights.java

```
   . . .

private void drawMyCard() {
   Card drewCard = deal();
   print();
   print("You drew " + drewCard);
   myHand.add(drewCard);

   // if I can play my drawn card, play it
   if (isValidPlay(_____) {
      print("You played " + drewCard);
      discardMyCard(_____);
   }
}
   . . .
```

Run the program. Try to enter something other than a D, a valid card, or a card in your hand. Try to enter a card that doesn't match the discard's suit or rank. In all these cases, the program should prompt you to try again and give you an appropriate message. If you draw a card that plays, the program should play it.

Lesson 16.9 – Crazy Eights: Computer's Turn

When it's the computer's turn, the program needs to play a valid card from the computer hand or draw a card.

Try It

It's time to let the computer play a card too. In order for us to see if the program works correctly, print the computer's hand in the *Console* pane.

First, create a method to discard the computer card.

1. Add a private method called *discardComputerCard()*. It should take one parameter, a Card called *computerCard*, and return nothing.

2. Remove the *computerCard* from the *computerHand*.

3. Add the current *discard* to the *discardPile*.

4. Assign the *computerCard* to be the new *discard*.

Listing 16-53, from CrazyEights.java

```
     . . .

_____ discardComputerCard(_____) {
   computerHand._____;
   discardPile._____;
   discard = _____;
}
     . . .
```

The computer can play a card if it has a card with the same suit or rank as the discard. The program will need to make a list of all the valid cards, then pick a random valid card and play it. If there are no valid cards in the computer's hand, it should draw a card.

1. Play the computer's card right after it plays the user's card in the constructor. (Hint: use *playComputerCard()*, which you will create next.)

2. Add a private method called *playComputerCard()*. It should take no parameters and return nothing.

3. Print *computerHand* to the *Console* pane. (Hint: use *System.out.println()*. Hint: use Hand's *toString()* method)

4. Create an ArrayList of type Card called *playableCards*.

5. Loop through each card in *computerHand*. Put the card in a new Card called *card*. If *card*'s suit or rank is equal to *discard*'s suit or rank, add it to *playableCards*.

6. If there are any *playableCards*, pick a random card from *playableCards*, put it in a new Card, and discard it. (Hint: use *discardComputerCard()*.)

7. Otherwise, if there are no *playableCards*, deal a new card and put it in *computerHand*. Then print a blank line and a message that the computer drew a card. If that card plays,

discard it. (Hint: use CrazyEight's *deal()*. Hint: compare the drawn card's suit and rank to the discard's suit and rank to determine if the card plays.)

Listing 16-54, from CrazyEights.java

```
    . . .

public CrazyEights() {

        . . .

    playMyCard();
    _____;
    showStatus();
}
        . . .

_____ playComputerCard(_____) {
    System.out.println(_____);
    ArrayList<Card> playableCards = _____;

    // make list of playable cards
    for(_____) {
        Card card = _____;
        // only cards of the same suit or rank are playable
        if (_____
                ||  _____) {
            playableCards._____;
        }
    }

    // pick a random playable card
    int numberOfPlayableCards = _____;
    if (_____) {
        int pick = _____;
        Card playedCard = playableCards._____;
        discardComputerCard(_____);
    }

    // if nothing could play, draw a card
    else {
        Card drewCard = _____;
        computerHand._____;
        print();
        print(_____);

        // if it plays, play it
        if (drewCard._____
                || drewCard._____) {
```

```
        discardComputerCard(_____);
      }
    }
  }
    . . .
```

Run the program. Take your turn, then see what happens for the computer's turn. If the computer had any cards that matched the discard in either suit or rank, you should see one of them as the discard in the status. Otherwise, a message will say the computer drew a card. If the computer drew a card, the status should show either one more card added to the computer hand or a different discard.

Lesson 16.10 – Crazy Eights: Taking Turns

To play the game, the program needs to alternate between the user's turn and the computer's turn. When either player runs out of cards, the program should announce the winner. The program should also choose who goes first.

Try It

You've called *playMyCard()* once and *playComputerCard()* once. To play a real game, you take turns until the game is over. When is the game over? When either player runs out of cards.

1. In the constructor, create a boolean called *done*, initially false, to tell if the game is done.

2. Move *playMyCard()* and *playComputerCard()* into a loop that repeats while not *done*.

3. After it plays the user's card, if *myHand* is empty, set *done* to true.

4. Otherwise, play the computer card and, if *ComputerHand* is empty, set *done* to true.

5. Remove the code that shows the status after it plays the computer card.

Listing 16-55, from CrazyEights.java

```
    . . .

public CrazyEights() {

    . . .

    else {
       activeSuit = ' ';
    }

    // play until either of us runs out of cards
    _____ done = _____;
```

```
    while(_____) {
        playMyCard();
        // are there any cards left in my hand?
        if (_____) {
            done = _____;
        }
        else {
            playComputerCard();
            // are there any cards left in the computer hand?
            if (_____) {
                done = _____;
            }
        }
    }
}
    . . .
```

It should play a pretty good game now. But when the game is done, the program just quits. Instead, it should tell the user if he/she won or lost.

1. In the constructor, after the game is done, print a blank line.

2. If *myHand* is empty, print a congratulations message saying how many cards are in *computerHand*.

3. Otherwise, print messages that say the user lost, how many cards and what cards he/she had left, and what the final *discard* was.

Listing 16-56, from CrazyEights.java

```
    . . .

public CrazyEights() {

        . . .

        if (computerHand.size() == 0) {
            done = true;
        }
    }
}
print(_____);
// who played all their cards?
if (_____) {
    print(_____);
}
else {
    print(_____);
    print("My Hand: " + _____);
```

```
        print("Discard: " + _____);
    }
}
    . . .
```

To make the game a little more fair, add code to randomly choose who gets to play first.

1. Add this code to the constructor, after the discard is dealt, and before it plays the cards:

    1. Create an integer called *turn*, initially a random value, either 0 or 1.

    2. If turn is 1, tell the user that the computer will go first, and play a computer card.

    3. Otherwise, tell the user that he/she will go first.

Listing 16-57, from CrazyEights.java

```
    . . .

public CrazyEights() {

    . . .

    else {
        activeSuit = ' ';
    }

    // who goes first?
    _____ turn = rand._____;
    if(_____) {
        print(_____);
        _____;
    }
    else {
        print(_____);
    }

    // play until either of us runs out of cards

    . . .
```

Lesson 16.11 – Crazy Eights: Playing Eights

One of the rules of Crazy Eights is that you can change the suit allowed on the discard pile by playing an 8. Any eight can be played on any suit. The player can then name any suit as the active suit.

Try It

First, update *isValidPlay()* to accept 8s.

1. Move the code that checks if the card matches the discard's suit or rank into a block of code that is only run if the card is not an 8. If the card is not an 8:

    1. If the discard is an 8, the card's suit must match the active suit. If not, print a message and mark it as not valid.

    2. Otherwise, if the discard isn't an 8, the card must match the discard rank or suit. (Hint: move the code that checked the card's rank and suit to the else block of the above condition.)

Listing 16-58, from CrazyEights.java

```
    . . .

    private boolean isValidPlay(String rankSuit) {

        . . .

    else if (!myHand.contains(card)) {
      print(rankSuit + " is not in your hand.");
      validPlay = false;
    }

    // 8s are always valid.  If the card is not an 8...
    else if (_____) {
      // is the discard an 8?
      if (discard._____) {
        // does the card match the active suit?
        if (card._____) {
          print(_____ + " cannot be played on " +
          + " because the suit was set to " + _____);
          validPlay = _____;
        }
      }

      // if the discard is not an 8,
      // does the discard match the rank or suit?
      else if (card.getSuit()!=discard.getSuit()
          && card.getRank()!=discard.getRank()) {
        print(rankSuit + " cannot be played on " + discard);
        validPlay = false;
      }
    }

    return validPlay;
```

Playing an 8 is now allowed as a valid play. If the user plays an 8, you'll have to prompt the user for what the new active suit should be. But suit is a character; you don't yet have a method in *MyWindow* to prompt for a character.

1. Add to the *MyWindow* class a protected method called *promptForChar()*. It should take one parameter, a String called *prompt*, and return a character.

2. Create a character called *c* with an initial value of a blank character. (Hint: use single-quotes around character values.)

3. Create a boolean called *valid*, initially false.

4. While *valid* is false, print the prompt, ask the user for input, and put the input into a String called *s*. If *s* is one character, put the first character of *s* into c and set *valid* to true. Otherwise, prompt for the character again, using the same *prompt*. (Hint: use String's *length()* to determine if it's one character. Hint: use String's *charAt()* to get the first character of the string.)

5. Return the value of *c*.

Listing 16-59, from MyWindow.java

```
. . .

_____ promptForChar(_____) {
        _____ c = _____;

    _____ valid = _____;
    while(_____) {
        print(_____);
        String s = _____;
        if (s._____) {
            c = _____;
            valid = _____;
        }
        else {
            c = _____;
        }
    }
    return _____;
}
. . .
```

Now, add a method to *CrazyEights* to prompt for a valid suit.

1. Add a private method called *promptForSuit()*. It should take no parameters and return a

character.

2. Create a character called *suit*, initially a blank character.

3. Create a boolean called *validSuit*, initially false.

4. While *validSuit* isn't true, prompt the user to enter a character for *suit*. Convert suit to uppercase. If the character entered is a valid suit, set *validSuit* accordingly. (Hint, use *promptForChar()*. Hint: to convert a character to uppercase, use Character's static method, *toUpperCase()*. Hint: to test if it's a valid suit, use Card's static method, *isValidSuit()*. Hint: use the class name and a period to call static methods.)

5. Return the *suit*.

Listing 16-60, from CrazyEights.java

```
    . . .

_____ promptForSuit(_____) {
    _____ suit = _____;
    _____ validSuit = _____;

    while (!validSuit) {
        suit = _____("Change the suit to H, D, C, or S?");
        suit = Character.toUpperCase(_____);
        if (Card._____) {
            validSuit = _____;
        }
    }

    return _____;
}
    . . .
```

If the user discarded an 8, ask for a new suit.

1. Add code to the *discardMyCard()* method so if the card is an 8, prompt the user for a suit and put his/her answer into *activeSuit*. (Hint: use *promptForSuit()*.)

Listing 16-61, from CrazyEights.java

```
    . . .

private void discardMyCard(Card myCard) {
    myHand.remove(myCard);
    discardPile.add(discard);
    discard = myCard;
    if (_____) {
        activeSuit = _____;
```

```
        }
    }
    . . .
```

Run the program. If you have an 8 in your hand, you should now be allowed to play it. If you play an 8, it should prompt you for a suit, though the computer's turn will not play correctly. That will be fixed in the next step. If you enter an invalid suit, it should prompt you for the suit again. If you enter a valid suit, it should change the active suit to the new suit.

Next, the computer must be able to play an 8 in its turn. It must also know how many cards it has in each suit, in case it should change the suit.

1. Create private integer instance variables called *countHearts, countDiamonds, countSpades,* and *countClubs,* initially 0. These variables will hold the number of hearts, diamonds, clubs, and spades.

Listing 16-62, from CrazyEights.java

```
    . . .

public class CrazyEights extends MyWindow {

    private Deck deck = new Deck();
    private Hand myHand = new Hand();
    private Hand computerHand = new Hand();
    private Card discard;
    private ArrayList<Card> discardPile = new ArrayList<Card>();
    private Random rand = new Random();
    private char activeSuit = ' ';
    _____ countHearts = ____;
    _____ countDiamonds = ____;
    _____ countClubs = ____;
    _____ countSpades = ____;

    . . .
```

Next, in *playComputerCard()*, keep track of the 8s and the number of cards in each suit, and handle playing when the discard is already an 8:

1. Create an ArrayList of Cards called *eights*, initialized by calling its constructor.

2. Set all the suit counts to 0.

3. Loop through all the computer cards. If the card is an eight, add it to the list of eights. Otherwise, increment the count of cards for that card's suit. (Hint: use a switch statement to increment the correct suit count based on the card's suit.)

4. When making the list of playable cards in the computer hand:

1. If the discard is an 8, and if the card matches the active suit, add it to the list of *playableCards*.

2. If the discard isn't an 8, and if the card's suit and rank match the discard's suit and rank, add it to the list of *playableCards*. (Hint: move the code that did this check into the new else block.)

5. If there were no playable cards and there's at least one 8, pick the first 8 and discard it.

Listing 16-63, from CrazyEights.java

```
. . .

private void playComputerCard() {
    System.out.println("Computer hand: " + computerHand);
    ArrayList<Card> playableCards = new ArrayList<Card>();
    _____ eights = _____ ;
    countHearts = ____ ;
    countDiamonds = ____ ;
    countClubs = ____ ;
    countSpades = ____ ;

    // count eights and number of each suit
    for(_____) {
        Card card = _____ ;

        // if it's an eight, save it
        if (_____) {
            eights._____ ;
        }
        // otherwise, count the number of each suit
        else {
            switch(card._____) {
            case '___' :
                _____ ;
                break;
            case '___' :
                _____ ;
                break;
            case '___' :
                _____ ;
                break;
            case '___' :
                _____ ;
                break;
            }
        }
    }
}
```

```
// make list of playable cards
for(int i=0; i<computerHand.size(); i++) {
  Card card = computerHand.cardAt(i);

  // if discard is an 8, all cards of active suit are playable
  if (discard._____) {
    if (card._____) {
      playableCards._____;
    }
  }

  // else, if discard is not an 8,
  // only cards of the same suit or rank are playable
  else if(card.getSuit() == discard.getSuit()
        || card.getRank() == discard.getRank()) {
    playableCards.add(card);
  }
}

// pick a random playable card
int numberOfPlayableCards = playableCards.size();
if (numberOfPlayableCards>0) {
  int pick = rand.nextInt(numberOfPlayableCards);
  Card playedCard = playableCards.get(pick);
  discardComputerCard(playedCard);
}

// otherwise, if have an eight, play an eight
else if(_____) {
  Card playedCard = eights._____;
  discardComputerCard(_____);
}

// if nothing could play, draw a card

  . . .
```

Finally, if the computer plays an 8, choose the suit to make the active suit.

1. Add code to *discardComputerCard()* so if it discards an 8, it should choose the suit of which it has the most and make that the active suit. (Hint: set the highest count to the number of hearts and set the active suit to hearts. If there are more diamonds than the highest count, set the highest count to the number of diamonds and set the active suit to diamonds. Repeat these steps for each suit.)

Listing 16-64, from CrazyEights.java

```
  . . .
```

```
private void discardComputerCard(Card computerCard) {
   computerHand.remove(computerCard);
   discardPile.add(discard);
   discard = computerCard;
   if (discard._____) {
      int highestCount = countHearts;
      activeSuit = 'H';
      if (countDiamonds > highestCount) {
         highestCount = _____;
         activeSuit = '___';
      }
      if (countClubs > _____) {
         highestCount = _____;
         activeSuit = '___';
      }
      if (countSpades > _____) {
         highestCount = _____;
         activeSuit = '___';
      }
   }
}
      . . .
```

1. Play the game several times to see if it's working correctly.

2. If you're satisfied with how the game is working, remove *System.out.println()* from *playComputerCard()*.

This is the end of the Crazy Eights program.

1. Export your Crazy Eights Project and Cards Project together to create your Crazy Eights program if you want to run it without Eclipse. (Hint: select both projects before you select the option to export.)

I Hope You Enjoyed this Book

My goal for this book was to give you a strong foundation in basic Java programming. I hope you have been inspired to explore more Java programming.

If you enjoyed this book:

- **Lend it** – This book is set up to allow lending. Please share it with a friend.

- **Recommend it** – Help others find this book by recommending it to friends, readers' groups, and discussion boards.

- **Review it** – Tell others why you liked this book. Review it on Amazon. If you do write a review, please send me a copy in an email at diyjava@godtlandsoftware.com so I can personally thank you.

If you liked this book, you might be interested in the next book in the series: *More Do-It-Yourself Java Games: An Introduction to Java Graphics and Event-driven Programming*. This second book will build on the Java programming skills you've learned in this book. It will use the same fill-in-the-blank approach to teach programming, but will leave the *DIYWindow* behind. Instead, it will use standard Java windows with images, buttons and input fields, and other mouse-click interactions. In this second book, you'll write more colorful and more interactive puzzle and game programs.

Other books planned for this series include: *Advanced Do-It-Yourself Java Games: An Introduction to Java Threads and Animated Video Games*, and *Do-It-Yourself Multi-Player Java Games: An Introduction to Java Sockets and Internet-Based Games*.

Good luck, and happy programming!

Annette Godtland

Questions, Comments, or Suggestions

To report problems, ask technical questions, or make comments or suggestions for future editions of this book, send e-mail to diyjava@godtlandsoftware.com.

Other Books I've Written

Do-It-Yourself Java Games Series

In the Do-It-Yourself Java Games series of books, I use a "discovery learning" approach to teach computer programming: learn Java programming techniques more by doing Java programming than by reading about them. Through extensive use of fill-in blanks, with easy access to answers, I guide you to write complete programs yourself, starting with the first lesson. You'll discover how, when, and why Java programs are written the way they are.

More Do-It-Yourself Java Games: An Introduction to Java Graphics and Event-Driven Programming

More Do-It-Yourself Java Games: An Introduction to Java Graphics and Event-Driven Programming is the second book of the Do-It-Yourself Java Games series. You'll learn to create windows and dialogs, to add buttons and input fields, to use images and drawings, and to respond to keyboard input and mouse clicks and drags. You'll create 10 more games including several puzzles, a dice game, a word game, and a card game. It's available at Amazon.com.

This book assumes you either have an understanding of basic Java programming or you have read the first book, Do-It-Yourself Java Games: An Introduction to Java Computer Programming.

This Little Program Went to Market

I also wrote the book "This Little Program Went to Market: Create, Deploy, Distribute, Sell, and Market Software and More on the Internet at Little or No Cost to You". In it, I compiled a detailed tutorial of all the tips, tools, and techniques I have learned for getting a program to market, and for selling almost anything on the Internet. It's available at Amazon.com, Barnes and Noble, and many other book retailers.

Appendix A - Glossary

ArithmeticException

An ArithmeticException is an <u>exception</u> thrown when you try to do arithmetic that is not allowed, such as divide by zero. See *Lesson 8.5 - Integer Subtraction, Multiplication, and Division.*

array

An array is a type of Java list. All items must be of the same <u>type</u>, either Java <u>primitives</u> or Java <u>objects</u>. The size of the array is set when it is <u>declared</u> and cannot be changed. See *Key Points and More* in *Lesson 12.4 - Arrays.* See *Key Points and More* in *Lesson 14.5 - Empty Array.*

ArrayList

An ArrayList is a type of Java list. An ArrayList can only hold Java <u>objects</u>, not Java <u>primitives</u>, and all items in the list must be of the same <u>type</u>. The size of the ArrayList can be changed at any time by adding or removing items. See *Key Points and More* in *Lesson 15.6 - Array Lists.*

block of code

A block of code is one or more lines of program <u>code</u>, grouped together as a unit, and surrounded by curly brackets, { }. See *Key Points and More* in *Lesson 1.2 - Classes, Superclasses and Programs.*

boolean

A boolean is a true or false <u>condition</u>. A boolean value must be typed as "true" or "false", without quotes. Boolean <u>variables</u> are <u>declared</u> in Java as "boolean". See *Key Points and More* in *Lesson 13.5 - Boolean Data Type.*

break

A break is used in a <u>switch statement</u> to break to the end of the <u>switch statement</u> instead of <u>running</u> the next line of <u>code</u>. See *Key Points and More* in *Lesson 6.2 - Switch Statements.*

build path

The build path is a list of all the <u>Java projects</u> and <u>libraries</u> containing code the current <u>Java project</u> needs to use. See *Lesson 8.7 - Extend the DIYWindow Class.*

byte

A byte is a Java <u>integer</u> <u>variable</u>. It can hold numbers between -128 and 128. See *Key Points and More* in *Lesson 8.1 - Integer Data Type and Addition.*

calculate

To calculate a number, you add, subtract, multiply, or divide other numbers. See *Key Points and More* in *Lesson 8.5 - Integer Subtraction, Multiplication, and Division*. See *Key Points and More* in *Lesson 10.1 - Order of Operation*. See *Key Points and More* in *Lesson 16.3 - Modulo*.

call

When you call a method, it means the program should run the code in that method before running the next line of code. See *Lesson 6.3 - Methods*.

case

A case label marks the code to run for one of the expected values of the variable used in the switch statement. See *Key Points and More* in *Lesson 6.2 - Switch Statements*. See *Key Points and More* in *Lesson 6.4 - Switch Default*. See *Key Points and More* in *Lesson 13.6 - Case without Break*. See *Key Points and More* in *Lesson 15.1 - Switch Statement with Integers*.

char

A char is a Java character variable. See *Key Points and More* in *Lesson 15.2 - Character Data Type*.

character

A character is always a single character. A character value must be typed with a single quote on each side of it. Character variables are declared in Java as "char". See *Key Points and More* in *Lesson 15.2 - Character Data Type*.

class

A class is a blueprint from which program objects are created. A class defines the information the object can hold (its instance variables) and what the object can do (its methods). See *Key Points and More* in *Lesson 1.2 - Classes, Superclasses and Programs*. See *Key Points and More* in *Lesson 8.7 - Extend the DIYWindow Class*.

code

Program code is a series of computer instructions that, when run in sequence, perform a desired task. See *Key Points and More* in *Lesson 1.2 - Classes, Superclasses and Programs*.

comment

Comments are notes you put in code to remind you of what you intended the code to do or to label sections of code. Comments are ignored when you run the program. See *Key Points and More* in *Lesson 12.1 - Comments*.

comment out

You can "comment out" lines of <u>code</u> by turning those lines into a <u>comment</u>. When you turn <u>code</u> into a <u>comment</u>, that <u>code</u> will be ignored since programs ignore <u>comments</u>. See *Key Points and More* in *Lesson 12.1 - Comments*.

condition

A condition is <u>code</u> which is either true or false. See *Key Points and More* in *Lesson 5.1 - If Statements, Strings that are Equal or Contain Letters*. See *Key Points and More* in *Lesson 9.1 - Comparing Numbers*. See *Key Points and More* in *Lesson 13.5 - Boolean Data Type*.

console

The console is where Java error messages, or your program System.out.println() messages, are displayed. In Eclipse, the console is usually in the bottom pane of the window. See *Key Points and More* in *Lesson 8.4 - Try/Catch Blocks and Exceptions*. See *Key Points and More* in *Lesson 12.3 - Print to the Console*.

constructor

A constructor is a special <u>method</u> called when an <u>instance</u> of the <u>class</u> (also known as an <u>object</u>) is created. See *Key Points and More* in *Lesson 16.2 - Constructors*.

convert

When you convert a <u>variable</u>, you change it using some form of <u>calculation</u>. For example, you can convert a <u>string</u> to an <u>integer</u>, or convert a <u>string</u> to all uppercase letters, or write a program to convert temperature from Fahrenheit to Celsius. See *Key Points and More* in *Lesson 8.2 - Convert a String to an Integer*. See Project 10 - Temperature Converter. See *Key Points and More* in *Lesson 14.4 - Convert a String to Uppercase*.

data

Data is another name for the information, or value, a <u>variable</u> can hold. See *Key Points and More* in *Lesson 1.3 - Variables and Strings*. See *Key Points and More* in *Lesson 13.1 - Write to a File*. See *Key Points and More* in *Lesson 13.2 - Read from a File, Catch Multiple Exceptions*.

decimal number

A decimal number is a <u>fractional</u> numeric value, with numbers after a decimal point, such as 1.25. Decimal number <u>variables</u> are <u>declared</u> in Java as "<u>double</u>" or "<u>float</u>". See *Key Points and More* in *Lesson 8.6 - Double Data Type*.

declare

When you declare a <u>variable</u>, you state that it exists, assign its properties, and optionally assign it an initial value. See *Key Points and More* in *Lesson 1.3 - Variables and Strings*.

decrement

To decrement a <u>variable</u>, you decrease its value by a small amount, usually 1. See *Key*

Points and More in *Lesson 9.3 - Increment Integers.*

define

When you define a <u>class</u> or <u>method</u>, you assign it its properties and provide <u>code</u> for what it does. See *Key Points and More* in *Lesson 1.2 - Classes, Superclasses and Programs.* See *Key Points and More* in *Lesson 6.3 - Methods.* See *Key Points and More* in *Lesson 7.1 - Methods with Parameters.* See *Key Points and More* in *Lesson 8.3 - Methods that Return a Value.* See *Key Points and More* in *Lesson 8.7 - Extend the DIYWindow Class.* See *Key Points and More* in *Lesson 12.5 – Static Methods.* See *Key Points and More* in *Lesson 13.3 – Methods with Multiple Parameters.*

double

A double is a Java <u>decimal number</u> <u>variable</u>. It can hold numbers with precision up to 16 decimal places. A double is typed with a decimal point, but without quotes. See *Key Points and More* in *Lesson 8.6 - Double Data Type.*

else block

An else block follows a <u>block of code</u> added to the end of an <u>if statement</u>. The else block <u>runs</u> only if the <u>condition</u> of the <u>if statement</u> is false. See *Key Points and More* in *Lesson 5.1 - If Statements, Strings that are Equal or Contain Letters.*

escape character

The escape character (backslash, \,) is used to mark special characters in a <u>string</u>. See *Key Points and More* in *Lesson 1.4 - Joining Strings, the Escape Character.*

equation

An equation is text that shows that a number or <u>calculation</u> is equal to another number or <u>calculation</u>.

exception

An exception is something unexpected that happens that Java doesn't know how to handle. For example, an exception will occur if you try to <u>convert</u> an alphabetic character into an <u>integer</u> or if you try to read from a file that does not exist. See *Key Points and More* in *Lesson 8.4 - Try/Catch Blocks and Exceptions.*

exclusive and operator

The exclusive and operator, &&, checks if both the <u>conditions</u> on either side of it are true. See *Key Points and More* in *Lesson 5.1 - If Statements, Strings that are Equal or Contain Letters.*

exclusive or operator

The exclusive or operator, ||, checks if at least one <u>condition</u> on either side of it is true. See *Key Points and More* in *Lesson 5.1 - If Statements, Strings that are Equal or Contain Letters.*

export

When you export a program, you take it out of Eclipse and put it in a separate JAR file. The program can then be run without Eclipse by double-clicking on the JAR file. See *Key Points and More* in *Lesson 2.2 - Export a Program*.

extend

When a class extends a second class, it makes the second class the superclass of the first class. In other words, it makes the first class a type of the second class and it can use all the public and protected methods and instance variables of the second class. See *Key Points and More* in *Lesson 8.7 - Extend the DIYWindow Class*.

extract

Extracting files is the process of copying the files stored in a ZIP file or JAR file into another folder on your computer. See *Download and Install Eclipse* in *Appendix C − Install Required Software and Files*.

FileNotFoundException

A FileNotFoundException is an exception thrown when you try to read from a file that doesn't exist. See *Key Points and More* in *Lesson 13.2 - Read from a File, Catch Multiple Exceptions*.

final

Final variables are those variables whose value is never changed by the program. See *Key Points and More* in *Lesson 14.6 - Static Final Variables*.

float

A float is a Java decimal number variable. It can hold numbers with precision up to about 7 decimal places. A float is typed without quotes and must have an "f" added to the end. See *Key Points and More* in *Lesson 8.6 - Double Data Type*.

for loop

A for loop is a block of code that repeats a set number of times. See *Key Points and More* in *Lesson 11.1 - For Loops*.

fraction

A fraction is a number that is part of a whole number, such as a half (1/2) or one and a quarter (1 1/4).

generate

When something is generated, it is created, usually by some sort of calculation. For example, Eclipse adds automatically-generated comments when you create a class or you generate <u>random</u> numbers for some programs. See *Key Points and More* in *Lesson 1.2 - Classes, Superclasses and Programs*. See *Key Points and More* in *Lesson 9.2 - Generate Random Numbers*.

hardware

Hardware is the physical part of a computer: the hard drive, keyboard, mouse, etc. The <u>operating system</u> allows <u>software</u> to interact with the computer hardware.

if statement

An if statement is a <u>block of code</u> that <u>runs</u> only if the <u>condition</u> is true. An if statement may also have an optional <u>else block</u>. See *Key Points and More* in *Lesson 5.1 - If Statements, Strings that are Equal or Contain Letters*.

import

Import <u>statements</u> are needed to link your <u>class</u> to any other <u>classes</u> used by your code. If Java does not recognize the name of a <u>class</u> used in your <u>code</u>, you must import that <u>class</u> at the beginning of the <u>class</u> <u>definition</u> with an import <u>statement</u>. Import <u>statements</u> must use the full, proper name of the <u>class</u>, which includes the <u>package</u> name. See *Key Points and More* in *Lesson 9.2 - Generate Random Numbers*.

increment

To increment a <u>variable</u>, you increase its value by a small amount, usually 1. See *Key Points and More* in *Lesson 9.3 - Increment Integers*.

index

An index is the position of an item in something else. For example, indexes are used to name the position of a <u>character</u> in a <u>string</u>, an item in a list, and the number of times through a <u>for loop</u>. See *Key Points and More* in *Lesson 13.4 - Index of Characters in a String*. See *Key Points and More* in *Lesson 15.3 - Index of Next Character*.

infinite loop

An infinite loop is a <u>block of code</u> that could repeat forever because an end <u>condition</u> is never met. You may have to use the Eclipse <u>terminate</u> button, or <u>reboot</u> the computer, to end an infinite loop. See *Key Points and More* in *Lesson 7.3 - Infinite Loops*.

initialize

To initialize a <u>variable</u>, you assign it its first value. See *Key Points and More* in *Lesson 1.3 - Variables and Strings*.

input

Input is a noun: <u>data</u> the <u>user</u> enters into the program while the program is <u>running</u>. Input is also a verb. The <u>user</u> inputs (enters) <u>data</u> into the program. Input is also the name of a <u>method</u>: input(). The program should <u>call</u> input() to wait for the <u>user</u> to enter <u>data</u>. See *Key Points and More* in *Lesson 4.1 - Input a String*. See *Key Points and More* in *Lesson 15.4 - Check User Input*.

instance

A <u>class</u> is a <u>definition</u> of an <u>object</u>. The instance of a <u>class</u> is what is created from a <u>class definition</u>. See *Key Points and More* in *Lesson 16.1 - Objects, Card*.

instance variable

An instance variable is a <u>variable</u> <u>declared</u> in the <u>class</u> <u>definition</u> instead of inside a <u>method</u>. Such a <u>variable</u> may be used by any of its <u>class</u> <u>methods</u> without being <u>passed</u> to the <u>methods</u> as a <u>parameter</u>. See *Key Points and More* in *Lesson 14.3 - Instance Variables*.

int

An int is a Java <u>integer</u> <u>variable</u>. It can hold numbers between -2,147,483,647 and 2,147,483,647. See *Key Points and More* in *Lesson 8.1 - Integer Data Type and Addition*.

integer

An integer is a numeric value; a <u>whole number</u>, either positive or negative. An integer is typed without quotes or a decimal point. Integer <u>variables</u> are <u>declared</u> in Java as "<u>int</u>", "<u>byte</u>", "<u>short</u>", or "<u>long</u>". See *Key Points and More* in *Lesson 8.1 - Integer Data Type and Addition*. See *Key Points and More* in *Lesson 8.2 - Convert a String to an Integer*. See *Key Points and More* in *Lesson 8.5 - Integer Subtraction, Multiplication, and Division*.

invalid

If something is invalid, it means it is not allowed. See *Key Points and More* in *Lesson 15.4 - Check User Input*.

IOException

An IOException is an <u>exception</u> thrown when reading from or writing to a file causes an error. For example, when a file that exists can't be opened. See *Key Points and More* in *Lesson 13.1 - Write to a File*. See *Key Points and More* in *Lesson 13.2 - Read from a File, Catch Multiple Exceptions*.

JAR file

A JAR file is a Java Archive file. It contains one or more folders or files of Java program <u>code</u>. A JAR file has ".jar" as its extension. If the JAR file is created as a Java executable file, you can <u>run</u> the program that is in the JAR file by simply double-clicking on it. See *Key Points and More* in *Lesson 1.1 - Java Projects and Packages*. See *Key Points and More* in *Lesson 2.2 - Export a Program*.

Java project

The Java project is the highest level of organization of Java <u>code</u> in Eclipse. Each program in this book is organized in a separate Java project in Eclipse. The Java project contains one or more <u>packages</u>, and each <u>package</u> contains one or more <u>classes</u>. Because the programs are small, most of the Java projects in this book contain only one <u>package</u>. See *Key Points and More* in *Lesson 1.1 - Java Projects and Packages*.

library

Eclipse refers to the external <u>JAR files</u> as libraries. For example, DIYJava.jar is a <u>JAR file</u> that must be added as a library to the <u>build path</u> of any <u>Java project</u>, using the DIYWindow <u>class</u>. See *Lesson 1.1 - Java Projects and Packages*.

listing

A program listing usually shows all the program <u>code</u> in a file. The listings in this book are only partial listings, showing an ellipsis, "...", where <u>code</u> from the file is not included. See *Lesson 1.2 - Classes, Superclasses and Programs*. See *Appendix B - Completed Listings*.

long

A long is a Java <u>integer</u> <u>variable</u>. It can hold numbers between -9,223,372,036,854,775,807 and 9,223,372,036,854,775,807. See *Key Points and More* in *Lesson 8.1 - Integer Data Type and Addition*.

main() method

The *main()* method is the first <u>method</u> called when a program starts. See *Key Points and More* in *Lesson 1.2 - Classes, Superclasses and Programs*.

maximum

A maximum value is the highest value allowed.

method

A method is a named <u>block of code</u> that can be <u>called</u> from anywhere in the program. See *Key Points and More* in *Lesson 6.3 - Methods*. See *Key Points and More* in *Lesson 7.1 - Methods with Parameters*. See *Key Points and More* in *Lesson 8.3 - Methods that Return a Value*. See *Key Points and More* in *Lesson 12.5 – Static Methods*. See *Key Points and More* in *Lesson 13.3 – Methods with Multiple Parameters*.

minimum

A minimum value is the lowest value allowed.

modulo

Modulo is an operation that starts like division. Instead of giving the <u>whole number</u> and dropping the remainder, modulo drops the <u>whole number</u> and gives the remainder. See

Key Points and More in *Lesson 16.3 - Modulo.*

mono-spaced font

A mono-spaced font is a font in which all the characters are the same width. In contrast, a proportional-spaced font is a font in which each character has a different width. For example, in a mono-spaced font, such as Courier New, the letters "i" and "W" are the same width. In a proportional-spaced font, such as Times New Roma", the letter "W" is much wider than the letter "i". See *Lesson 1.2 - Classes, Superclasses and Programs.*

not operator

The not operator, !, returns the opposite of a <u>condition</u>. For example, !true returns false. See *Key Points and More* in *Lesson 5.1 - If Statements, Strings that are Equal or Contain Letters.*

null

Null means something has no value, not even a blank or a 0. You will receive an error if you try to use a <u>variable</u> with no value.

NumberFormatException

An NumberFormatException is an <u>exception</u> thrown if you try to <u>convert</u> something to a number that cannot be <u>converted</u> into a number. For example, if you try to <u>convert</u> "abc" into a number, you will receive a NumberFormatException. See *Lesson 8.4 - Try/Catch Blocks and Exceptions.*

object

An object is an <u>instance</u> of a <u>class</u>. The object holds the information <u>defined</u> in the <u>class</u> and can <u>call</u> its <u>methods</u>. See *Key Points and More* in *Lesson 16.1 - Objects, Card.*

operating system

The operating system is the <u>software</u> on the computer that manages how other programs interact with the <u>hardware</u> of the computer. Examples of operating systems include Windows, Mac, or Linux. See *Appendix C – Install Required Software and Files.*

package

Packages contain one or more <u>class</u> files typically used together. See *Key Points and More* in *Lesson 1.1 - Java Projects and Packages.*

parameter

A parameter is a value <u>passed</u> into a <u>method</u> when the <u>method</u> is <u>called</u>. The <u>method</u> may then use that value in its <u>code</u>. See *Key Points and More* in *Lesson 7.1 - Methods with Parameters.* See *Key Points and More* in *Lesson 13.3 - Methods with Multiple Parameters.*

pass

Passing a value to a <u>method</u> means you send it to the <u>method</u> as a <u>parameter</u>. See *Lesson 7.1 - Methods with Parameters*.

primitive

The Java primitive types are <u>int</u>, <u>double</u>, <u>char</u>, <u>boolean</u>, <u>byte</u>, <u>short</u>, <u>long</u>, and <u>float</u>. They have no <u>class</u> definition nor do they have any <u>methods</u> that may be <u>called</u> from them. See *Key Points and More* in *Lesson 15.6 - Array Lists*.

private

A <u>variable</u> or <u>method</u> may be <u>declared</u> as private. A private <u>declaration</u> means only the <u>class</u> that <u>declared</u> it may see it and use it. See *Key Points and More* in *Lesson 6.3 - Methods*. See *Key Points and More* in *Lesson 8.7 - Extend the DIYWindow Class*. See *Key Points and More* in *Lesson 12.5 - Static Methods*. See *Key Points and More* in *Lesson 14.3 - Instance Variables*.

programmer

A programmer is a person who writes computer program <u>code</u>.

prompt

You prompt a <u>user</u> to enter something by asking him/her a question and then waiting for the answer. See *Key Points and More* in *Lesson 8.3 - Methods that Return a Value*. See *Key Points and More* in *Lesson 8.6 - Double Data Type*. See *Key Points and More* in *Lesson 14.1 - Prompt for Yes or No*.

protected

A <u>variable</u> or <u>method</u> may be <u>declared</u> as protected. A protected <u>declaration</u> means only the <u>class</u> that <u>declared</u> it, or any <u>class</u> that <u>extends</u> the <u>class</u> that declared it, may see it and use it. See *Key Points and More* in *Lesson 8.7 - Extend the DIYWindow Class*.

public

A <u>variable</u> or <u>method</u> may be <u>declared</u> as public. A public <u>declaration</u> means any <u>class</u> in the same <u>build path</u> may see it and use it. See *Key Points and More* in *Lesson 8.7 - Extend the DIYWindow Class*. See *Key Points and More* in *Lesson 12.5 - Static Methods*. See *Key Points and More* in *Lesson 14.3 - Instance Variables*.

Quick Fix

You can use the Quick Fix option of Eclipse to view a list of ways Eclipse thinks a <u>syntax error</u> could be fixed. When you select one of those options, Eclipse will fix the <u>code</u> for you, in the way you selected. See *Key Points and More* in *Lesson 1.2 - Classes, Superclasses and Programs*.

random

If something is chosen at random, it means any item in a list can be chosen. It is just a likely for any one of the items to be chosen as any other. See *Key Points and More* in *Lesson 9.2 - Generate Random Numbers*.

reboot

You reboot a computer by shutting it down and then turning it back on again.

resolved

When you receive an error that a <u>variable</u> name cannot be resolved, it means Java doesn't know what the <u>variable</u> is. This error is usually fixed by <u>declaring</u> the <u>variable</u> before it is used. When you receive an error that a <u>class</u> name cannot be resolved, it means Java doesn't know what the <u>class</u> is. This error is usually fixed by using <u>Quick Fix</u> to <u>import</u> the needed <u>class</u>. See *Lesson 7.1 - Methods with Parameters*. See *Lesson 9.2 - Generate Random Numbers*.

return

When a <u>method</u> returns a value, it gives that value back to the <u>calling</u> <u>method</u>. Not all <u>methods</u> return a value. If a <u>method</u> returns a value, the <u>code</u> that <u>called</u> the <u>method</u> may assign the results of that <u>call</u> to a <u>variable</u> of the same <u>type</u> as the returned value. See *Key Points and More* in *Lesson 8.3 - Methods that Return a Value*.

run

When you run a program, Java <u>calls</u> the program's *main()* <u>method</u> and does the instructions of each line of <u>code</u> in sequence. See *Key Points and More* in *Lesson 1.2 - Classes, Superclasses and Programs*.

scramble

To scramble a group of items, you rearrange them in a <u>random</u> order. See *Key Points and More* in *Lesson 12.1 - Comments*.

short

A short is a Java <u>integer</u> <u>variable</u>. It can hold numbers between -32,768 and 32,768. See *Key Points and More* in *Lesson 8.1 - Integer Data Type and Addition*.

shortcut

A shortcut is a shorter way to make something happen. For example, you can create a shortcut icon on your computer desktop to start a program that may otherwise take more steps to start. See *Key Points and More* in *Lesson 13.8 - Data File with the Jar File*. See *Download and Install Eclipse* in *Appendix C – Install Required Software and Files*.

software

Software is another name for a computer program. Software is created from program code written by programmers.

statement

A statement is a complete line of code, usually up to and including the ending semicolon, ;. Some statements, such as if statements and switch statements, include a block of code. Such statements end after the block of code instead of after a semicolon. See *Key Points and More* in *Lesson 1.2 - Classes, Superclasses and Programs*. See *Key Points and More* in *Lesson 5.1 - If Statements, Strings that are Equal or Contain Letters*. See *Key Points and More* in *Lesson 6.2 - Switch Statements*. See *Key Points and More* in *Lesson 7.2 - While Loops*. See *Key Points and More* in *Lesson 11.1 - For Loops*.

static

Static methods are self-contained. They can only use the data passed in as its parameters. A static method may be called by using its class name, followed by the method name. Static variables are shared by every object created from the class. If one object updates the value of a static variable, all objects created from that class see the same new value for that variable. See *Key Points and More* in *Lesson 12.5 - Static Methods*. See *Key Points and More* in *Lesson 14.6 - Static Final Variables*.

string

A string is text with zero or more characters of any kind. A string value must start and end with double quotes. String variables are declared in Java as "String". See *Key Points and More* in *Lesson 1.3 - Variables and Strings*. See *Key Points and More* in *Lesson 8.2 - Convert a String to an Integer*. See *Key Points and More* in *Lesson 10.1 - Order of Operation*. See *Key Points and More* in *Lesson 12.2 - String Length and Substring*. See *Key Points and More* in *Lesson 13.4 - Index of Characters in a String*. See *Key Points and More* in *Lesson 14.2 - Replace Characters in a String*.

stub

Stub code is an automatically-generated method with a valid declaration. The contents of the method is left empty for you to program yourself.

superclass

Every class must have a superclass, any Java class to which it adds functionality. A class is considered to be a type of its superclass, and may use any of the public or protected instance variables or methods of its superclass. For example, a class which names *DIYWindow* as its superclass is a type of *DIYWindow* and may use the *print()* and *input()* methods in *DIYWindow*. See *Key Points and More* in *Lesson 1.2 - Classes, Superclasses and Programs*. See *Key Points and More* in *Lesson 8.7 - Extend the DIYWindow Class*.

switch statement

A switch statement is a block of code that runs different code for each expected value of a variable. See *Key Points and More* in *Lesson 6.2 - Switch Statements*. See *Key Points and More* in *Lesson 6.4 - Switch Default*. See *Key Points and More* in *Lesson 13.6 - Case without Break*. See *Key Points and More* in *Lesson 15.1 - Switch Statement with Integers*.

syntax error

A syntax error occurs when the program code does not meet the minimum order or contents as required by Java. All syntax errors must be fixed before you can run the program. Eclipse provides a Quick Fix tool to make it easy to find and fix syntax errors. See *Key Points and More* in *Lesson 1.2 - Classes, Superclasses and Programs*.

terminate

If you terminate a program, you stop it. See *Key Points and More* in *Lesson 7.3 - Infinite Loops*.

try/catch block

A try/catch block consists of a *try* block and one or more *catch* blocks. Wrap code that might throw an exception in a *try* block. Place *catch* blocks at the end of the *try* block for each expected exception. Put code inside the *catch* block to run when that exception is caught. The program will then be able to continue with the code after the try/catch block. See *Key Points and More* in *Lesson 8.4 - Try/Catch Blocks and Exceptions*.

type

In Java, the type of something is usually its class or its superclass. For example, the HelloWorld class is a type of DIYWindow; or a variable declared as a string has string as its type. See *Key Points and More* in *Lesson 1.2 - Classes, Superclasses and Programs*.

unhandled exception

An unhandled exception is an exception not handled by any code. Add a try/catch block to handle exceptions. A program will stop if it runs into an unhandled exception. See *Key Points and More* in *Lesson 8.4 - Try/Catch Blocks and Exceptions*.

unscramble

To unscramble a group of items, you put them back into their proper order.

unzip

Unzip is the process of extracting files from a ZIP file. See *Download and Install Eclipse* in *Appendix C – Install Required Software and Files*.

user

The user is the person running the program. See *Key Points and More* in *Lesson 4.1 - Input a String*.

valid

If something is valid, it means it is allowed. See *Key Points and More* in *Lesson 15.4 - Check User Input*.

variable

A variable is a named piece of <u>data</u>, whose value you can change. See *Key Points and More* in *Lesson 1.3 - Variables and Strings*. See *Key Points and More* in *Lesson 3.1 - Reuse Strings*.

visible

If a <u>variable</u> or <u>method</u> is visible, it means it can be seen. The three different visibility settings are <u>private</u>, <u>protected</u>, and <u>public</u>. See *Key Points and More* in *Lesson 6.3 - Methods*. See *Key Points and More* in *Lesson 8.7 - Extend the DIYWindow Class*. See *Key Points and More* in *Lesson 12.5 - Static Methods*. See *Key Points and More* in *Lesson 14.3 - Instance Variables*.

while loop

A while loop is a <u>block of code</u> that repeats until a <u>condition</u> is met. See *Key Points and More* in *Lesson 7.2 - While Loops*.

whole number

A whole number is a numeric value, with no additional fractional or decimal part. Whole number <u>variables</u> are <u>declared</u> in Java as "<u>byte</u>", "<u>short</u>", "<u>int</u>" or "<u>long</u>". See *Key Points and More* in *Lesson 8.1 - Integer Data Type and Addition*.

work folder

You will create a work folder to contain all the Java <u>code</u> and other files needed for your programs. See *Create a Java Work Folder* in *Setup*. See *Key Points and More* in *Lesson 1.1 - Java Projects and Packages*. See *Create a Java Work Folder* in *Appendix C – Install Required Software and Files*.

wrapper

Wrappers exist for each of the Java <u>primitives</u> and may be used to <u>convert</u> the Java <u>primitives</u> into <u>objects</u>. For example, Integer is a wrapper for <u>integers</u>. You can create an Integer <u>object</u> called *obj* from an <u>int</u> called *num* by using *Integer obj = new Integer(num)*. See *Key Points and More* in *Lesson 15.6 - Array Lists*.

ZIP file

A ZIP file contains one or more folders or files. A ZIP file has an extension of ".zip". You must <u>extract</u> the files from the ZIP file to use them. See *Download and Install Eclipse* in *Setup*. See *Download and Install Eclipse* in *Appendix C – Install Required Software and Files*.

Appendix B - Completed Listings

These completed listings show what every listing in the book should look like after all changes have been made, blanks filled in, and code removed.

Project 1 – Hello World

Listing 1-1, from HelloWorld.java

```java
package annette.godtland.helloworld;

import com.godtsoft.diyjava.DIYWindow;

public class HelloWorld extends DIYWindow {

    public HelloWorld() {
        // TODO Auto-generated constructor stub
    }

    public static void main(String[] args) {
        // TODO Auto-generated method stub

    }

}
```

Listing 1-2, from HelloWorld.java

```java
package annette.godtland.helloworld;

import com.godtsoft.diyjava.DIYWindow;

public class HelloWorld extends DIYWindow {

    public HelloWorld() {

    }

    public static void main(String[] args) {

    }

}
```

Listing 1-3, from HelloWorld.java

```java
package annette.godtland.helloworld;

import com.godtsoft.diyjava.DIYWindow;

public class HelloWorld extends DIYWindow {

   public HelloWorld() {
      print("Hello World");
   }

   public static void main(String[] args) {
      new HelloWorld();
   }

}
```

Listing 1-4, from HelloWorld.java

```java
      . . .

   public HelloWorld() {
      print("Hello Annette");
   }
      . . .
```

Listing 1-5, from HelloWorld.java

```java
      . . .

   public HelloWorld() {
      printttt("Hello Annette");
   }
      . . .
```

Listing 1-6, from HelloWorld.java

```java
      . . .

   public HelloWorld() {
      print("Hello, earthling.");
      print("Take me to your leader.");
   }
      . . .
```

Listing 1-7, from HelloWorld.java

```
    . . .

  public HelloWorld() {
    print("Hello, earthling.");
    print();
    print("Take me to your leader.");
  }
    . . .
```

Listing 1-8, from HelloWorld.java

```
    . . .

  public HelloWorld() {
    String word1 = "Jeff's";
    String word2 = "awesome";
    String word3 = "dog";
    print(word1);
    print(word2);
    print(word3);
  }
    . . .
```

Listing 1-9, from HelloWorld.java

```
    . . .

  public HelloWorld() {
    String word1 = "Jeff's";
    String word2 = "awesome";
    String word3 = "dog";
    print(word2);
    print(word1);
    print(word3);
  }
    . . .
```

Listing 1-10, from HelloWorld.java

```
    . . .

  public HelloWorld() {
    String word1 = "Jeff's";
    print(word1);
    String word2 = "awesome";
    print(word2);
```

```
    String word3 = "dog";
    print(word3);
  }
    ...
```

Listing 1-11, from HelloWorld.java

```
    ...

  public HelloWorld() {
    print(word1);
    String word1 = "Jeff's";
    String word2 = "awesome";
    print(word2);
    String word3 = "dog";
    print(word3);
  }
    ...
```

Listing 1-12, from HelloWorld.java

```
    ...

  public HelloWorld() {
    String word1 = "Jeff's";
    String word2 = "awesome";
    String word3 = "dog";
    print(word2);
    print(word1);
    print(word2);
    print(word3);
  }
    ...
```

Listing 1-13, from HelloWorld.java

```
    ...

  public HelloWorld() {
    String word1 = "Jeff's";
    String word2 = "awesome";
    String word3 = "dog";
    String statement = word1 + word2 + word3;
    print(statement);
  }
    ...
```

Listing 1-14, from HelloWorld.java

```java
    . . .

public HelloWorld() {
    String word1 = "Jeff's";
    String word2 = "awesome";
    String word3 = "dog";
    String statement = word1 + " " + word2 + " " + word3;
    print(statement);
}
    . . .
```

Listing 1-15, from HelloWorld.java

```java
    . . .

public HelloWorld() {
    String greeting = "Hello, Annette.\nHow are you?";
    print(greeting);
}
    . . .
```

Listing 1-16, from HelloWorld.java

```java
    . . .

public HelloWorld() {
    String greeting = "Hello, Annette.\n\nHow are you?";
    print(greeting);
}
    . . .
```

Listing 1-17, from HelloWorld.java

```java
    . . .

public HelloWorld() {
    print("Annette said to say "hi".");
}
    . . .
```

Listing 1-18, from HelloWorld.java

```java
    . . .

public HelloWorld() {
    print("Annette said to say \"hi\".");
```

```
    }
    ...
```

Listing 1-19, from HelloWorld.java

```
    ...

  public HelloWorld() {
    print("My user folder is \"c:\\Users\\Annette\".");
  }
    ...
```

Project 2 – ASCII Art

Listing 2-1, from ASCIIArt.java

```
package annette.godtland.asciiart;

import com.godtsoft.diyjava.DIYWindow;

public class ASCIIAart extends DIYWindow {

  public ASCIIArt() {
  }

  public static void main(String[] args) {
    new ASCIIArt();
  }
}
```

Listing 2-2, from ASCIIArt.java

```
    ...

  public ASCIIArt() {
    print("H   H");
    print("H   H");
    print("HHHH");
    print("H   H");
    print("H   H");
  }
    ...
```

Listing 2-3, from ASCIIArt.java

```
    ...
```

```
public ASCIIArt() {
  print(" A    M    M   GGG ");
  print(" A A   MM MM  G     ");
  print("AAAAA  M M M  G GGG");
  print("A   A  M   M  G   G");
  print("A   A  M    M   GGG ");
}
    ...
```

Listing 2-4, from ASCIIArt.java

    ...

```
public ASCIIArt() {
  print("   @@@@@@@@");
  print("  |        |");
  print("  | (o)(o)");
  print("  C      _)");
  print("  |    ___|");
  print("  |    /");
  print("  /     \\");
}
    ...
```

Listing 2-5, from ASCIIArt.java

    ...

```
public ASCIIArt() {
  print("        /\\       ___#_               O");
  print("       //\\\\\\   /\\\____\\        +-(.)-+");
  print("_____||___|_|___|_____(_:_)_____");
}
    ...
```

Project 3 – Name Game

Listing 3-1, from NameGame.java

```
package annette.godtland.namegame;

import com.godtsoft.diyjava.DIYWindow;

public class NameGame extends DIYWindow {

  public NameGame() {
  }
```

```
   public static void main(String[] args) {
      new NameGame();
   }
}
```

Listing 3-2, from NameGame.java

```
      . . .

   public NameGame() {
      print("Jack be nimble,");
      print("Jack be quick,");
      print("Jack jump over the candlestick.");
   }
      . . .
```

Listing 3-3, from NameGame.java

```
      . . .

   public NameGame() {
      String name = "Jack";
      print(name + " be nimble,");
      print("Jack be quick,");
      print("Jack jump over the candlestick.");
   }
      . . .
```

Listing 3-4, from NameGame.java

```
      . . .

   public NameGame() {
      String name = "Annette";
      print(name + " be nimble,");
      print("Jack be quick,");
      print("Jack jump over the candlestick.");
   }
      . . .
```

Listing 3-5, from NameGame.java

```
      . . .

   public NameGame() {
      String name = "Annette";
      print(name + " be nimble,");
```

```
      print(name + " be quick,");
      print(name + " jump over the candlestick.");
   }
   ...
```

Listing 3-6, from NameGame.java

```
   ...

   public NameGame() {
      String name = "Annette";
      print(name + " be nimble,");
      print(name + " be quick,");
      print(name + " jump over the candlestick.");
      print();
      print("Way to go, " + name + "!");
   }
   ...
```

Project 4 – Silly Story

Listing 4-1, from SillyStory.java

```
package annette.godtland.sillystory;

import com.godtsoft.diyjava.DIYWindow;

public class SillyStory extends DIYWindow {

   public SillyStory() {
      print("Mary had a little lamb,");
      print("Whose fleece was white as snow.");
      print("And everywhere that Mary went,");
      print("The lamb was sure to go.");
   }

   public static void main(String[] args) {
      new SillyStory();
   }
}
```

Listing 4-2, from SillyStory.java

```
   ...

   public SillyStory() {
      String name = "Annette";
```

```
      print(name + " had a little lamb,");
      print("Whose fleece was white as snow.");
      print("And everywhere that " + name + " went,");
      print("The lamb was sure to go.");
   }
   ...
```

Listing 4-3, from SillyStory.java

```
   ...

   public SillyStory() {
      String name = input();
      print(name + " had a little lamb,");
      print("Whose fleece was white as snow.");
      print("And everywhere that " + name + " went,");
      print("The lamb was sure to go.");
   }
   ...
```

Listing 4-4, from SillyStory.java

```
   ...

   public SillyStory() {
      print("Enter a name");
      String name = input();
      print();
      print(name + " had a little lamb,");
      print("Whose fleece was white as snow.");
      print("And everywhere that " + name + " went,");
      print("The lamb was sure to go.");
   }
   ...
```

Listing 4-5, from SillyStory.java

```
   ...

   public SillyStory() {
      print("Enter a name");
      String name = input();
      print("Enter an animal");
      String animal = input();
      print("Enter a part of that animal");
      String animalPart = input();
      print("Enter a color");
      String color = input();
```

```
    print("Enter something that is " + color);
    String thing = input();
    print("Enter an action");
    String action = input();
    print();
    print(name + " had a little " + animal + ",");
    print("Whose " + animalPart + " was " + color + " as " + thing +
".");
    print("And everywhere that " + name + " went,");
    print("The " + animal + " was sure to " + action + ".");
    }
    . . .
```

Project 5 – Name Game Revisited

Listing 5-1, from NameGame.java

```
    . . .

public NameGame() {
    print("Enter a name");
    String name = input();
    print(name + " be nimble,");
    print(name + " be quick,");
    print(name + " jump over the candlestick.");
    print("");
    print("Way to go, " + name + "!");
}
    . . .
```

Listing 5-2, from NameGame.java

```
    . . .

public NameGame() {

    . . .

    print("Way to go, " + name + "!");

    if (name.equals("Jack")) {
        print(name + ", your jumping skills are famous!");
    }
    else {
        print(name + ", I've never heard of you.");
    }
    . . .
```

Listing 5-3, from NameGame.java

```
   . . .

 public NameGame() {

     . . .

    print(name + ", I've never heard of you.");
  }

  if (name.equals("Annette")) {
    print(name + " is a Java programmer.");
  }
  else {
    print(name + ", are you a Java programmer?");
  }
    . . .
```

Listing 5-4, from NameGame.java

```
   . . .

 public NameGame() {

      . . .

    print(name + ", are you a Java programmer?");
  }

  if (name.startsWith("King")) {
    print("Your highness!");
  }
    . . .
```

Listing 5-5, from NameGame.java

```
   . . .

 public NameGame() {

      . . .

    print("Your highness!");
  }

  if (!name.equals("Billy")) {
```

```
        print("I'm waiting for Billy.");
    }
        . . .
```

Listing 5-6, from NameGame.java

```
    . . .

public NameGame() {

        . . .

    print("I'm waiting for Billy.");
    }

    if (!name.contains(" ")) {
      print("Don't you have a first and last name?");
    }
        . . .
```

Listing 5-7, from NameGame.java

```
    . . .

public NameGame() {

        . . .

    if (name.startsWith("King") || name.startsWith("Queen")) {
      print("Your highness!");
    }
        . . .
```

Listing 5-8, from NameGame.java

```
    . . .

public NameGame() {

        . . .

    print("Don't you have a first and last name?");
    }

    if (name.startsWith("Dr.") && !name.equals("Dr. Frankenstein")) {
      print("Doctor, this may be a medical emergency!");
    }
    else if (name.equals("Dr. Frankenstein")) {
```

```
    print("Dr. Frankenstein, no help is needed here.");
  }
  else {
    print("Is there a doctor in the house?");
  }
    . . .
```

Project 6 – Choose an Adventure

Listing 6-1, from ChooseAnAdventure.java

```java
package annette.godtland.chooseanadventure;

import com.godtsoft.diyjava.DIYWindow;

public class ChooseAnAdventure extends DIYWindow {

  public ChooseAnAdventure() {
  }

  public static void main(String[] args) {
    new ChooseAnAdventure();
  }
}
```

Listing 6-2, from ChooseAnAdventure.java

```java
    . . .

  public ChooseAnAdventure() {
    String story = "I woke up in unfamiliar woods.";
    story = story + " I was hungry and tired.";
    story = story + " I didn't know where I was.";
    story = story + " In my pocket were three beans.";
    story = story + " Up the hill was a well.";
    story = story + " To the right was a small cottage.";
    print(story);
  }
    . . .
```

Listing 6-3, from ChooseAnAdventure.java

```java
    . . .

  public ChooseAnAdventure() {

    . . .
```

```
      print(story);
      print("Should I:");
      print("a) Go up the hill?");
      print("b) Check out the cottage?");
      print("c) Plant the beans?");
   }
      ...
```

Listing 6-4, from ChooseAnAdventure.java

```
      ...

   public ChooseAnAdventure() {

         ...

      print("c) Plant the beans?");
      String choice = input();

         ...
```

Listing 6-5, from ChooseAnAdventure.java

```
      ...

   public ChooseAnAdventure() {

         ...

      String choice = input();

      switch(choice) {
      case "a" :
        print ("Going up the hill.");
        break;
      case "b" :
        print ("Checking the cottage.");
        break;
      case "c" :
        print ("Planting beans.");
        break;
      }
         ...
```

Listing 6-6, from ChooseAnAdventure.java

```
         ...
```

```
   }

   private void goUpTheHill() {

   }

   public static void main(String[] args) {

      ...
```

Listing 6-7, from ChooseAnAdventure.java

```
      ...

   private void goUpTheHill() {
      print("Going up the hill");
   }
      ...
```

Listing 6-8, from ChooseAnAdventure.java

```
      ...
   }

   private void checkTheCottage() {
      print("Checking the cottage.");
   }

   private void plantTheBeans() {
      print("Planting the beans.");
   }

   public static void main(String[] args) {

      ...
```

Listing 6-9, from ChooseAnAdventure.java

```
      ...

   public ChooseAnAdventure() {

         ...

      switch(choice) {
      case "a" :
         goUpTheHill();
         break;
```

```
      case "b" :
        checkTheCottage();
        break;
      case "c" :
        plantTheBeans();
        break;
      }
   }
      ...
```

Listing 6-10, from ChooseAnAdventure.java

```
         ...

   public ChooseAnAdventure() {
      startStory();
   }

   private void startStory() {
      String story = "I woke up in unfamiliar woods.";

         ...

   }
      ...
```

Listing 6-11, from ChooseAnAdventure.java

```
         ...

   public void startStory() {

         ...

      case "c" :
        plantTheBeans();
        break;
      default :
        startStory();
      }
         ...
```

Listing 6-12, from ChooseAnAdventure.java

```
         ...

   private void startStory() {
      print();
      String story = "I woke up in unfamiliar woods.";
```

Listing 6-13, from ChooseAnAdventure.java

. . .

```java
private void goUpTheHill() {
    print();
    String story = "On my way up the hill, a girl joined me.";
    story = story + " She told me her name was Jill.";
    story = story + " She was carrying a pail.";
    story = story + " There's also a trail of breadcrumbs going down
another path.";
    print(story);
    print("Should I:");
    print("a) Ask Jill to join me?");
    print("b) Follow the trail of bread crumbs?");

    String choice = input();

    switch(choice) {
    case "a" :
        goWithJill();
        break;
    case "b" :
        followBreadCrumbs();
        break;
    default :
        goUpTheHill();
    }
}
    ...

private void plantTheBeans() {
    print("Planting the beans.");
}

private void goWithJill() {
    print("Going with Jill.");
}

private void followBreadCrumbs() {
    print("Following the bread crumbs.");
}

public static void main(String[] args) {
    new ChooseAnAdventure();
```

```
    }
        . . .
```

Listing 6-14, from ChooseAnAdventure.java

```
        . . .

    private void goWithJill() {
        print();
        String story = "I was so much enjoying listening to Jill's
stories.";
        story = story + " I didn't notice the branch across the path.";
        story = story + " I fell down.";
        print(story);
        print("What happened next?");
        print("a) I broke my crown and Jill came tumbling after.");
        print("b) The beans fell out of my pocket and immediately sprouted
a bean stalk.");

        String choice = input();

        switch(choice) {
        case "a" :
            brokeMyCrown();
            break;
        case "b" :
            sproutedABeanstalk();
            break;
        default :
            goWithJill();
        }
    }
        . . .

    private void brokeMyCrown() {
        print("Broke my crown.");
    }

    private void sproutedABeanstalk() {
        print("Sprouted a beanstalk.");
    }

    public static void main(String[] args) {
        new ChooseAnAdventure();
    }
        . . .
```

Listing 6-15, from ChooseAnAdventure.java

```
    . . .
  private void followBreadCrumbs() {
    print();
    String story = "I followed the bread crumbs for awhile.";
    story = story + " Jill had to go to her grandmother's house.";
    story = story + " Before she left, Jill warned me about the cottage
in the woods.";
    print(story);
    print("Should I:");
    print("a) Go with Jill?");
    print("b) Check out the cottage in the woods?");

    String choice = input();

    switch(choice) {
    case "a" :
      goWithJill();
      break;
    case "b" :
      checkTheCottage();
      break;
    default :
      followBreadCrumbs();
    }
  }
    . . .
```

Project 7 – Finish the Name Game

Listing 7-1, from NameGame.java

```
    . . .
  public NameGame() {
    print("Enter a name:");
    String name = input();
    checkName();
  }

  private void checkName() {
    print(name + " be nimble,");
    print(name + " be quick,");
    print(name + " jump over the candlestick.");
    print();
```

```
      print("Way to go, " + name + "!");

         ...

      if (name.startsWith("Dr.") && !name.equals("Dr. Frankenstein")) {
         print("Doctor, this may be a medical emergency!");
      }
      else if (name.equals("Dr. Frankenstein")) {
         print("Dr. Frankenstein, no help is needed here.");
      }
      else {
         print("Is there a doctor in the house?");
      }
   }
      ...
```

Listing 7-2, from NameGame.java

```
      ...

   public NameGame() {
      print("Enter a name:");
      String name = input();
      checkName();
   }

   private void checkName() {
      print(name + " be nimble,");

         ...

   }
      ...
```

Listing 7-3, from NameGame.java

```
      ...

   private void checkName() {
      String name = "";
      print(name + " be nimble,");

         ...

   }
      ...
```

Listing 7-4, from NameGame.java

```
    ...

public NameGame() {
   print("Enter a name:");
   String name = input();
   checkName(name);
}

private void checkName(String name) {
   print(name + " be nimble,");
   print(name + " be quick.");
   print(name + " jump over the candlestick.");

      ...

}
   ...
```

Listing 7-5, from NameGame.java

```
    ...

public NameGame() {
   while (true) {
      print("Enter a name:");
      String name = input();
      checkName(name);
   }
}
```

Listing 7-6, from NameGame.java

```
    ...

public NameGame() {
   while (true) {
      print("Enter a name:");
      String name = input();
      print();
      checkName(name);
      print();

      ...
```

Listing 7-7, from NameGame.java

```
   ...

   public NameGame() {
      while (true)

         ...
      }
      print("Thank you for playing my game!");

         ...
```

Listing 7-8, from NameGame.java

```
      ...

   public NameGame() {
      while (!name.equals("quit"))
         print("Enter a name:");

         ...
```

Listing 7-9, from NameGame.java

```
      ...

   public NameGame() {
      print("Enter a name:");
      String name = input();
      while (!name.equals("quit")) {
         print();
         checkName(name);
         print();
         print("Enter another name:");
         name = input();
      }
      print("Thank you for playing my game!");
   }
      ...
```

Listing 7-10, from NameGame.java

```
      ...

   public NameGame() {
      print("Enter a name:");
      String name = input();
      while (!name.equals("quit")) {
         print();
```

```
        checkName(name);
        print();
        print("Enter another name");

    }
        ...
```

Listing 7-11, from NameGame.java

```
        ...

    public NameGame() {
        print("Enter a name:");
        String name = input();
        while (!name.equals("quit")) {
            print();
            checkName(name);
            print();
            print("Enter another name");
            name = input();
        }
        ...
```

Project 8 – Calculator

Listing 8-1, from Calculator.java

```
package annette.godtland.calculator;

import com.godtsoft.diyjava.DIYWindow;

public class Calculator extends DIYWindow {

    public Calculator() {
    }

    public static void main(String[] args) {
        new Calculator();
    }
}
```

Listing 8-2, from Calculator.java

```
        ...

    public Calculator() {
        print(5);
```

```
    }
    . . .
```

Listing 8-3, from Calculator.java

```
    . . .

    public Calculator() {
        int a = 5;
        print(a);
    }
    . . .
```

Listing 8-4, from Calculator.java

```
    . . .

    public Calculator() {
        int a = 5;
        print("a is " + a);
    }
    . . .
```

Listing 8-5, from Calculator.java

```
    . . .

    public Calculator() {
        int a = 5;
        print("a is " + a);
        int b = 7;
        print("b is " + b);
    }
    . . .
```

Listing 8-6, from Calculator.java

```
    . . .

    public Calculator() {
        int a = 5;
        print("a is " + a);
        int b = 7;
        print("b is " + b);
        int c = 5 + 7;
        print("c is " + c);
    }
    . . .
```

Listing 8-7, from Calculator.java

```
   . . .

public Calculator() {
   int a = 5;
   print("a is " + a);
   int b = 7;
   print("b is " + b);
   int c = a + b;
   print("c is " + c);
}
   . . .
```

Listing 8-8, from Calculator.java

```
   . . .

public Calculator() {
   int a = input();
   print("a is " + a);
   int b = 7;
   print("b is " + b);
   int c = a + b;
   print("c is " + c);
}
   . . .
```

Listing 8-9, from Calculator.java

```
   . . .

public Calculator() {
   String s = input();
   int a = Integer.parseInt(s);
   print("a is " + a);

   . . .
```

Listing 8-10, from Calculator.java

```
   . . .

public Calculator() {
   print("Enter a number:");
   String s = input();
   int a = Integer.parseInt(s);
```

```
    print("a is " + a);

        . . .
```

Listing 8-11, from Calculator.java

```
        . . .

    public Calculator() {
        print("Enter a number:");
        String s = input();
        int a = Integer.parseInt(s);
        print("a is " + a);
        print("Enter another number:");
        s = input();
        int b = Integer.parseInt(s);
        print("b is " + b);
        int c = a + b;
        print("c is " + c);
    }
        . . .
```

Listing 8-12, from Calculator.java

```
        . . .

    public Calculator() {
        print("Enter a number:");
        String s = input();
        int a = Integer.parseInt(s);
        print("Enter another number:");
        s = input();
        int b = Integer.parseInt(s);
        int c = a + b;
        print(a + " + " + b + " = " + c);
    }
        . . .
```

Listing 8-13, from Calculator.java

```
        . . .

    public Calculator() {

        . . .

        print(a + " + " + b + " = " + c);
        print("Do you want to do another?");
```

```
      s = input();

         . . .
```

Listing 8-14, from Calculator.java

```
         . . .

   public Calculator() {
      while (s.startsWith("Y") || s.startsWith("y")) {
         print("Enter a number");
         String s = input();
         int a = Integer.parseInt(s);
         print("Enter another number:");
         s = input();
         int b = Integer.parseInt(s);
         int c = a + b;
         print(a + " + " + b + " = " + c);
         print("Do you want to do another?");
         s = input();
      }
   }
         . . .
```

Listing 8-15, from Calculator.java

```
         . . .

   public Calculator() {
      String s = "Y";
      while (s.startsWith("Y") || s.startsWith("y")) {
         print("Enter a number");
         String s = input();

            . . .
```

Listing 8-16, from Calculator.java

```
         . . .

   public Calculator() {
      String s = "Y";
      while (s.startsWith("Y") || s.startsWith("y")) {
         print("Enter a number");
         s = input();

            . . .
```

Listing 8-17, from Calculator.java

```
   . . .

private int promptForInt(String prompt) {
   int i = 0;

   return i;
}
   . . .
```

Listing 8-18, from Calculator.java

```
   . . .

private int promptForInt(String prompt) {
   int i = 0;
   print(prompt);
   String s = input();
   i = Integer.parseInt(s);
   return i;
}
   . . .
```

Listing 8-19, from Calculator.java

```
   . . .

public Calculator() {
   String s = "Y";
   while (s.startsWith("Y") || s.startsWith("y")) {
      int a = promptForInt("Enter a number");
      print("Enter another number:");

      . . .
```

Listing 8-20, from Calculator.java

```
   . . .

public Calculator() {
   String s = "Y";
   while (s.startsWith("Y") || s.startsWith("y")) {
      int a = promptForInt("Enter a number");
      int b = promptForInt("Enter another number");
      int c = a + b;

      . . .
```

Listing 8-21, from Calculator.java

```java
      . . .

   private String promptForString(String prompt) {
      print(prompt);
      String s = input();
      return s;
   }
      . . .
```

Listing 8-22, from Calculator.java

```java
      . . .

   public Calculator() {
      String s = "Y";
      while (s.startsWith("Y") || s.startsWith("y")) {
         int a = promptForInt("Enter a number");
         int b = promptForInt("Enter another number");
         int c = a + b;
         print(a + " + " + b + " = " + c);
         s = promptForString("Do you want to do another?");
      }
   }
      . . .
```

Listing 8-23, from Calculator.java

```java
      . . .

   private int promptForInt(String prompt) {
      int i = 0;
      print(prompt);
      String s = input();
      try {
         i = Integer.parseInt(s);
      }
      catch(NumberFormatException e) {
         print(s + " is not a valid number. Try again.");
         i = promptForInt(prompt);
      }
      return i;
   }
      . . .
```

Listing 8-24, from Calculator.java

```
    . . .

  public Calculator() {
     String s = "Y";
     while (s.startsWith("Y") || s.startsWith("y")) {
        int a = promptForInt("Enter a number");
        int b = promptForInt("Enter another number");
        int c = a - b;
        print(a + " - " + b + " = " + c);
        s = promptForString("Do you want to do another?");
     }
  }
     . . .
```

Listing 8-25, from Calculator.java

```
    . . .

  public Calculator() {
     String s = "Y";
     while (s.startsWith("Y") || s.startsWith("y")) {
        int a = promptForInt("Enter a number");
        int b = promptForInt("Enter another number");
        int c = a * b;
        print(a + " * " + b + " = " + c);
        s = promptForString("Do you want to do another?");
     }
  }
     . . .
```

Listing 8-26, from Calculator.java

```
    . . .

  public Calculator() {
     String s = "Y";
     while (s.startsWith("Y") || s.startsWith("y")) {
        int a = promptForInt("Enter a number");
        int b = promptForInt("Enter another number");
        int c = a / b;
        print(a + " / " + b + " = " + c);
        s = promptForString("Do you want to do another?");
     }
  }
     . . .
```

Listing 8-27, from Calculator.java

```
    . . .

  public Calculator() {
     String s = "Y";
     while (s.startsWith("Y") || s.startsWith("y")) {
        int a = promptForInt("Enter a number");
        String operation = promptForString("Enter +, - , *, or /");
        int b = promptForInt("Enter another number");
        int c = 0;
        switch(operation) {
           case "+" :
              c = a + b;
              print(a + " + " + b + " = " + c);
              break;
           case "-" :
              c = a - b;
              print(a + " - " + b + " = " + c);
              break;
           case "*" :
              c = a * b;
              print(a + " * " + b + " = " + c);
              break;
           case "/" :
              c = a / b;
              print(a + " / " + b + " = " + c);
              break;
           default:
              print(operation + " is not a valid operation.");
        }
        s = promptForString("Do you want to do another?");
     }
        . . .
```

Listing 8-28, from Calculator.java

```
    . . .

  public Calculator() {

           . . .

        case "/" :
           try {
              c = a / b;
              print(a + " / " + b + " = " + c);
           }
```

```
        catch (ArithmeticException e) {
          print("Division by zero is not allowed.");
        }
        break;

          . . .
```

Listing 8-29, from Calculator.java

```
    . . .

  public Calculator() {
    String s = "Y";
    while (s.startsWith("Y") || s.startsWith("y")) {
      double a = promptForInt("Enter a number");
      String operation = promptForString("Enter +, - , *, or /");
      double b = promptForInt("Enter another number");
      double c = 0;
      switch(operation) {
        case "+" :

      . . .
```

Listing 8-30, from Calculator.java

```
    . . .

  private double promptForDouble(String prompt) {
    double d = 0;
    print(prompt);
    String s = input();
    try {
      d = Double.parseDouble(s);
    }
    catch(NumberFormatException e) {
      print(s + " is not a valid number. Try again.");
      d = promptForDouble(prompt);
    }
    return d;
  }
    . . .
```

Listing 8-31, from Calculator.java

```
    . . .

  public Calculator() {
    String s = "Y";
```

```
while (s.startsWith("Y") || s.startsWith("y")) {
    double a = promptForDouble("Enter a number");
    String operation = promptForString("Enter +, - , *, or /");
    double b = promptForDouble("Enter another number");
    double c = 0;
    switch(operation) {
        ...
```

Listing 8-32, from MyWindow.java

```
package annette.godtland.mywindow;

import com.godtsoft.diyjava.DIYWindow;

public class MyWindow extends DIYWindow {

}
```

Listing 8-33, from MyWindow.java

```
    ...

public class MyWindow extends DIYWindow {

  private double promptForDouble(String prompt) {
    double d = 0;
    print(prompt);
    String s = input();
    try {
      d = Double.parseDouble(s);
    }
    catch(NumberFormatException e) {
      print(s + " is not a valid number. Try again.");
      d = promptForDouble(prompt);
    }
    return d;
  }

  private int promptForInt(String prompt) {
    int i = 0;
    print(prompt);
    String s = input();
    try {
      i = Integer.parseInt(s);
    }
    catch(NumberFormatException e) {
      print(s + " is not a valid number. Try again.");
      i = promptForInt(prompt);
```

```
        }
        return i;
    }

    private String promptForString(String prompt) {
        print(prompt);
        String s = input();
        return s;
    }
}
```

Listing 8-34, from Calculator.java

```
package annette.godtland.calculator;

import annette.godtland.mywindow.MyWindow;

public class Calculator extends MyWindow {

    ...
```

Listing 8-35, from MyWindow.java

```
    ...

    protected double promptForDouble(String prompt) {
        double d = 0;

        ...

        return d;
    }

    protected int promptForInt(String prompt) {
        int i = 0;

        ...

        return i;
    }

    protected String promptForString(String prompt) {
        print(prompt);
        String s = input();
        return s;
    }
    ...
```

Project 9 – Guess My Number

Listing 9-1, from GuessMyNumber.java

```
package annette.godtland.guessmynumber;

import annette.godtland.mywindow.MyWindow;

public class GuessMyNumber extends MyWindow {

  public GuessMyNumber() {
  }

  public static void main(String[] args) {
    new GuessMyNumber();
  }
}
```

Listing 9-2, from GuessMyNumber.java

```
    . . .

  public GuessMyNumber() {
    int myNumber = 56;
    int myGuess = promptForInt("Guess my number, between 0 and 100.");
  }
    . . .
```

Listing 9-3, from GuessMyNumber.java

```
    . . .

  public GuessMyNumber() {
    int myNumber = 56;
    int myGuess = promptForInt("Guess my number, between 0 and 100.");
    if(myGuess == myNumber) {
      print("You guessed it!");
    }
  }
    . . .
```

Listing 9-4, from GuessMyNumber.java

```
    . . .

  public GuessMyNumber() {
    int myNumber = 56;
    int myGuess = promptForInt("Guess my number, between 0 and 100.");
```

```
      if(myGuess != myNumber) {
        print("Sorry, that's not it.");
      }
  }
      ...
```

Listing 9-5, from GuessMyNumber.java

```
      ...

  public GuessMyNumber() {
      int myNumber = 56;
      int myGuess = promptForInt("Guess my number, between 0 and 100.");
      if(myGuess != myNumber) {
        myGuess = promptForInt("Sorry, that's not it. Try again.");
      }
  }
      ...
```

Listing 9-6, from GuessMyNumber.java

```
      ...

  public GuessMyNumber() {
      int myNumber = 56;
      int myGuess = promptForInt("Guess my number, between 0 and 100.");
      while(myGuess != myNumber) {
        myGuess = promptForInt("Sorry, that's not it. Try again.");
      }
  }
      ...
```

Listing 9-7, from GuessMyNumber.java

```
      ...

  public GuessMyNumber() {
      int myNumber = 56;
      int myGuess = promptForInt("Guess my number, between 0 and 100.");
      while(myGuess != myNumber) {
        myGuess = promptForInt("Sorry, that's not it. Try again.");
      }
      print("You guessed it!");
  }
      ...
```

Listing 9-8, from GuessMyNumber.java

```
    ...

  public GuessMyNumber() {

      ...

    while(myGuess != myNumber) {
      if (myGuess < myNumber) {
        myGuess = promptForInt("You guessed too low, try again.");
      }
      else if (myGuess > myNumber) {
        myGuess = promptForInt("You guessed too high, try again.");
      }
    }
    print("You guessed it!");

      ...
```

Listing 9-9, from GuessMyNumber.java

```
      ...

  public GuessMyNumber() {
    Random rand = new Random();
    int myNumber = 56;
    int myGuess = promptForInt("Guess my number, between 0 and 100.");
    while(myGuess != myNumber) {

      ...
```

Listing 9-10, from GuessMyNumber.java

```
      ...

  public GuessMyNumber() {
    Random rand = new Random();
    int myNumber = rand.nextInt(101);
    int myGuess = promptForInt("Guess my number, between 0 and 100.");
    while(myGuess != myNumber) {

      ...
```

Listing 9-11, from GuessMyNumber.java

```
      ...
```

```
public GuessMyNumber() {
   Random rand = new Random();
   int myNumber = rand.nextInt(101);
   int myGuess = promptForInt("Guess my number, between 0 and 100.");
   int count = 1;
   while(myGuess != myNumber) {

      . . .
```

Listing 9-12, from GuessMyNumber.java

```
   . . .

public GuessMyNumber() {

   . . .

   while(myGuess != myNumber) {
      if (myGuess < myNumber) {
         myGuess = promptForInt("You guessed too low, try again.");
      }
      else if (myGuess > myNumber) {
         myGuess = promptForInt("You guessed too high, try again.");
      }
      count = count + 1;
   }
   . . .
```

Listing 9-13, from GuessMyNumber.java

```
   . . .

public GuessMyNumber() {

   . . .

   while(myGuess != myNumber) {
      if (myGuess < myNumber) {
         myGuess = promptForInt("You guessed too low, try again.");
      }
      else if (myGuess > myNumber) {
         myGuess = promptForInt("You guessed too high, try again.");
      }
      count = count + 1;
   }
   print("You guessed it in " + count + " tries!");
}
   . . .
```

Listing 9-14, from GuessMyNumber.java

```
        . . .

    public GuessMyNumber() {

            . . .

        else if (myGuess > myNumber) {
          myGuess = promptForInt("You guessed too high, try again.");
        }
        count += 1;

            . . .
```

Listing 9-15, from GuessMyNumber.java

```
        . . .

    public GuessMyNumber() {

            . . .

        else if (myGuess > myNumber) {
          myGuess = promptForInt("You guessed too high, try again.");
        }
        count++;

            . . .
```

Project 10 – Fahrenheit to Celsius Converter

Listing 10-1, from TemperatureConverter.java

```
package annette.godtland.temperatureconverter;

import annette.godtland.mywindow.MyWindow;

public class TemperatureConverter extends MyWindow {

  public TemperatureConverter() {
    print(1 + 2 + 3);
  }

  public static void main(String[] args) {
    new TemperatureConverter();
```

Listing 10-2, from TemperatureConverter.java

```
    . . .

  public TemperatureConverter() {
    print(1 + 2 * 3);
  }
    . . .
```

Listing 10-3, from TemperatureConverter.java

```
    . . .

  public TemperatureConverter() {
    double f = promptForDouble("Enter degrees Fahrenheit.");
    print((f - 32) * 5 / 9);
  }
    . . .
```

Listing 10-4, from TemperatureConverter.java

```
    . . .

  public TemperatureConverter() {
    double f = promptForDouble("Enter degrees Fahrenheit");
    print((f - 32) * 5 / 9 + " degrees Celsius");
  }
    . . .
```

Listing 10-5, from TemperatureConverter.java

```
    . . .

  public TemperatureConverter() {
    double f = promptForDouble("Enter degrees Fahrenheit");
    print((f - 32) * 5 / 9 + " degrees Celsius");
    double c = promptForDouble("Enter degrees Celsius");
    print(1.8 * c + 32);
  }
    . . .
```

Listing 10-6, from TemperatureConverter.java

```
    . . .
```

```
public TemperatureConverter() {
   double f = promptForDouble("Enter degrees Fahrenheit");
   print((f - 32) * 5 / 9 + " degrees celsius");
   double c = promptForDouble("Enter degrees Celsius");
   print("Fahrenheit = " + 1.8 * c + 32);
}
   ...
```

Listing 10-7, from TemperatureConverter.java

```
   ...

public TemperatureConverter() {
   double f = promptForDouble("Enter degrees Fahrenheit");
   print((f - 32) * 5 / 9 + " degrees celsius");
   double c = promptForDouble("Enter degrees Celsius");
   print("Fahrenheit = " + (1.8 * c + 32));
}
   ...
```

Project 11 – Ten Little Chocolates

Listing 11-1, from TenLittleChocolates.java

```
package annette.godtland.tenlittlechocolates;

import annette.godtland.mywindow.MyWindow;

public class TenLittleChocolates extends MyWindow {

   public TenLittleChocolates() {

   }

   public static void main(String[] args) {
      new TenLittleChocolates();
   }
}
```

Listing 11-2, from TenLittleChocolates.java

```
   ...

public TenLittleChocolates() {
   for(int i=1; i<4; i++) {
      print(i + " little");
   }
```

```
      print("chocolates.");
   }
   ...
```

Listing 11-3, from TenLittleChocolates.java

```
   ...

public TenLittleChocolates() {
   for(int i=1; i<4; i++) {
      print(i + " little");
   }
   print("chocolates.");
   for(int i=4; i<7; i++) {
      print(i + " little");
   }
   print("chocolates.");
}
   ...
```

Listing 11-4, from TenLittleChocolates.java

```
   ...

public TenLittleChocolates() {

   ...

   for(int i=4; i<7; i++) {
      print(i + " little");
   }
   print("chocolates.");
   for(int i=7; i<10; i++) {
      print(i + " little");
   }
   print("chocolates.");
   print("10 little chocolate bars");
}
   ...
```

Listing 11-5, from TenLittleChocolates.java

```
   ...

public TenLittleChocolates() {

   ...
```

```
   print("10 little chocolate bars");
   for(int i=10; i>7; i--) {
      print(i + " little");
   }
   print("chocolates.");

      ...
```

Listing 11-6, from TenLittleChocolates.java

```
   ...

public TenLittleChocolates() {

   ...

   for(int i=10; i>7; i--) {
      print(i + " little");
   }
   print("chocolates.");
   for(int i=7; i>4; i--) {
      print(i + " little");
   }
   print("chocolates.");
   for(int i=4; i>1; i--) {
      print(i + " little");
   }
   print("chocolates.");
   print("1 little chocolate bar");

   ...
```

Project 12 – Word Scramble

Listing 12-1, from WordScramble.java

```
package annette.godtland.wordscramble;

import annette.godtland.mywindow.MyWindow;

public class WordScramble extends MyWindow {

   public WordScramble() {

   }

   public static void main(String[] args) {
```

```
      new WordScramble();
   }
}
```

Listing 12-2, from WordScramble.java

```
      ...

   private String scramble(String word) {
      String scrambled = "";

      return scrambled;
   }
      ...
```

Listing 12-3, from WordScramble.java

```
      ...

   public WordScramble() {
      String word = "ANIMALS";
      String scrambled = scramble(word);
      print(scrambled);
   }
      ...
```

Listing 12-4, from WordScramble.java

```
      ...

   private String scramble(String word) {
      String scrambled = "";

      // pick a random letter from the original word

      // remove that letter from the original word

      // add that letter to a new word

      // repeat these steps until all the letters have been removed from
the original word

      return scrambled;
   }
      ...
```

Listing 12-5, from WordScramble.java

```
    . . .

private String scramble(String word) {
    String scrambled = "";
    Random rand = new Random();

    // pick a random letter from the original word

        . . .
```

Listing 12-6, from WordScramble.java

```
    . . .

private String scramble(String word) {

        . . .

    // pick a random letter from the original word
    int length = word.length();
    int index = rand.nextInt(length);

        . . .
```

Listing 12-7, from WordScramble.java

```
    . . .

private String scramble(String word) {

        . . .

    // pick a random letter from the original word
    int length = word.length();
    int index = rand.nextInt(length);
    String letter = word.substring(index, index+1);

        . . .
```

Listing 12-8, from WordScramble.java

```
    . . .

private String scramble(String word) {

        . . .

    // remove that letter from the original word
```

```
    String firstString = word.substring(0,index);
    String secondString = word.substring(index+1);
    word = firstString + secondString;

        . . .
```

Listing 12-9, from WordScramble.java

```
        . . .

    private String scramble(String word) {

            . . .

        // pick a random letter from the original word
        int length = word.length();
        int index = rand.nextInt(length);
        System.out.println("index = " + index);
        String letter = word.substring(index, index+1);
        System.out.println("letter = " + letter);

        // remove that letter from the original word
        String firstString = word.substring(0,index);
        String secondString = word.substring(index+1);
        word = firstString + secondString;
        System.out.println("word = " + word);

            . . .
```

Listing 12-10, from WordScramble.java

```
        . . .

    private String scramble(String word) {

            . . .

        // add that letter to a new word
        scrambled += letter;
        System.out.println("scrambled = " + scrambled);

            . . .
```

Listing 12-11, from WordScramble.java

```
        . . .

    private String scramble(String word) {
```

```
        . . .

    // repeat these steps until all the letters have been removed from
the original word
    while (word.length()>0) {
        // pick a random letter from the original word
        int length = word.length();

        . . .

        // add that letter to a new word
        scrambled += letter;
        System.out.println("scrambled = " + scrambled);

    }
    return scrambled;

        . . .
```

Listing 12-12, from WordScramble.java

```
        . . .

    public WordScramble() {

        // create a list of words
        String words[] = {"ANIMALS", "ELEPHANT", "GIRAFFE", "PENGUIN",
            "GORIALLA", "HIPPOPOTAMUS", "COUGAR", "KANAGAROO", "OSTRICH",
            "BUFFALO", "LEOPARD", "OCTOPUS"};

        String scrambled = scramble(word);
        print(scrambled);

        . . .
```

Listing 12-13, from WordScramble.java

```
        . . .

    public WordScramble() {

        String words[] = {"ANIMALS", "ELEPHANT", "GIRAFFE", "PENGUIN",
            "GORIALLA","HIPPOPOTAMUS", "COUGAR", "KANAGAROO", "OSTRICH",
            "BUFFALO", "LEOPARD", "OCTOPUS"};

        String scrambled = scramble(words[0]);
        print(scrambled);
```

...

Listing 12-14, from WordScramble.java

...

```java
public WordScramble() {

    ...

    int numberOfWords = words.length;
    String scrambled = scramble(words[numberOfWords-1]);
    print(scrambled);

    ...
```

Listing 12-15, from WordScramble.java

...

```java
public WordScramble() {

    ...

    int numberOfWords = words.length;

    // for each word in the list, scramble the word and print it
    for (int i=0; i<numberOfWords; i++) {
      String scrambled = scramble(words[i]);
      print(scrambled);
    }
    ...
```

Listing 12-16, from MyStringMethods.java

```java
package annette.godtland.mystringmethods;

public class MyStringMethods {

}
```

Listing 12-17, from MyStringMethods.java

...

```java
public class MyStringMethods {
```

```
    private String scramble(String word) {
        String scrambled = "";
        Random rand = new Random();
        // repeat these steps until all the letters have been removed from
the original word
        while (word.length()>0) {
            // pick a random letter from the original word
            int length = word.length();
            int index = rand.nextInt(length);
            String letter = word.substring(index, index+1);

            // remove that letter from the original word
            String firstString = word.substring(0,index);
            String secondString = word.substring(index+1);
            word = firstString + secondString;

            // add that letter to a new word
            scrambled += letter;
        }
        return scrambled;
    }
}
```

Listing 12-18, from MyStringMethods.java

```
        . . .

    public String scramble(String word) {
        String scrambled = "";
        Random rand = new Random();

        . . .
```

Listing 12-19, from MyStringMethods.java

```
        . . .

    public static String scramble(String word) {
        String scrambled = "";
        Random rand = new Random();

        . . .
```

Listing 12-20, from WordScramble.java

```
        . . .

    public WordScramble() {
```

```
    . . .

    // for each word in the list, scramble the word and print it
    for (int i=0; i<numberOfWords; i++) {
       String scrambled = MyStringMethods.scramble(words[i]);

       . . .
```

Listing 12-21, from WordScramble.java

```
package annette.godtland.wordscramble;

import annette.godtland.mystringmethods.MyStringMethods;
import annette.godtland.mywindow.MyWindow;

    . . .
```

Project 13 – Secret Code

Listing 13-1, from SecretCodeKey.java

```
package annette.godtland.secretcodekey;

import annette.godtland.mywindow.MyWindow;

public class SecretCodeKey extends MyWindow {

   public SecretCodeKey() {

   }

   public static void main(String[] args) {
      new SecretCodeKey();
   }
}
```

Listing 13-2, from SecretCodeKey.java

```
    . . .

   public SecretCodeKey() {
      String alphabet =
"ABCDEFGHIJKLMNOPQRSTUVWXYZabcdefghijklmnopqrstuvwxyz";
   }
    . . .
```

Listing 13-3, from SecretCodeKey.java

```
    . . .

  public SecretCodeKey() {
     String alphabet =
"ABCDEFGHIJKLMNOPQRSTUVWXYZabcdefghijklmnopqrstuvwxyz";
     String scrambled = MyStringMethods.scramble(alphabet);
  }
    . . .
```

Listing 13-4, from SecretCodeKey.java

```
    . . .

  public SecretCodeKey() {
     String alphabet =
"ABCDEFGHIJKLMNOPQRSTUVWXYZabcdefghijklmnopqrstuvwxyz";
     String scrambled = MyStringMethods.scramble(alphabet);
     print(alphabet);
     print(scrambled);
  }
    . . .
```

Listing 13-5, from SecretCodeKey.java

```
    . . .

  public SecretCodeKey() {

       . . .

     print(alphabet);
     print(scrambled);

     String fileName = "key.txt";
     BufferedWriter out = new BufferedWriter(new FileWriter(new
File(fileName)));
     out.write(alphabet);
     out.newLine();
     out.write(scrambled);
     out.close();

       . . .
```

Listing 13-6, from SecretCodeKey.java

```
    . . .
```

```java
    public SecretCodeKey() {

        ...

    String fileName = "key.txt";
    try {
        BufferedWriter out = new BufferedWriter(new FileWriter(new
File(fileName)));
        out.write(alphabet);
        out.newLine();
        out.write(scrambled);
        out.close();
    }
    catch (IOException e) {
        print("Could not open file " + fileName);
    }
        ...
```

Listing 13-7, from SecretCode.java

```java
package annette.godtland.secretcode;

import annette.godtland.mywindow.MyWindow;

public class SecretCode extends MyWindow {

    public SecretCode() {

    }

    public static void main(String[] args) {
        new SecretCode();
    }
}
```

Listing 13-8, from SecretCode.java

```java
        ...

    public SecretCode() {
        String fileName = "key.txt";
        // read the alphabet and key from the file
        BufferedReader in = new BufferedReader(new FileReader(new
File(fileName)));
        String alphabet = in.readLine();
        String key = in.readLine();
        in.close();
```

```
   }
      . . .
```

Listing 13-9, from SecretCode.java

```
      . . .

   public SecretCode() {
      String fileName = "key.txt";
      try {
         // read the alphabet and key from the file
         BufferedReader in = new BufferedReader(new FileReader(new
File(fileName)));
         String alphabet = in.readLine();
         String key = in.readLine();
         in.close();
      }
      catch (FileNotFoundException e) {
         print("Could not find file " + fileName + ".");
      }
      catch (IOException e) {
         print("Could not open file " + fileName + ".");
      }
   }
      . . .
```

Listing 13-10, from SecretCode.java

```
      . . .

   public SecretCode() {

         . . .

      in.close();

      print(alphabet);
      print(key);
   }
      . . .
```

Listing 13-11, from SecretCode.java

```
      . . .

   private String encode(String message, String fromAlphabet, String
toAlphabet) {
      String newMessage = "";
```

```
        return newMessage;
    }
    ...
```

Listing 13-12, from SecretCode.java

```
        ...

    public SecretCode() {

        ...

        String key = in.readLine();
        in.close();

        String messageToEncode = promptForString("Enter a message:");
        String encodedMessage = encode(messageToEncode, alphabet, key);

        print(encodedMessage);
    }
    ...
```

Listing 13-13, from SecretCode.java

```
        ...

    private String encode(String message, String fromAlphabet, String
toAlphabet) {
        String newMessage = "";

        // take the first letter of the message

        // find the index of that letter in the "from alphabet"

        // if it is in the "from alphabet", find the letter in the same
position
        // in the "to alphabet" and add that new letter to the new message.

        // if it is not in the "from alphabet", add that letter to the new
message.

        // repeat these steps with each letter in the message.

        return newMessage;
    }
    ...
```

Listing 13-14, from SecretCode.java

```
    . . .

  private String encode(String message, String fromAlphabet, String
toAlphabet) {

      . . .

    // take the first letter of the message
    String letter = message.substring(0, 1);

    // find the index of that letter in the "from alphabet"
    int letterPos = fromAlphabet.indexOf(letter);

      . . .
```

Listing 13-15, from SecretCode.java

```
    . . .

  private String encode(String message, String fromAlphabet, String
toAlphabet) {

      . . .

    // if it is in the "from alphabet", find the letter in the same
position
    // in the "to alphabet" and add that new letter to the new message.
    if (letterPos>-1) {
       String newLetter = toAlphabet.substring(letterPos, letterPos+1);
       newMessage += newLetter;
    }
      . . .
```

Listing 13-16, from SecretCode.java

```
    . . .

  private String encode(String message, String fromAlphabet, String
toAlphabet) {

      . . .

    // if it is not in the "from alphabet", add that letter to the new
message.
    else {
        newMessage += letter;
```

```
        }
        . . .
```

Listing 13-17, from SecretCode.java

```
    . . .

    private String encode(String message, String fromAlphabet, String
toAlphabet) {

        . . .

        // repeat these steps with each letter in the message.
        for(int i=0; i<message.length(); i++) {
            // take the next letter of the message
            String letter = message.substring(i,i+1);

            . . .

            // if it is not in the "from alphabet", add that letter to the
new message.
            else {
                newMessage += letter;
            }
        }
        . . .
```

Listing 13-18, from SecretCode.java

```
    . . .

    public SecretCode() {

        . . .

        String messageToEncode = promptForString("Enter a message:");
        String encodedMessage = encode(messageToEncode, alphabet, key);

        print(encodedMessage);
        String decodedMessage = encode(encodedMessage, key, alphabet);
        print(decodedMessage);

        . . .
```

Listing 13-19, from SecretCode.java

```
    . . .
```

```java
public SecretCode() {

        ...

      String key = in.readLine();
      in.close();

      boolean quit = false;
      while (!quit) {
          String option = promptForString("Do you want to encode(E) or
decode(D) a message, or quit(Q)?");
      }
   }
     ...
```

Listing 13-20, from SecretCode.java

```java
    ...

  public SecretCode() {

        ...

        String option = promptForString("Do you want to encode(E) or
decode(D) a message, or quit(Q)?");

        switch(option) {
        // quit
        case "Q" :
          quit = true;
          break;
        }
        ...
```

Listing 13-21, from SecretCode.java

```java
    ...

  public SecretCode() {

        ...

        case "Q" :
          quit = true;
          break;
        // encode a message
        case "E" :
          String messageToEncode = promptForString("Enter a
```

```
message:");
            String encodedMessage = encode(messageToEncode, alphabet,
key);
            print(encodedMessage);
            break;
        }
        . . .
```

Listing 13-22, from SecretCode.java

```
    . . .

  public SecretCode() {

        . . .

        print(encodedMessage);
        break;
    // decode a message
    case "D" :
        String messageToDecode = promptForString("Enter a message:");
        String decodedMessage = encode(messageToDecode, key,
alphabet);
        print(decodedMessage);
        break;

        . . .
```

Listing 13-23, from SecretCode.java

```
    . . .

  public SecretCode() {

        . . .

        print(decodedMessage);
        break;
    // anything else
    default :
        print(option + " is not a valid option.");

        . . .
```

Listing 13-24, from SecretCode.java

```
    . . .
```

```
    public SecretCode() {

            ...

        case "E" :
           String messageToEncode = promptForString("Enter a message:");
           String encodedMessage = encode(messageToEncode, alphabet,
key);
           print(encodedMessage + "\n");
           break;
        // decode a message
        case "D" :
           String messageToDecode = promptForString("Enter a message:");
           String decodedMessage = encode(messageToDecode, key,
alphabet);
           print(decodedMessage + "\n");
           break;

            ...
```

Listing 13-25, from SecretCode.java

```
    ...

  public SecretCode() {

        ...

    switch(option) {
       // quit
       case "Q" :
       case "q" :
          quit = true;
          break;
       // encode a message
       case "E" :
       case "e" :
          String messageToEncode = promptForString("Enter a message:");
          String encodedMessage = encode(messageToEncode, alphabet,
key);
          print(encodedMessage + "\n");
          break;
       // decode a message
       case "D" :
       case "d" :
          String messageToDecode = promptForString("Enter a message:");
          String decodedMessage = encode(messageToDecode, key,
alphabet);
```

```
            print(decodedMessage + "\n");
            break;
        // anything else
        default :
            print(option + " is not a valid option.");
    }
    ...
```

Listing 13-26, from SecretCode.java

```
    ...

  public SecretCode() {

        ...

      boolean quit = false;
      while (!quit) {

          ...

      }
      System.exit(0);
    }
    catch (FileNotFoundException e) {

        ...
```

Project 14 – Word Mastermind

Listing 14-1, from MyWindow.java

```
    ...

  protected boolean promptForYesNo(String prompt) {
      boolean yes = true;
      return yes;
  }
    ...
```

Listing 14-2, from WordMastermind.java

```
package annette.godtland.wordmastermind;

import annette.godtland.mywindow.MyWindow;

public class WordMastermind extends MyWindow {
```

```
    public WordMastermind() {

    }

    public static void main(String[] args) {
        new WordMastermind();
    }
}
```

Listing 14-3, from WordMastermind.java

```
        . . .

    public WordMastermind() {
        boolean repeat = true;
        while(repeat) {
            print("Hello");
        }
    }
        . . .
```

Listing 14-4, from WordMastermind.java

```
        . . .

    public WordMastermind() {
        boolean repeat = true;
        while(repeat) {
            print("Hello");
            repeat = promptForYesNo("Should I repeat this?");
        }
        . . .
```

Listing 14-5, from MyWindow.java

```
        . . .

    protected boolean promptForYesNo(String prompt) {
        boolean yes = true;
        boolean valid = false;
        while(!valid) {
            String YorN = promptForString(prompt);
            switch (YorN) {
                case "Y" :
                case "y" :
                    yes = true;
                    valid = true;
```

```
          break;
        case "N" :
        case "n" :
          yes = false;
          valid = true;
          break;
        default :
          print("Enter Y for yes, or N for no.");
          valid = false;
      }
    }
    return yes;
  }
    . . .
```

Listing 14-6, from MyStringMethods.java

```
    . . .

  public static String replaceStringAt(String originalString, int
index, String replaceString) {
    String newString = originalString;
    return newString;
  }
    . . .
```

Listing 14-7, from MyStringMethods.java

```
    . . .

  public static String replaceStringAt(String originalString, int
index, String replaceString) {
    String newString = originalString;
    String firstString = originalString.substring(0,index);
    String secondString = originalString.substring(index +
replaceString.length());
    newString = firstString + replaceString + secondString;
    return newString;
  }
    . . .
```

Listing 14-8, from WordMastermind.java

```
    . . .

  public WordMastermind() {
    String word = "book";
    word = MyStringMethods.replaceStringAt(word, 3, "t");
```

```
      print(word);
   }
      . . .
```

Listing 14-9, from WordMastermind.java

```
      . . .

   public WordMastermind() {
      String word = "book";
      word = MyStringMethods.replaceStringAt(word, 1, "an");
      print(word);
   }
      . . .
```

Listing 14-10, from WordMastermind.java

```
      . . .

   public WordMastermind() {
      String word = "book";
      word = MyStringMethods.replaceStringAt(word, 4, "s");
      print(word);
   }
      . . .
```

Listing 14-11, from MyStringMethods.java

```
      . . .

   public static String replaceStringAt(String originalString, int
index, String replaceString) {
      String newString = originalString;
      // only replace the string if the index is inside the original
string
      if (index <= originalString.length()) {
         String firstString = originalString.substring(0,index);
         String secondString = originalString.substring(index +
replaceString.length());
         newString = firstString + replaceString + secondString;
      }
      return newString;
   }
      . . .
```

Listing 14-12, from WordMastermind.java

```
      . . .
```

```
public WordMastermind() {
   String word = "book";
   word = MyStringMethods.replaceStringAt(word, 2, "ating");
   print(word);
}
   ...
```

Listing 14-13, from MyStringMethods.java

```
   ...

  public static String replaceStringAt(String originalString, int
index, String replaceString) {
     String newString = originalString;
     // only replace the string if the index is inside the original
string
     if (index <= originalString.length()) {
        // if replaceString is too long to fit, truncate it.
        int roomAvailable = originalString.length()-index;
        if(replaceString.length() > roomAvailable) {
           replaceString = replaceString.substring(0, roomAvailable);
        }
        String firstString = originalString.substring(0,index);

        ...
```

Listing 14-14, from WordMastermind.java

```
   ...

  public WordMastermind() {
     String word = "quit";
     String guess = "lint";
     String clue = "----";
  }
     ...
```

Listing 14-15, from WordMastermind.java

```
   ...

  private void findRightPlaceLetters(String guess) {

  }

  private void findWrongPlaceLetters(String guess) {
```

```
    }
    . . .
```

Listing 14-16, from WordMastermind.java

```
    . . .

  public WordMastermind() {
     String word = "quit";
     String guess = "lint";
     String clue = "----";

     findRightPlaceLetters(guess);
     findWrongPlaceLetters(guess);

     print(clue);
  }
    . . .
```

Listing 14-17, from WordMastermind.java

```
    . . .

  private void findRightPlaceLetters(String guess) {
     // loop through all the letters of the guess
     for(int i=0; i<guess.length(); i++) {
        // get the letter in that position of the guess and word
        String guessLetter = guess.substring(i, i+1);
        String wordLetter = word.substring(i, i+1);
        // if guess letter is same as word letter, set clue to O and
word to -
        if (guessLetter.equals(wordLetter)) {
           clue = MyStringMethods.replaceStringAt(clue, i, "O");
           word = MyStringMethods.replaceStringAt(word, i, "-");
        }
     }
  }
    . . .
```

Listing 14-18, from WordMastermind.java

```
    . . .

public class WordMastermind extends MyWindow {

    . . .

  public WordMastermind() {
```

```
        String word = "quit";
        String guess = "lint";
        String clue = "----";

            . . .

    }

    private void findRightPlaceLetters(String guess) {

        . . .

    }

        . . .
}
```

Listing 14-19, from WordMastermind.java

```
    . . .

public class WordMastermind extends MyWindow {
    private String word;
    private String clue;

        . . .

    public WordMastermind() {
        word = "quit";
        String guess = "lint";
        clue = "----";

            . . .

    }
        . . .
```

Listing 14-20, from WordMastermind.java

```
    . . .

    private void findWrongPlaceLetters(String guess) {
        // loop through all the letters of the guess
        for(int i=0; i<guess.length(); i++) {
            // get the guess letter at position i
            String letter = guess.substring(i, i+1);
            // if letter is in word (indexOf > -1)
            int letterLoc = word.indexOf(letter);
```

```
     if (letterLoc > -1) {
        // replace letter in word with -
        word = MyStringMethods.replaceStringAt(word, letterLoc, "-");
        // set clue at the loop index to X if it is still -
        String clueLetter = clue.substring(i, i+1);
        if (clueLetter.equals("-")) {
           clue = MyStringMethods.replaceStringAt(clue, i, "X");
        }
     }
   }
  }
  ...
```

Listing 14-21, from WordMastermind.java

```
   ...

public WordMastermind() {
   word = "quit";

   // Prompt user for a guess
   String guess = promptForString("Guess my word.");
   String originalWord = word;
   boolean solved = false;

   // Repeat while not solved
   while (!solved) {
      // reset word and clue for each guess
      word = originalWord;
      clue = "----";

      // set the clue
      findRightPlaceLetters(guess);
      findWrongPlaceLetters(guess);

      // did he guess it?
      if(guess.equals(originalWord)) {
         solved = true;
      }
      else {
         guess = promptForString(clue);
      }
   }

   // congratulate the user
   print("OOOO");
   print("You guessed it!");
}
```

. . .

Listing 14-22, from WordMastermind.java

```
    . . .

  public WordMastermind() {

      . . .

    while (!solved) {
      if (guess.length()==4) {
        // reset word and clue for each guess
        word = originalWord;
        clue = "----";

          . . .

        else {
          guess = promptForString(clue);
        }
      }
      else {
        guess = promptForString("Your guess must contain 4 letters.");
      }
    }
      . . .
```

Listing 14-23, from WordMastermind.java

```
    . . .

  public WordMastermind() {
    word = "quit";
    word = word.toUpperCase();

    // Prompt user for a guess
    String guess = promptForString("Guess my word");
    guess = guess.toUpperCase();
    String originalWord = word;

        . . .

        else {
          guess = promptForString(clue);
          guess = guess.toUpperCase();
        }
      }
```

338 | Appendix B - Completed Listings

```
      else {
         guess = promptForString("Your guess must contain 4 letters.");
         guess = guess.toUpperCase();
      }
   }
      ...
```

Listing 14-24, from WordMastermind.java

```
   ...

public WordMastermind() {

   ...

   // prompt the user for a guess
   print("I'm thinking of a 4 letter word.");
   print("  I will give you clues:");
   print("  An \"O\" means you guessed the correct letter in the
correct position.");
   print("  An \"X\" means you guessed the correct letter but in
the wrong position.");
   String guess = promptForString("Guess my word");
   guess = guess.toUpperCase();

   ...
```

Listing 14-25, from WordMastermind.java

```
   ...

public WordMastermind() {

   ...

   String guess = promptForString("Guess my word");
   guess = guess.toUpperCase();
   int count = 1;

      ...

      // did he guess it?
      if(guess.equals(originalWord)) {
         solved = true;
      }
      else {
         guess = promptForString(clue);
         guess = guess.toUpperCase();
```

```
            count++;
        }

        . . .

    // congratulate the user
    print("OOOO");
    print("You guessed it in " + count + " tries!");
    }

    . . .
```

Listing 14-26, from WordMastermind.java

```
    . . .

public WordMastermind() {
    int numberOfWords = 342;
    String words[] = new String[numberOfWords];

    word = "quit";

        . . .
```

Listing 14-27, from WordMastermind.java

```
    . . .

public WordMastermind() {

        . . .

    String words[] = new String[numberOfWords];
    String fileName = "wordMastermind.txt";

    // read a list of words from the file
    BufferedReader in = new BufferedReader(new FileReader(new
File(fileName)));
    for (int i=0; i<numberOfWords; i++) {
        words[i] = in.readLine();
    }
    in.close();

        . . .
```

Listing 14-28, from WordMastermind.java

```
    . . .

    public WordMastermind() {
```

```
        ...

    String fileName = "wordMastermind";

    try {
      // read a list of words from the file

        ...

      print("You guessed it in " + count + " tries!");
    }
    catch(FileNotFoundException e) {
      print("Could not find file " + fileName);
    }
    catch(IOException e) {
      print("Could not read from file " + fileName);
    }
  }
    ...
```

Listing 14-29, from WordMastermind.java

```
    ...

  public WordMastermind() {

      ...

    String fileName = "wordMastermind.txt";
    Random rand = new Random();

    try {
      // read a list of words from the file
      BufferedReader in = new BufferedReader(new FileReader(new
File(fileName)));
      for (int i=0; i<numberOfWords; i++) {
        words[i] = in.readLine();
      }
      in.close();

      int pick = rand.nextInt(numberOfWords);
      word = words[pick];
      word = word.toUpperCase();

      // Prompt user for a guess

        ...
```

Listing 14-30, from WordMastermind.java

```
    ...

   public WordMastermind() {

       ...

      in.close();

      boolean repeat = true;
      while(repeat) {
         int pick = rand.nextInt(numberOfWords);

            ...

         print("You guessed it in " + count + " tries!\n");

         repeat = promptForYesNo("Do you want to play again?");
         print();
      }
      System.exit(0);

         ...
```

Listing 14-31, from WordMastermind.java

```
    ...

public class WordMastermind extends MyWindow {
   private String clue;
   private String word;
   private static final int numberOfWords = 342;
   private static final String fileName = "wordMastermind.txt";

   public WordMastermind() {
      String words[] = new String[numberOfWords];
      Random rand = new Random();

         ...
```

Listing 14-32, from WordMastermind.java

```
    ...

   private String word;
   private String clue;
   private static final int NUMBEROFWORDS = 342;
```

```java
   private static final String FILENAME = "wordMastermind.txt";

   public WordMastermind() {
      String words[] = new String[NUMBEROFWORDS];
      Random rand = new Random();

      try {
         // read a list of words from the file
         BufferedReader in = new BufferedReader(new FileReader(new
File(FILENAME)));
         for (int i=0; i<NUMBEROFWORDS; i++) {
            words[i] = in.readLine();
         }
         in.close();

         boolean repeat = true;
         while(repeat) {
            int pick = rand.nextInt(NUMBEROFWORDS);


               ...
      }
      catch(FileNotFoundException e) {
         print("Could not find the file " + FILENAME);
      }
      catch(IOException e) {
         print("Could not read from file " + FILENAME);
      }
      ...
```

Project 15 – Hangman

Listing 15-1, from Hangman.java

```java
package annette.godtland.hangman;

import annette.godtland.mywindow.MyWindow;

public class Hangman extends MyWindow {

   public Hangman() {

   }

   public static void main(String[] args) {
      new Hangman();
   }
}
```

Listing 15-2, from Hangman.java

```
package annette.godtland.hangman;

import annette.godtland.mywindow.MyWindow;

public class Hangman extends MyWindow {
   private String phrase;
   private String clue;
   private String wrongLetters;

   public Hangman() {

   }
   ...
```

Listing 15-3, from Hangman.java

```
   ...

   public Hangman() {
      printPuzzle();
   }

   private void printPuzzle() {
      print("_____");
      print("|   O");
      print("| --|--    ");
      print("| _/ \\_");
      print("|");
   }
   ...
```

Listing 15-4, from Hangman.java

```
   ...

   public Hangman() {
      wrongLetters = "ABC";
      printPuzzle();
   }

   private void printPuzzle() {
      print("_____");
      print("|   O");
      print("| --|--    " + wrongLetters);
      print("| _/ \\_");
```

```
        print("|");
    }
    ...
```

Listing 15-5, from Hangman.java

```
    ...

    private void printPuzzle() {
        switch (wrongLetters.length()) {
            case 0:
                break;
            case 1:
                break;
            case 2:
                break;
            case 3:
                break;
            case 4:
                break;
            case 5:
                break;
            case 6:
                break;
            case 7:
                break;
            case 8:
                break;
            case 9:
                break;
            case 10:
                break;
        }
        print("_____");
        print("|    O");
        print("|  --|--    " + wrongLetters);
        print("|  _/ \\_");
        print("|");
    }
    ...
```

Listing 15-6, from Hangman.java

```
    ...

    private void printPuzzle() {
        print("_____");
        switch (wrongLetters.length()) {
```

```
        case 0:
           break;
        case 1:
           break;
        case 2:
           break;
        case 3:
           break;
        case 4:
           break;
        case 5:
           break;
        case 6:
           break;
        case 7:
           break;
        case 8:
           break;
        case 9:
           break;
        case 10:
        print("|   O");
        print("| --|--    " + wrongLetters);
        print("| _/ \\_");
           break;
      }
      print("|");
   }
      ...
```

Listing 15-7, from Hangman.java

```
      ...

   private void printPuzzle() {
      print("_____");
      switch (wrongLetters.length()) {
      case 0:
         print("|");
         print("|           " + wrongLetters);
         print("|");
         break;
      case 1:
         print("|   O");
         print("|           " + wrongLetters);
         print("|");
         break;
      case 2:
```

```java
      print("|   O");
      print("|   |       " + wrongLetters);
      print("|");
      break;
    case 3:
      print("|   O");
      print("|  -|       " + wrongLetters);
      print("|");
      break;
    case 4:
      print("|   O");
      print("| --|       " + wrongLetters);
      print("|");
      break;
    case 5:
      print("|   O");
      print("| --|-      " + wrongLetters);
      print("|");
      break;
    case 6:
      print("|   O");
      print("| --|--     " + wrongLetters);
      print("|");
      break;
    case 7:
      print("|   O");
      print("| --|--     " + wrongLetters);
      print("|  /");
      break;
    case 8:
      print("|   O");
      print("| --|--     " + wrongLetters);
      print("| _/");
      break;
    case 9:
      print("|   O");
      print("| --|--     " + wrongLetters);
      print("| _/ \\");
      break;
    case 10:
      print("|   O");
      print("| --|--     " + wrongLetters);
      print("| _/ \\_");
      break;
  }
  print("|");
}
  ...
```

Listing 15-8, from Hangman.java

```
    ...

  public Hangman() {
     wrongLetters = "ABCD";
     printPuzzle();
  }
    ...
```

Listing 15-9, from Hangman.java

```
    ...

  public Hangman() {
     phrase = "HELLO WORLD";
     blankOutClue();

     wrongLetters = "ABC";
     printPuzzle();
  }

  private void blankOutClue() {

  }
    ...
```

Listing 15-10, from Hangman.java

```
    ...

  private void blankOutClue() {
     // start with an empty clue
     // for each letter in the phrase
     // if the letter is a blank, add a blank to the clue
     // if it is anything else, add a dash to the clue
  }
    ...
```

Listing 15-11, from Hangman.java

```
    ...

  private void blankOutClue() {
     // start with an empty clue
     clue = "";
     // for each letter in the phrase
     for(int i=0; i<phrase.length(); i++) {
```

```
    char letter = phrase.charAt(i);
    // if the letter is a blank, add a blank to the clue
    if (letter == ' ') {
       clue += ' ';
    }
    // if it is anything else, add a dash to the clue
    else {
       clue += '-';
    }
  }
}
  ...
```

Listing 15-12, from Hangman.java

```
  ...

private void printPuzzle() {

    ...

  }
  print("|            " + clue);
}
  ...
```

Listing 15-13, from Hangman.java

```
  ...

public Hangman() {
   phrase = "HELLO WORLD";
   blankOutClue();

   wrongLetters = "ABC";
   printPuzzle();

   // find the first occurrence of the guessed letter in the phrase
   // as long as it finds the guessed letter
   // replace the dash in the same position of the clue with the
letter
   // find the next occurrence of the guessed letter
   // print the puzzle again
}
  ...
```

Listing 15-14, from Hangman.java

```
    ...

public Hangman() {

    ...

    String guess = "L";
    // find the first occurrence of the guessed letter in the phrase
    int index = phrase.indexOf(guess);
    // as long as it finds the guessed letter
    while(index>-1) {
       // replace the dash in the same position of the clue with the
letter
       clue = MyStringMethods.replaceStringAt(clue, index, guess);
       // find the next occurrence of the guessed letter
       index = phrase.indexOf(guess,index+1);
    }
    // print the puzzle again
    printPuzzle();

    ...
```

Listing 15-15, from Hangman.java

```
    ...

public Hangman() {

    ...

    wrongLetters = "";
    printPuzzle();

    String guess = "L";
    boolean found = false;
    // find the first occurrence of the guessed letter in the phrase
    int index = phrase.indexOf(guess);
    // as long as it finds the guessed letter
    while(index>-1) {
       found = true;
       // replace the dash in the same position of the clue with the
letter
       clue = MyStringMethods.replaceStringAt(clue, index, guess);
       // find the next occurrence of the guessed letter
       index = phrase.indexOf(guess,index+1);
    }
    if (!found) {
       wrongLetters += guess;
```

```
        }
        // print the puzzle again
        printPuzzle();

            . . .
```

Listing 15-16, from Hangman.java

```
        . . .

    public Hangman() {

            . . .

        // repeat until phrase solved or hangman complete (10 tries)
        while(clue.contains("-") && wrongLetters.length() < 10) {
            String guess = promptForString("Guess a letter");
            boolean found = false;

                . . .

            // print the puzzle again
            printPuzzle();
        }
    }
        . . .
```

Listing 15-17, from Hangman.java

```
        . . .

    public Hangman() {

            . . .

        String guess = promptForString("Guess a letter");
        guess = guess.toUpperCase();
        // must be one letter
        if (guess.length()!=1) {
            print("Your guess must contain only 1 letter. Guess again.");
        }
        // guess must not have been tried before
        else if (clue.contains(guess) || wrongLetters.contains(guess)) {
            print("You already guessed " + guess + ". Guess again.");
        }
        else {
            boolean found = false;
            // find the first occurrence of the guessed letter
```

```
        ...

        // print the puzzle again
        printPuzzle();
    }
        ...
```

Listing 15-18, from Hangman.java

```
    ...

  public Hangman() {

        ...

    // repeat until phrase solved or hangman complete (10 tries)
    while(clue.contains("-") && wrongLetters.length() < 10) {

        ...

    }
    if (!clue.contains("-")) {
       print ("Congratulations! You guessed it before you were
hanged!");
    }
    else {
       print ("Sorry, you lose. The phrase was " + phrase);
    }
  }
    ...
```

Listing 15-19, from Hangman.java

```
    ...

  private String phrase;
  private String clue;
  private String wrongLetters;

  private static final String FILENAME = "phrases.txt";

  public Hangman() {

    try {
       BufferedReader in = new BufferedReader(new FileReader(new
File(FILENAME)));
       String s = in.readLine();
```

```
      while (s != null) {
         s = in.readLine();
      }
      in.close();

      phrase = "HELLO WORLD";
      blankOutClue();

         ...

      else {
         print ("Sorry, you lose. The phrase was " + phrase);
      }
   }
   catch(FileNotFoundException e) {
      print("Could not find file " + FILENAME);
   }
   catch(IOException e) {
      print("Could not read from file " + FILENAME);
   }
      ...
```

Listing 15-20, from Hangman.java

```
   ...

public Hangman() {
   ArrayList<String> phrases = new ArrayList<String>();

   try {
      BufferedReader in = new BufferedReader(new FileReader(new
File(FILENAME)));
      String s = in.readLine();
      while (s != null) {
         phrases.add(s);
         s = in.readLine();
      }
         ...
```

Listing 15-21, from Hangman.java

```
   ...

public Hangman() {
   ArrayList<String> phrases = new ArrayList<String>();
   Random rand = new Random();

   try {
```

```
        . . .

        in.close();
        int numberOfPhrases = phrases.size();

        int pick = rand.nextInt(numberOfPhrases);
        phrase = phrases.get(pick);
        phrase = phrase.toUpperCase();
        blankOutClue();

        . . .
```

Listing 15-22, from Hangman.java

```
    . . .

  public Hangman() {

        . . .

    int numberOfPhrases = phrases.size();

    boolean again = true;
    while (again) {
      int pick = rand.nextInt(numberOfPhrases);
      phrase = phrases.get(pick);

        . . .

      print("Sorry, you lose. The phrase was " + phrase);
    }
    again = promptForYesNo("Do you want to play again?");
    }
    System.exit(0);

  } catch (FileNotFoundException e) {

        . . .
```

Project 16 – Crazy Eights

Listing 16-1, from Card.java

```
package annette.godtland.cards;

public class Card {
```

```
}
```

Listing 16-2, from Card.java

```
package annette.godtland.cards;

public class Card {
   private char rank = '8';
   private char suit = 'H';
}
```

Listing 16-3, from Card.java

```
      ...

   public String toString() {
      String rs = "" + rank + suit;
      return rs;
   }
}
```

Listing 16-4, from CrazyEights.java

```
package annette.godtland.crazyeights;

import annette.godtland.mywindow.MyWindow;

public class CrazyEights extends MyWindow {

   public CrazyEights() {

   }

   public static void main(String[] args) {
      new CrazyEights();
   }
}
```

Listing 16-5, from CrazyEights.java

```
      ...

public class CrazyEights extends MyWindow {

   public CrazyEights() {
      Card card = new Card();
      print(card.toString());
```

```
  }

  public static void main(String[] args) {
    new CrazyEights();
  }
}
```

Listing 16-6, from Card.java

```
    . . .

  private char rank = ' ';
  private char suit = ' ';

  public Card(String rs) {
    rank = rs.charAt(0);
    suit = rs.charAt(1);
  }
    . . .
```

Listing 16-7, from CrazyEights

```
    . . .

  public CrazyEights() {
    Card card = new Card("7S");
    print(card.toString());
  }
    . . .
```

Listing 16-8, from Card.java

```
    . . .

  private char rank = ' ';
  private char suit = ' ';

  private static final String RANKS = "A23456789TJQK";
  private static final String SUITS = "HDCS";

  public Card(String rs) {

    . . .
```

Listing 16-9, from Card.java

```
    . . .
```

```
public Card(int id) {

}

public Card(String rs) {

    . . .
```

Listing 16-10, from Card.java

```
    . . .

public Card(int id) {
   rank = RANKS.charAt(id%13);
   suit = SUITS.charAt(id/13);
}
    . . .
```

Listing 16-11, from Card.java

```
    . . .

public Card(int id) {
   id = id%52;
   if(id<0) {
      id = id * -1;
   }
   rank = RANKS.charAt(id%13);
   suit = SUITS.charAt(id/13);
}
    . . .
```

Listing 16-12, from Card.java

```
    . . .

public Card(String rs) {
   if(rs.length()==2) {
      char r = rs.charAt(0);
      char s = rs.charAt(1);
      int ri = RANKS.indexOf(r);
      int si = SUITS.indexOf(s);
      if (ri>-1 && si>-1) {
         rank = r;
         suit = s;
      }
   }
}
```

. . .

Listing 16-13, from CrazyEights.java

. . .

```java
public CrazyEights() {
    Card card = new Card(0);
    print(card.toString());
}
```

. . .

Listing 16-14, from Card.java

. . .

```java
public char getRank() {
    return rank;
}

public char getSuit() {
    return suit;
}
```

. . .

Listing 16-15, from Card.java

. . .

```java
public boolean isValid() {
    boolean valid = false;
    if (suit != ' ') {
        valid = true;
    }
    return valid;
}
```

. . .

Listing 16-16, from Card.java

. . .

```java
public boolean equals(Card card) {
    boolean equals = false;
    if ((card.getSuit()==suit) && (card.getRank()==rank)) {
        equals = true;
    }
    return equals;
```

```
    }
    ...
```

Listing 16-17, from Card.java

```
    ...

public boolean isGreaterThan(Card card) {
   boolean greaterThan = false;
   char cardSuit = card.getSuit();
   char cardRank = card.getRank();
   if (SUITS.indexOf(suit) > SUITS.indexOf(cardSuit)) {
      greaterThan = true;
   }
   else if(suit==cardSuit) {
      if (RANKS.indexOf(rank) > RANKS.indexOf(cardRank)) {
         greaterThan = true;
      }
   }
   return greaterThan;
}
   ...
```

Listing 16-18, from Card.java

```
    ...

public static boolean isValidSuit(char c) {
   boolean valid = false;
   if (SUITS.indexOf(c)>-1) {
      valid = true;
   }
   return valid;
}
   ...
```

Listing 16-19, from CrazyEights.java

```
    ...

public CrazyEights() {
   Card card1 = new Card("QH");
   print(card1.toString());
   Card card2 = new Card("QC");
   print(card2.toString());
   if (!card1.isValid()) {
      print("The first card is not valid");
   }
```

```
      if (!card2.isValid()) {
         print("The second card is not valid");
      }
      if (card1.equals(card2)) {
         print("The cards are equal.");
      }
      else {
         print("The cards are not equal.");
      }
      if (card1.isGreaterThan(card2)) {
         print("The first card is greater.");
      }
      else {
         print("The first card is not greater.");
      }
      char c = 'X';
      if (Card.isValidSuit(c)) {
         print(c + "is a valid suit");
      }
      else {
         print(c + "is not a valid suit");
      }
   }
   ...
```

Listing 16-20, from Deck.java

```
package annette.godtland.cards;

public class Deck {

   public Deck() {

   }

}
```

Listing 16-21, from Deck.java

```
   ...

public class Deck {
   private ArrayList<Card> cards = new ArrayList<Card>();
   private Random rand = new Random();

   public Deck() {

      ...
```

Listing 16-22, from Deck.java

```
    . . .

public Deck() {
    for(int i=0; i<52; i++){
        Card card = new Card(i);
        cards.add(card);
    }
}
    . . .
```

Listing 16-23, from Deck.java

```
    . . .

public String toString() {
    String deckString = "";
    for(int i=0; i<cards.size(); i++) {
        Card card = cards.get(i);
        deckString += card + " ";
    }
    return deckString;
}
    . . .
```

Listing 16-24, from CrazyEights.java

```
    . . .

public CrazyEights() {
    Deck deck = new Deck();
    print(deck.toString());
}
    . . .
```

Listing 16-25, from Deck.java

```
    . . .

public void shuffle() {
    ArrayList<Card> shuffled = new ArrayList<Card>();
    int numberOfTimes = cards.size();
    for(int i=0; i<numberOfTimes; i++){
        int deckSize = cards.size();
        int pick = rand.nextInt(deckSize);
        Card card = cards.remove(pick);
```

```
      shuffled.add(card);
    }
    cards = shuffled;
  }
    . . .
```

Listing 16-26, from Deck.java

```
    . . .

  public Deck() {
    for(int i=0; i<52; i++){
      Card card = new Card(i);
      cards.add(card);
    }
    shuffle();
  }
    . . .
```

Listing 16-27, from Deck.java

```
    . . .

  public Card deal(){
    Card card = cards.remove(0);
    return card;
  }
    . . .
```

Listing 16-28, from Deck.java

```
    . . .

  public void reuse(ArrayList<Card> newCards) {
    cards = newCards;
  }
    . . .
```

Listing 16-29, from Deck.java

```
    . . .

  public int size() {
    return cards.size();
  }
    . . .
```

Listing 16-30, from CrazyEights.java

```java
    . . .

  public CrazyEights() {
    Deck deck = new Deck();
    print(deck.toString());
    print(deck.size());
    ArrayList<Card> discardPile = new ArrayList<Card>();
    for(int i=0; i<10; i++) {
      Card card = deck.deal();
      print(card.toString());
      discardPile.add(card);
    }
    print(deck.size());
    deck.reuse(discardPile);
    print(deck.toString());
    print(deck.size());

  }
    . . .
```

Listing 16-31, from Hand.java

```java
package annette.godtland.cards;

public class Hand {
   private ArrayList<Card> cards = new ArrayList<Card>();
}
```

Listing 16-32, from Hand.java

```java
    . . .

  public void add(Card card){
    int index = 0;
    boolean done = false;
    while (!done && index<cards.size()) {
      Card cardInHand = cards.get(index);
      if (card.isGreaterThan(cardInHand)) {
        index++;
      }
      else {
        done = true;
      }
    }
    cards.add(index,card);
  }
```

```
}
```

Listing 16-33, from Hand.java

```
      . . .

   public String toString() {
      String string = "";
      for (int i=0; i<cards.size(); i++) {
         Card card = cards.get(i);
         string += card.toString() + " ";
      }
      return string;
   }
}
```

Listing 16-34, from Hand.java

```
      . . .

   public String toString() {
      String string = "";
      for (int i=0; i<cards.size(); i++) {
         Card card = cards.get(i);
         // if this is not the first card, compare it with the
         // previous card.  If the suits are different add a
         // couple extra spaces
         if (i>0) {
            Card priorCard = cards.get(i-1);
            char priorSuit = priorCard.getSuit();
            char currentSuit = card.getSuit();
            if (priorSuit != currentSuit) {
               string += "   ";
            }
         }
         string += card.toString() + " ";

      . . .
```

Listing 16-35, from CrazyEights.java

```
      . . .

   public CrazyEights() {
      Hand hand = new Hand();
      Card card1 = new Card("KC");
      Card card2 = new Card("7H");
```

```
      Card card3 = new Card("JC");
      hand.add(card1);
      hand.add(card2);
      hand.add(card3);
      print(hand.toString());
   }
      . . .
```

Listing 16-36, from Hand.java

```
      . . .

   public void remove(Card card) {
      int index = 0;
      boolean found = false;
      while(!found && index < cards.size()) {
         Card compareCard = cards.get(index);
         if(compareCard.equals(card)) {
            cards.remove(index);
            found = true;
         }
         else {
            index++;
         }
      }
   }
}
```

Listing 16-37, from Hand.java

```
      . . .

   public boolean contains(Card card) {
      int index = 0;
      boolean contains = false;
      while(!contains && index < cards.size()) {
         Card compareCard = cards.get(index);
         if(compareCard.equals(card)) {
            contains = true;
         }
         else {
            index++;
         }
      }
      return contains;
   }
}
```

Listing 16-38, from Hand.java

```java
    ...

  public Card cardAt(int i) {
    return cards.get(i);
  }
}
```

Listing 16-39, from Hand.java

```java
    ...

  public int size() {
    return cards.size();
  }
}
```

Listing 16-40, from CrazyEights.java

```java
    ...

  public CrazyEights() {
    Hand hand = new Hand();
    Card card1 = new Card("KC");
    Card card2 = new Card("7H");
    Card card3 = new Card("JC");
    Card card4 = new Card("2D");
    hand.add(card1);
    hand.add(card2);
    hand.add(card3);
    print(hand.toString());
    print(hand.size());
    if (hand.contains(card3)){
      print("Found Jack of Clubs");
    }
    if (hand.contains(card4)){
      print("Found 2 of Diamonds");
    }
    hand.remove(card2);
    hand.remove(card4);
    print(hand.toString());
    print(hand.size());
  }
    ...
```

Listing 16-41, from CrazyEights.java

```
   . . .

public class CrazyEights extends MyWindow {

   private Deck deck = new Deck();
   private Hand myHand = new Hand();
   private Hand computerHand = new Hand();
   private Card discard;
   private ArrayList<Card> discardPile = new ArrayList<Card>();
   private Random rand = new Random();
   private char activeSuit = ' ';

   public CrazyEights() {

   }
   . . .
```

Listing 16-42, from CrazyEights.java

```
   . . .

   private Card deal() {
      // if end of deck, reuse the discard pile and shuffle it.
      if (deck.size()==0) {
         deck.reuse(discardPile);
         deck.shuffle();
         discardPile.clear();
         print();
         print("Reshuffled the discard pile.");
      }

      // deal a card from the deck
      Card card = deck.deal();
      return card;
   }
}
```

Listing 16-43, from CrazyEights.java

```
   . . .

   public CrazyEights() {
      // deal 7 cards to each of us
      for (int i=0; i<7; i++) {
         Card card1 = deal();
         myHand.add(card1);
```

```
      Card card2 = deal();
      computerHand.add(card2);
   }

   // turn up the discard
   discard = deal();

   // if discard is an 8, set the active suit
   if (discard.getRank()=='8') {
      activeSuit = discard.getSuit();
   }
   else {
      activeSuit = ' ';
   }

}
   ...
```

Listing 16-44, from CrazyEights.java

```
   ...

private void showStatus() {
   print();
   print("Computer has " + computerHand.size() + " cards.");
   print("My Hand: " + myHand);
   print("Discard: " + discard);
   if(discard.getRank()=='8') {
      print("Suit is " + activeSuit);
   }

}
   ...
```

Listing 16-45, from CrazyEights.java

```
   ...

public CrazyEights() {

   ...

   else {
      activeSuit = ' ';
   }

   showStatus();
}
```

. . .

Listing 16-46, from CrazyEights.java

. . .

```java
private void drawMyCard() {
   Card drewCard = deal();
   print();
   print("You drew " + drewCard);
   myHand.add(drewCard);
}
```
. . .

Listing 16-47, from CrazyEights.java

. . .

```java
private void discardMyCard(Card myCard) {
   myHand.remove(myCard);
   discardPile.add(discard);
   discard = myCard;
}
```
. . .

Listing 16-48, from CrazyEights.java

. . .

```java
private void playMyCard() {
   showStatus();
   String rankSuit = promptForString("Which card do you want to play
(or D to draw)?");
   rankSuit = rankSuit.toUpperCase();
   // if draw, draw a card
   if (rankSuit.equals("D")) {
     drawMyCard();
   }
   // else play the card
   else {
     Card selectedCard = new Card(rankSuit);
     discardMyCard(selectedCard);
   }
}
```
. . .

Listing 16-49, from CrazyEights.java

```
      ...

   public CrazyEights() {

         ...

      else {
         activeSuit = ' ';
      }

      playMyCard();
      showStatus();
   }
      ...
```

Listing 16-50, from CrazyEights.java

```
         ...

   private boolean isValidPlay(String rankSuit) {
      boolean validPlay = true;
      Card card = new Card(rankSuit);

      // is it a valid card?
      if (!card.isValid()) {
         print(rankSuit + " is not a valid card");
         validPlay = false;
      }

      // is that card in my hand?
      else if(!myHand.contains(card)) {
         print(rankSuit + " is not in your hand");
         validPlay = false;
      }

      // does the discard match the rank or suit?
      else if ((card.getSuit()!=discard.getSuit())
          && (card.getRank()!=discard.getRank())) {
         print(rankSuit + " cannot be played on " + discard + ".");
         validPlay = false;
      }

      return validPlay;
   }
      ...
```

Listing 16-51, from CrazyEights.java

```
      . . .

   private void playMyCard() {
      showStatus();
      boolean validPlay = false;
      // repeat until a valid play has been entered
      while (!validPlay) {
         String rankSuit = promptForString("Which card do you want to
play (or D to draw)?");
         rankSuit = rankSuit.toUpperCase();
         // if draw, draw a card
         if (rankSuit.equals("D")) {
            drawMyCard();
            validPlay = true;
         }
         // if valid play, play the card
         else if (isValidPlay(rankSuit)) {
            Card selectedCard = new Card(rankSuit);
            discardMyCard(selectedCard);
            validPlay = true;
         }
      }
   }
      . . .
```

Listing 16-52, from CrazyEights.java

```
      . . .

   private void drawMyCard() {
      Card drewCard = deal();
      print();
      print("You drew " + drewCard);
      myHand.add(drewCard);

      // if I can play my drawn card, play it
      if (isValidPlay(drewCard.toString())) {
         print("You played " + drewCard);
         discardMyCard(drewCard);
      }
   }
      . . .
```

Listing 16-53, from CrazyEights.java

```
      . . .

   private void discardComputerCard(Card computerCard) {
```

```
      computerHand.remove(computerCard);
      discardPile.add(discard);
      discard = computerCard;
   }
      ...
```

Listing 16-54, from CrazyEights.java

```
      ...

   public CrazyEights() {

         ...

      playMyCard();
      playComputerCard();
      showStatus();
   }
      ...

   private void playComputerCard() {
      System.out.println("Computer hand: " + computerHand);
      ArrayList<Card> playableCards = new ArrayList<Card>();

      // make a list of playable cards
      for(int i=0; i<computerHand.size(); i++) {
         Card card = computerHand.cardAt(i);
         // only cards of same suit or rank are playable
         if (card.getSuit()==(discard.getSuit())
               || card.getRank()==(discard.getRank())){
            playableCards.add(card);
         }
      }

      // pick a random playable card
      int numberOfPlayableCards = playableCards.size();
      if (numberOfPlayableCards>0) {
         int pick = rand.nextInt(numberOfPlayableCards);
         Card playedCard = playableCards.get(pick);
         discardComputerCard(playedCard);
      }

      // if nothing could play, draw a card
      else {
         Card drewCard = deal();
         computerHand.add(drewCard);
         print();
         print("Computer drew a card.");
```

```
      // if it plays, play it
      if (drewCard.getSuit()==discard.getSuit()
          || drewCard.getRank()==discard.getRank()) {
        discardComputerCard(drewCard);
      }
    }
  }
    ...
```

Listing 16-55, from CrazyEights.java

```
    ...

  public CrazyEights() {

      ...

    else {
      activeSuit = ' ';
    }

    // play until either of us runs out of cards
    boolean done = false;
    while(!done) {
      playMyCard();
      // are there any cards left in my hand?
      if (myHand.size()==0) {
        done = true;
      }
      else {
        playComputerCard();
        // are there any cards left in the computer hand?
        if (computerHand.size()==0) {
          done = true;
        }
      }
    }
  }
    ...
```

Listing 16-56, from CrazyEights.java

```
    ...

  public CrazyEights() {

        ...
```

```
            if (computerHand.size() == 0) {
               done = true;
            }
         }
      }
      print();
      // who played all their cards?
      if (myHand.size()==0) {
         print("Congratulations! You won! The computer still had " +
computerHand.size() + " cards.");
      }
      else {
         print("Sorry, you lost. You still had " + myHand.size() + "
cards.");
         print("My Hand: " + myHand);
         print("Discard: " + discard);
      }
   }
   ...
```

Listing 16-57, from CrazyEights.java

```
      ...

   public CrazyEights() {

         ...

      else {
         activeSuit = ' ';
      }

      // who goes first?
      int turn = rand.nextInt(2);
      if(turn==1) {
         print("Computer goes first.");
         playComputerCard();
      }
      else {
         print("You go first.");
      }

      // play until either of us runs out of cards

         ...
```

Listing 16-58, from CrazyEights.java

```
    ...

private boolean isValidPlay(String rankSuit) {

        ...

    else if (!myHand.contains(card)) {
      print(rankSuit + " is not in your hand.");
      validPlay = false;
    }

    // 8s are always valid.  If the card is not an 8...
    else if (card.getRank()!='8') {
      // is the discard an 8?
      if (discard.getRank()=='8') {
        // does the card match the active suit?
        if (card.getSuit()!=activeSuit) {
          print(rankSuit + " cannot be played on " + discard
          + " because the suit was set to " + activeSuit);
          validPlay = false;
        }
      }

      // if the discard is not an 8,
      // does the discard match the rank or suit?
      else if (card.getSuit()!=discard.getSuit()
          && card.getRank()!=discard.getRank()) {
        print(rankSuit + " cannot be played on " + discard);
        validPlay = false;
      }
    }

    return validPlay;

        ...
```

Listing 16-59, from MyWindow.java

```
    ...

protected char promptForChar(String prompt) {
    char c = ' ';

    boolean valid = false;
    while(!valid) {
      print(prompt);
```

```
      String s = input();
      if (s.length()==1) {
         c = s.charAt(0);
         valid = true;
      }
      else {
         c = promptForChar(prompt);
      }
   }
   return c;
}
   . . .
```

Listing 16-60, from CrazyEights.java

```
   . . .

private char promptForSuit() {
   char suit = ' ';
   boolean validSuit = false;

   while(!validSuit) {
      suit = promptForChar("Change the suit to H, D, C, or S?");
      suit = Character.toUpperCase(suit);
      if (Card.isValidSuit(suit)) {
         validSuit = true;
      }
   }

   return suit;
}
   . . .
```

Listing 16-61, from CrazyEights.java

```
   . . .

private void discardMyCard(Card myCard) {
   myHand.remove(myCard);
   discardPile.add(discard);
   discard = myCard;
   if (myCard.getRank()=='8') {
      activeSuit = promptForSuit();
   }
}
   . . .
```

Listing 16-62, from CrazyEights.java

```
    . . .

public class CrazyEights extends MyWindow {

    private Deck deck = new Deck();
    private Hand myHand = new Hand();
    private Hand computerHand = new Hand();
    private Card discard;
    private ArrayList<Card> discardPile = new ArrayList<Card>();
    private Random rand = new Random();
    private char activeSuit = ' ';
    private int countHearts = 0;
    private int countDiamonds = 0;
    private int countClubs = 0;
    private int countSpades = 0;

        . . .
```

Listing 16-63, from CrazyEights.java

```
        . . .

    private void playComputerCard() {
        System.out.println("Computer hand: " + computerHand);
        ArrayList<Card> playableCards = new ArrayList<Card>();
        ArrayList<Card> eights = new ArrayList<Card>();
        countHearts = 0;
        countDiamonds = 0;
        countClubs = 0;
        countSpades = 0;

        // count eights and number of each suit
        for(int i=0; i<computerHand.size(); i++) {
            Card card = computerHand.cardAt(i);

            // if it's an eight, save it
            if (card.getRank()=='8') {
                eights.add(card);
            }
            // otherwise, count the number of each suit
            else {
                switch(card.getSuit()) {
                case 'H' :
                    countHearts++;
                    break;
                case 'D' :
```

```
        countDiamonds++;
        break;
     case 'C' :
        countClubs++;
        break;
     case 'S' :
        countSpades++;
        break;
     }
   }
}

// make list of playable cards
for(int i=0; i<computerHand.size(); i++) {
  Card card = computerHand.cardAt(i);

   // if discard is an 8, all cards of active suit are playable
   if (discard.getRank()=='8') {
     if (card.getSuit()==activeSuit) {
        playableCards.add(card);
     }
   }

   // else, if discard is not an 8,
   // only cards of the same suit or rank are playable
   else if(card.getSuit() == discard.getSuit()
        || card.getRank() == discard.getRank()) {
     playableCards.add(card);
   }
}

// pick a random playable card
int numberOfPlayableCards = playableCards.size();
if (numberOfPlayableCards>0) {
  int pick = rand.nextInt(numberOfPlayableCards);
  Card playedCard = playableCards.get(pick);
  discardComputerCard(playedCard);
}

// otherwise, if have an eight, play an eight
else if(eights.size()>0) {
  Card playedCard = eights.get(0);
  discardComputerCard(playedCard);
}

// if nothing could play, draw a card

   ...
```

Listing 16-64, from CrazyEights.java

```
   . . .

private void discardComputerCard(Card computerCard) {
   computerHand.remove(computerCard);
   discardPile.add(discard);
   discard = computerCard;
   if (discard.getRank()=='8') {
      int highestCount = countHearts;
      activeSuit = 'H';
      if (countDiamonds > highestCount) {
         highestCount = countDiamonds;
         activeSuit = 'D';
      }
      if (countClubs > highestCount) {
         highestCount = countClubs;
         activeSuit = 'C';
      }
      if (countSpades > highestCount) {
         highestCount = countSpades;
         activeSuit = 'S';
      }
   }
}
   . . .
```

Appendix C – Install Required Software and Files

These installation and setup instructions are for Microsoft Windows. The programs you'll download, install, and create could run on any computer with a Windows, Mac, or Linux operating system. However, this book doesn't provide instructions for how to do installation and setup on those computers.

Create a Java Work Folder Detailed Instructions

Create your own Java work folder on your computer. It's recommended that you put your Java work folder in your Windows user folder, but you can put it anywhere on your computer. I called mine *java* and put it in my user folder, *c:\Users\Annette*. Therefore, my Java work folder is *c:\Users\Annette\java*.

To create a folder in Windows 7, first click *Start / Computer* to open *Windows Explorer*. To create a folder in Windows 10, first click *Start / File Explorer*. Then go to the folder in which you want to create the new folder, and click the *New folder* button. Enter a name for your new folder.

If you share your computer with someone else who also wants to do java programming, create a different Java work folder for each of you. Your Java work folders must either have different names or be in different folders.

1. Create a Java work folder on your computer now.

Download and Install Java Detailed Instructions

You'll be writing your computer programs in the Java programming language. Your computer needs the free Java Development Kit to generate programs from Java program code.

The Java Development Kit only needs to be installed one time on your computer, no matter how many people plan to do Java programming on it.

To install the Java Development Kit:

1. Go to *http://www.oracle.com/technetwork/java/javase/downloads/index.html*.

2. Click the download button, as shown in Figure C.1, to download the latest version of the *Java Development Kit (JDK)* for *Java Standard Edition (SE)*.

Java Platform (JDK) 8u65 / 8u66

Figure C.1 – Download Java

3. Accept the license agreement, as shown in Figure C.2. Download either the Windows x86 or Windows x64 version of the Java Development Kit, depending on which version of Windows you have. Windows x86 is for 32-bit Windows; Windows x64 is for 64-bit Windows.

   1. How do you know if you have 32-bit or 64-bit Windows? In Windows 7, click *Start / Control Panel* and double-click on *System*. In Windows 10, click *Start / Settings / System / About*. The *System Type* indicates whether you have the 32-bit or 64-bit operating system. If your *Control Panel* doesn't have the *System* icon, you might have to click the *View by* drop down list in the top right corner of the *Control Panel* and choose *Small Icons*.

4. Double-click the downloaded .exe file name to install Java. You should be able to take all the installation defaults.

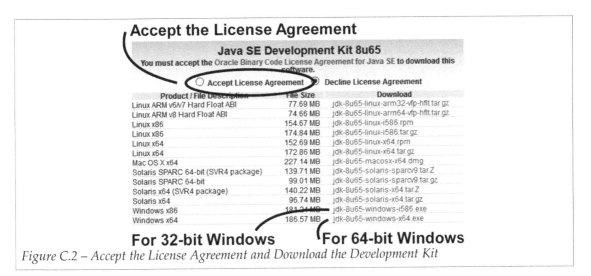

Figure C.2 – Accept the License Agreement and Download the Development Kit

Download and Install Eclipse Detailed Instructions

Eclipse is a free Java development environment. Eclipse simplifies typing program code, identifies programming errors, and even suggests ways to fix those errors.

It's recommended that you install Eclipse in your Windows user folder, but you can put it anywhere on your computer. I put mine in my user folder, *c:\Users\Annette*.

1. Download the latest version of *Eclipse IDE for Java Developers* from *http://www.eclipse.org/downloads/*. Download either the 32-bit or 64-bit version, depending on which version of Windows you have, to any location on your computer.

2. To <u>unzip</u> the downloaded .zip file, right-click on its name, choose *Extract all...*, and browse to the folder to which you want install Eclipse. I extracted mine to my user folder, *c:/Users/Annette*.

    1. If you share your computer with someone else who also wants to do java programming, extract each person's copy of Eclipse to a different folder.

Create a shortcut on your desktop for Eclipse. These instructions are for Windows 7 and 10:

1. Open the *eclipse* folder that was created when you extracted the files from the downloaded .zip file. My *eclipse* folder is in *c:/Users/Annette*.

2. Right-click on *eclipse.exe* and choose *copy*.

3. Right-click on your desktop and choose *Paste shortcut*.

4. If you aren't the only one who will use Eclipse for programming on your computer, right-click on the shortcut you just created and rename it for your use. For example, I renamed mine *Eclipse for Annette*.

Download DIYJava.zip Detailed Instructions

The lessons require a few additional data files. Those files are included in a free .zip file on the Godtland Software website:

1. Download *DIYJava.zip* from *http://www.godtlandsoftware.com/DIYJava/*.

2. To unzip *DIYJava.zip*, right-click on it and choose *Extract all....* Use the *Browse* button to extract the files into your Java work folder. I extracted mine to *c:/Users/Annette/java*.

You've now installed everything you need for creating the programs in this book. Follow the *Set up Eclipse* instructions at the beginning of this book to complete the setup needed for the lessons.